D1452815

ISLAMIC POLITICS
IN PALESTINE

Library of Modern Middle East Studies
Series ISBN 1 86064 077 X

ISLAMIC POLITICS IN PALESTINE

Beverley Milton-Edwards

I.B.Tauris *Publishers*

LONDON • NEW YORK

Paperback edition published in 1999 by I.B.Tauris & Co Ltd
Victoria House, Bloomsbury Square, London WC1B 4DZ
175 Fifth Avenue, New York NY 10010
Website: http://www.ibtauris.com

In the United States and Canada distributed by St. Martin's Press
175 Fifth Avenue, New York NY 10010

First published in 1996 by Tauris Academic Studies
an imprint of I.B.Tauris & Co Ltd

ISBN 1 86064 475 9

A full CIP record for this book is available from the British Library
A full CIP record for this book is available from the Library of
Congress

Library of Congress catalog card: available

Typeset in Monotype Garamond by Philip Armstrong, Sheffield
Printed and bound in Great Britain by WBC Ltd, Bridgend

For Graham and Cara

Contents

Acronyms

ANM	Arab National Movement
CIA	Central Intelligence Agency
DFLP	Democratic Front for the Liberation of Palestine
DOP	Declaration of Principles
FBIS	Foreign Broadcast Information Service
HAC	Higher Arab Committee
HIC	Higher Islamic Council
IAF	Islamic Action Front
IDF	Israel Defence Force
IRM	Islamic Resistance Movement (Hamas)
IUG	Islamic University Gaza
LP	Liberation Party
MYA	Muslim Youth Association
PFLP	Popular Front for the Liberation of Palestine
PFLP–GC	Popular Front for the Liberation of Palestine – General Command
PLA	Palestine Liberation Army
PLO	Palestine Liberation Organisation
PNA	Palestinian National Authority
PNC	Palestine National Council
PPF	Palestinian Police Force
PRC	Palestine Red Crescent
PRO	Public Record Office (Kew)
RCC	Revolutionary Command Council
SMC	Supreme Muslim Council
UN	United Nations
UNLU	United National Leadership of the Uprising
UNRWA	United Nations Relief and Works Agency
WMC	World Muslim Conference

Preface

The rise of political Islam among the Palestinians of the West Bank and Gaza Strip is part of a challenging new wave of Islamic life in the region. The influence of political Islam in Palestine has, in the 1990s, intensified to the point where it has brought Palestinian politics to the threshold of a new era. Political Islam now constitutes a formidable challenge to the Palestinian national movement. In the years since the Oslo Accords, signed between Israel and the Palestinian Liberation Organisation on 13 September 1993, Islamist groups like Hamas and Islamic Jihad have come to constitute a threat to the present peace process. Islamist intransigence over the issue of peace with Israel has led to an intensification of the campaign of armed attacks on Israel.

The spectre of confrontation between Hamas and the Palestinian National Authority (PNA) is also present. PNA–Hamas relations are already tense and the decision of the latter to boycott the presidential and legislative elections for the PNA in January 1996 has exacerbated the situation. The Hamas boycott paved the way for a landslide victory for Yasser Arafat in the presidential election and has in this way legitimated the PNA. Political Islam in Palestine is, at the time of writing, engaged in the most important struggle for power in its history.

My aim in this book is to chart the evolution of Islam's political response to the political changes in Palestine since the 1920s and the days of British mandate. I have sought to explain a number of trends and to debunk or modify the following assumptions about this history:

1. *That the Islamic movement in Palestine is essentially 'fundamentalist' and terrorist.* The Western and Israeli media have both played a part in typifying the contemporary Islamic movement in this alarmist fashion, but this crude reduction plays more on ignorance and fear than on knowledge and facts and erodes the prospect for a

peaceful and long-lasting resolution of the Israeli–Palestinians conflict in the West Bank and Gaza Strip.

2. *That politically active Muslims in Palestine belong to one monolithic group.* I seek to explain and illustrate that Palestinian Islamic groups have embraced a number of perspectives that cover a broad political spectrum, from traditional conservatives, to mystic-influenced radicals, and moderate reformers, to modernists all intent on an Islamic transformation (not necessarily revolutionary) of their own society.

3. *That the decline of Arab secularism triggered the rise of political Islam.* It is my contention that the articulation of political Islam in Palestine has not been tightly bound to the 'failure' of secularism and modernism. Among the main themes of 'resurgence theory', which has dominated much of the recent thinking about political Islam, is the assertion that the decline of Arab secularism triggered its increasing importance in the Middle East. In the case of Palestine, however, the opposite was true: the period after 1967 saw political Islam eclipsed by an increasingly flourishing secular nationalism. Furthermore, the contemporary movement, including groups like Hamas, has appeared as a result of a very specific set of political circumstances primarily linked to the Israeli occupation of the West Bank and Gaza Strip. The political circumstances of a sustained foreign military occupation and the threat of annexation triggered the Palestinian uprising or Intifada in 1987, which in turn encouraged the formation of the Hamas movement as a wing of the Muslim Brotherhood. Resurgence theory does not account for this pattern of transformation in the internal political dynamic of the Palestinian community nor can it truly take account of the deeply dialectical relationship which grew between the Israeli occupier and Palestinian subject. Resurgence theory falters when applied to a deeply divided society where conflict is ethnic and class based, where a settler state develops a neo-colonial and internal-colonial relationship with the subordinate community, and where sectarian-religious politics become paramount.

4. *That the strategy of the contemporary Islamist groups in Palestine has been solely dedicated to armed struggle as the means to achieve its political objectives.* While it is true that a commitment to armed struggle, blessed by Qur'anic interpretation, has been present among elements in the Islamic trend since the 1930s, this does not mean that Palestinian advocates of political Islam are all murderers intent on the physical annihilation of their opponents, whether Israeli or secular-

nationalist. In this book, political Islam's strategy of social transformation in Palestine is examined over a seventy-five year period
(1920–95). For much of this time Islamic groups have engaged
largely in activities which promote the peaceful transformation
of society. Political violence has been a product of unusual
circumstances and external influences; thus it is important to
examine the motives for the recent armed campaign to which
contemporary Islamic groups like Hamas and Islamic Jihad are
committed. To ask, in other words, what has caused them to
forsake the olive branch for the gun.

My study adopts a political-ethnographic approach which relies
on oral evidence and testimony, extensive interviews and the collation
of large amounts of primary-source material. As a result I may have
gone into more detail than is customary for a text of this kind. But
I have wanted to bring alive the personalities behind the thinking
that has shaped political Islam in Palestine and recreate for the reader
the events and struggles that have formed and are continuing to
form the background to that thinking. My work has also been shaped
by the political circumstances which prevailed during the period of
my fieldwork, particularly the closure of Palestinian universities by
the Israeli authorities which restricted my access to a whole variety
of sources.

The specific subject of my study, the individuals and organisations
of the Palestinian Islamic movement, was even harder to research.
Members of the Muslim Brotherhood, Hamas, Islamic Jihad and
other groups were often wary of foreigners, while Israeli crackdowns
on Hamas and Islamic Jihad made it increasingly difficult to reach
leaders and activists alike. Other Islamic groups, for example the
Liberation Party, expressly forbade their members from passing on
information about their organisation to outsiders of any sort. Given
such limitations, I can make no apology for writing this study from
a Western point of view.

Over fifty interviews with the activists of the Islamic and national
movements have nevertheless provided the basis for a comprehensive
history of the Palestinian Islamic movement since the 1920s. They
include the testimony of men who were boys at the time of the first
Arab–Israeli war, who remembered the upheaval in their own society
– how they fled from their rural village life and settled in Gaza as
refugees. The interviewees, often learned men who have dedicated
themselves to theological study, have proffered considered opinions

and views on the nature of the Islamic struggle against the state of
Israel and the forces of secularism in their own society. Protecting
the identity of these men was very important to the success of this
work. For the most part they would agree to be interviewed only on
the condition of anonymity, a condition which I have been careful
to respect.

In addition to personal interviews, I have made use of a large
number of *bayanat* (leaflets) issued by Hamas and Islamic Jihad, as
well as books, pamphlets, cassettes of sermons and photos of Islamic
graffiti. I have also consulted a wealth of secondary sources from
newspapers, journals, magazines, news agencies and government
documents. These written sources, both primary and secondary, have
been useful in clarifying chronology, political rhetoric and ideology
but have brought with them the constant need to interpret information and contextualise rhetoric.

My study is thus drawn from a wide variety of sources. From the
Public Record Office in Kew, London, to the cramped breeze-block
refugee shelters of Islamists in Khan Yunis, I have engaged in my
own personal odyssey following the trials and tribulations of a unique
Islamic movement. I hope that my journey has been transformed
into an account of political Islam in Palestine that will inform and
intrigue the Western reader.

Chapter One highlights the diversity of political Islam in Palestine
in its infancy, looking at both radical and conservative approaches
through an account of the activities of two Islamic leaders: Sheikh
Izz ad-Din al-Qassam and Haj Amin al-Husseini. Chapters Two and
Three illustrate the conservative reformist nature of political Islam
and its varied fortunes under the administrations of Egypt, Jordan
and the Israel. In Chapter Four the decline of secularism and
resurgency myth is challenged through a portrayal of the political
situation in the Gaza Strip and West Bank during the second decade
of Israeli occupation. The Palestinian uprising and the subsequent
peace process with Israel is investigated in Chapter Five. The strategy
of armed struggle and political contest against Palestinian nationalism
is here contextualised in the wider debate about the rising force of
political Islam. Chapter Six examines the ideology of Hamas and
Islamic Jihad looking at their ideas about politics, violence and
religion. Finally, a short Epilogue draws the themes of the book
together and ends with a discussion of likely scenarios facing
Palestinian Islamists in the next decade.

The list of those who have helped me is endless and while I have mentioned as many as possible I would like to add my profound thanks to all those who, for security and other reasons, remain anonymous in the pages of this book. I am grateful to Professor Tim Niblock who was my supervisor for my initial study of the subject and Professor James Piscatori for his encouragement and whose own work on the subject of political Islam inspired me. The following are but some of the figures who have assisted me over the years: Paul Adams, Atef from Azoun, Sam Banga, Said Barzin, Mr Ibrahim Dakkak (Abu Azzam), Bob Eccleshall and the colleagues and staff in the School of Politics at The Queen's University of Belfast, Ismaen Fagawi, Nabil Feidy, Ismaen Habash, Rema Hammami, Mahmoud Hawari, Saleh Abdel Jawad, Mousa Keilani, Ali Khashan, Bashir Nafe, Mohammad Nairab, Nasir from Kalandia camp, Alex Pollock, Mark Power-Stevens, Tanya Power-Stevens, Mr Mohammad al-Radwan (Abu Zaki), Bryan Robson, Eugene Rogan, Reem Saad, Haider Abdel Shaffi, Ramadan Shallah, Walid Abu Srour, Suha Taji-Farouqi, Salim Tamari, Graham Usher, Majd Yassin, staff of the Arab Thought Forum, and staff of the British School of Archaeology in Jerusalem and staff at the Centre for Research and Documentation of Palestinian Society at Birzeit University. My appreciation also to my family for their constant interest and encouragement. Anna Enayat deserves special thanks for the time, effort and guidance she has given me over the years and for transforming this project into a worthwhile publication. I also wish to extend my gratitude to Meg Howarth who helped with copy editing of this book. Appreciation also to my husband Graham whom I met in Jerusalem during my fieldwork and who has supported me throughout. Finally my thanks to Cara, born in Bethlehem and whose first years of life have been shared with this book on Islamic politics in Palestine. The royalties from this book will be donated to Save the Children.

BME
Belfast, Northern Ireland
February 1996.

Introduction

In recent decades Islamic groups, from Morocco to Iran, have been engaged in a political struggle to change the prevailing order and install Islamic states based on *shari'a* law. They are widely perceived as mounting a formidable challenge to the government and political systems of the Arab world. So far, however, the main achievement of this region-wide phenomenon has been to alter the nature of societies from the bottom upwards. Under its influence the place of religion in people's lives has increased, either voluntarily or through coercion, and Arab society has become increasingly Islamic. An Islamic state system and the resurrection of a caliphate (government with a Muslim leader) has the potential to alter the nature of the region. Although this change need not necessarily be viewed as a negative development, it is the fear of revolutionary Islam that has motivated the current Western fascination with Islamic movements in the region.

Political Islam, or 'Islamic fundamentalism' as it is popularly referred to, has become central to current analyses of Middle Eastern politics. Whether scholars are trying to assess the impact of economic change, ethnic configuration or the likelihood of a lasting peace deal in the region, the Islamic factor is always addressed. This fascination, however, is largely negative. Images of Islam, whether received from television, radio, newspapers or books are normally associated with terrorism, violence, barbarian and intolerant social agendas and complete intolerance of other faiths. Whether these images are accurate or representative is often immaterial, for the attempt is to underline the urgency of the measures the West should take to confront and vanquish the Islamic fundamentalist threat. Militant Islam and its political agenda is often portrayed in the West as the biggest threat since the demise of communism.

There are a number of commonly cited reasons for the current revival of political Islam in the Middle East. These include the deterioration of socio-economic conditions, the collapse of prevailing political systems and the rejection of foreign influence and cultural hegemony. Any study of the history of political Islam in Palestine must examine these explanations. More particularly, debates surrounding the definition of terms like Islamic fundamentalism and Islamic resurgence should be critically assessed since these terms have radically affected the manner in which the Islamic phenomenon is analysed, both in historical and contemporary contexts. It is my contention that, as they are used in current work, these terms often lack perspective and that the typology or classificatory criteria currently associated with their use is too rigid.

Islamic Fundamentalism

The ebb and flow of Islamic fundamentalism throughout history reveals an ongoing dialectic between Islam and its socio-economic political environment. [H. Dekmejian, *Islam in Revolution*, New York, 1985]

Islamic fundamentalism in the 1990s is often perceived as a region-wide product of the 1979 Iranian revolution. It is also frequently portrayed as an enraged mass movement engaged in a social uprising which abhors the symbols of the West and Western influence in the Arab world. As it is popularly understood, Islamic fundamentalism is an anti-modern trend that champions a return to an uncivilised age with a social and political order based on despotic rule and barbarian practices. Yet, as Aziz Al-Azmeh notes, 'Islamist revanchism in the Arab world is not a "return" to a primitivist utopia', although this, Al-Azmeh argues, is how Islam in the 1990s appears to 'present itself'.[1] Nevertheless, Islamic fundamentalism's relationship with the West continues to be the subject of intense analysis, and alarm. The West feels threatened and the spectre of hostility between the Christian West and Muslim East has been raised again with wide repercussions. As John Esposito remarks:

Fear of Islam is not new. The tendency to judge the actions of Muslims in splendid isolation, to generalize from the actions of the few to the many, to disregard similar excesses committed in the name of other religions and ideologies, is also not new.[2]

Political Islam in the 1990s, however, is much more complex than this simplified presentation suggests. In the Arab world it is a socio-religious phenomenon that represents both popular discontent and stable political order. The Islam which serves as the backbone of the Saudi Arabian order is the same as that used by al-Gama Islamiyya in Egypt to promote the overthrow of the government of President Hosni Mubarak. Islam both legitimates and opposes political rule in the Arab world. This heterogeneous and contradictory nature is found also in the West Bank and Gaza Strip, where political Islam represents at one and the same time a segment of a dis-enchanted refugee population, the aspiring urban classes and the continuation of a social order which bears allegiance to both Yasser Arafat as president of the Palestinian National Authority (PNA) and the late King Hussein of Jordan as custodian of the Holy Shrine of al-Aqsa (the third most holy site in Islam). Fundamentalism as a concept or term has become tainted and distorted. It fails to characterise those who are truly 'fundamentalist' and is often ascribed to groups and organisations which in fact promote or purvey an ideology that, while claiming a link to the Islam of the Prophet's time, is in fact an invented tradition based on certain political objectives, strategies and interpretations. How, therefore, has Islam as a political phenomenon come to be ascribed with universal fundamentalist characteristics?

In the context of the Palestinian case the term Islamic fundament-alism both aids and distorts the analysis of a group like Hamas. There is always an element of a call to a return to the fundamental values of Islam in the ideologies of such groups and yet, in its most literal sense, as Sami Zubaida and Yousef Choueri both point out, Islamic fundamentalism has 'become a catch-phrase which is sup-posed to define and describe all active involvement of Muslims in politics.'[3] Under this definition the current Islamic groups in the West Bank and Gaza, from Islamic Jihad to the Liberation Party, are all fundamentalist. Yet used in this way the term obscures as much as it clarifies and is certainly inappropriate if it is used to argue the existence of a religio-political monolith not influenced by the society in which it is based. The term fundamentalism deployed in this way has become part of the political language of those who seek to halt that which they do not truly understand.

The ideas of the Islamic movement in Palestine are as much a reflection socially, economically and politically of contemporary Palestinian society as of an invented tradition inspired by a seventh-century model of Islam. Palestinian Islamists are calling for an end to the Israeli occupation, the creation of an Islamic state system, for national leaders to represent all Palestinians and for a social order that permits the free practice of religion and respects the religious rights of the majority population. The Islamists of Palestine are modern day activists who represent many types of people, and their ideology reflects this. Their Islam has become generic and acculturated, reflecting a specific political circumstance. As one avowedly partisan Fatah nationalist commented on reading the Hamas Covenant (the main ideological document of Hamas organisation): 'They cannot fail to appeal to me, because I am a Muslim, if not by spiritual choice then by the very nature of my Palestinian culture, my socialisation, my struggle.'[4] By the same token, the leaders of Hamas or Islamic Jihad are not the only groups to claim a right to raise the banner of Islam over Palestine; the leadership of the nationalist movement, particularly Fatah, has also used Islamic symbols and slogans in the struggle for national liberation from Israeli rule.

In short, Hamas and other Palestinian Islamic groups active today are not the reincarnation of the Khomeini-style rhetoric of the early 1980s, nor are they like the Wahhabi fundamentalists of Arabia, nor do they mirror the activities of the Muslim Brotherhood in Egypt. They are unique Islamic organisations located in the West Bank and Gaza Strip which are creating their own political and social programmes. Their political Islam is shaped by the British colonisation of Palestine in 1917, Zionist immigration, the refugee experience of 1948, the heritage of Jordanian and Egyptian rule from 1948–67, the Israeli occupation in 1967, and the Palestinian nationalist experience of the 1970s and 1980s. Political Islam in Palestine has also been shaped by the Intifada and the climate that has transformed Palestinian politics since 1987. The term 'fundamentalism' does not help explain the heterogeneity of the Palestinian Islamic movement, even in terms of its ultimate goal. How can such a diverse trend, developed in response to the calamities that have befallen the Palestinians, be correctly defined simply as 'fundamentalist'?

Islamic Resurgence

Does the idea of an 'Islamic resurgence' better describe the Palestinian case? Is the message of Hamas and Islamic Jihad the same as that preached by the Islamic movements of Egypt or Algeria? Has the Islamic movement in the West Bank arisen from the same circumstances as its counterparts in Jordan or Tunisia? Are Hamas and Islamic Jihad part of a resurgence of Islam defined by Hilal

Dessouki as 'the increasing prominence and politicisation of Islamic ideology and symbols in Muslim societies and in the public life of Muslim individuals'?[5] At first glance 'resurgence theory' appears appropriate to the Palestinian case; but a deeper examination of the context in which resurgence (or revival) is triggered leads to the conclusion that it is only partially useful.

In itself, the phenomenon of Islamic resurgence is of course not new. The history of Islam has always been one of the ebb and flow of revivalist movements dating back to the Kharijites of Medina who rose against Ali, the Prophet's nephew. However, current writers on the subject of resurgent Islam contend that the contemporary Islamic resurgence is significantly different from these historical cases.

According to such writers, the factor that has most profoundly affected the emergence of Islamic groups in the twentieth century, and makes them different from their earlier counterparts, is colonialism – or in other words the development of an economic and social order in the Middle East that can be traced to European capitalist exploitation of Arab labour and markets and the influence of Western-inspired political ideologies like socialism, communism and free-market capitalism. The ensuing modernisation and industrialisation of the region encouraged urban migration and traditional agrarian modes of production were abandoned. The drive to literacy encouraged the development of an education system which neglected traditional Islamic-based learning in favour of the technological skills of the twentieth century. Under these conditions Arab identity was challenged by Western notions of social order. Even when colonial rule (direct or indirect) over the region ended, its legacy, in the form of Western systems of government and policies that encouraged economic and social modernisation, continued under Arab rule in the 1950s and 1960s. Arab political elites of this period were consciously or unconsciously a product of, and saddled with, the socio-political and cultural baggage of the colonial experience and its ideological trappings.

Thus theorists of resurgence argue that the current Islamic revival differs from its predecessors because of the twentieth-century and Western-influenced context in which it has arisen. According to Bassam Tibi, contemporary political Islam 'must be seen as a product of modern acculturation, shaped by factors and forces of the modern world to which it responds while attempting to develop an idiom in which to do so.'[6] Acculturation has inevitably impacted on the ideology of political Islam. Attempts to return ideologically to Islamic fundamentals are modified by the cultural experience of all Muslim thinkers in the contemporary era. The resurgence theorists seem to want it both ways; acknowledging past revivals but seeking out modern and unique attributes to the contemporary phenomenon.

The Crisis of Identity:
Arab Defeat and Islam Ascendant

Colonialism, then, played its part in the manifestation of the current Islamic political revival through the imposition of particular political systems in the Middle East and the creation of artificial nation-states like Iraq, Jordan, Syria, Lebanon and Israel. Arab political leaders not only worked and articulated power in these artificial systems but also embraced alien Western ideologies to legitimate their rule. The inevitable failure of this process, according to resurgence literature, caused a societal, cultural and identity crisis after 1967, with the mass of the Arab population alienated from its political rulers and systems. The military forces of the state of Israel had vanquished in less than six days the combined military might of Egypt, Jordan and Syria supported by the armies of Iraq and other Arab states. This humiliating military defeat, it is argued, not only signalled the end of the political pan-Arab ideal promoted by President Gamal Abdel Nasser of Egypt but also the bankruptcy of the Western-inspired approach to politics and power in the Middle East. The masses, resurgence theorists explain, turned away from the secular nation-state and the ideology of the West, and Islam began to fill the vacuum, empowering people, through their faith, with a sense of identity. As a result of this crisis of identity new approaches to politics and systems of government in the Arab world emerged.

The writers on Islamic resurgence continue their discourse by noting that the response to the crisis of identity, to the loss of Muslim mores and values, has not been uniform but differs from one socio-political context to another. Nevertheless, they continue to identify common threads that run through all the examples. These include:

> ... a sense that existing political, economic, and social systems had failed; a disenchantment with, and at times a rejection of, the West ... the conviction that Islam provides a self-sufficient ideology for state and society, a valid alternative to secular nationalism, socialism and capitalism.[7]

According to resurgence theorists, political Islam arose offering a solution, more active than traditional Islam and yet still embracing every other aspect of Muslim identity. The ideology of political Islam associated the crisis of identity with the crisis of the Muslim soul that had lost touch with its religion. If Muslims would return to the practice of their religion and embrace the accompanying political ideology, the nation of Islam would rise, unified and triumphant, to seize political power.

Historic and Contemporary Palestine

In turning to the case of Palestine, there are some problems with a theory that builds an equation between the defeat of 1967, the Arab crisis of identity, the rejection of Western ideology and Islamic resurgence. The resurgence model fits Palestine in some ways but not in others. It fits in that it points to the ebbs and flows of resurgence, with organisations and groups dedicated to attaining political power or achieving political change for Islamic reasons. In the 1930s Palestine witnessed just such a resurgence, which declined subsequently until the contemporary revival of the 1980s.

However, the model raises a number of issues in other areas. For example, can it be argued that a crisis of identity really occurred and that a resurgence of Islam took place in the newly-occupied territories of the West Bank and Gaza Strip after 1967? Did the Islamic movement revive naturally in response to disenchantment with Palestinian secular nationalism? Did the ideology of the new Islamic groups, when they emerged, reflect a political/theological agenda that was a valid alternative to secular nationalism, socialism and capitalism? The answer to all these questions is, in short, no.

Following the war of 1967 and the Israeli capture of Jerusalem and the al-Aqsa mosque, no political vacuum appeared because Palestinians did not abandon nationalism. Nationalism, in both its pan-Arab and Palestinian form, was still regarded by the Palestinians as their solution. Palestinians embraced a secular national response, supported the Palestine Liberation Organisation (PLO) and its constituent members from Fatah to the Popular Front for the Liberation of Palestine and the communists. Furthermore, Palestinians took up arms in the name of the nationalist struggle, and their fedayeen forces fought for the creation of an independent Palestinian state, secular, not sectarian or Islamic. The Palestinian population was encouraged to adopt a strategy of national resistance against the

Israeli occupation through the nationalist secular agenda. As the Islamist figures interviewed for this book admitted, even they did not turn to their religion to provide a political solution for their problems. Instead they looked to Marxist, Leninist, Maoist and liberal-democratic doctrines as alternatives to Israeli occupation.

The resurgence of Islam in the occupied territories occurred under peculiar and specific conditions which somewhat surprisingly were not related primarily to the defeat of 1967. The factors that gave rise to the revival of Islam in Gaza and the West Bank both support resurgence theory and call it into question for the following reasons:

1. The revival of Islam in the occupied territories really took off after the defeat of PLO national forces in Lebanon in 1982. The resulting disarray and internal conflict within the national movement presented an opportunity for nascent Islamists to mount a political challenge in the West Bank and Gaza arena.

2. The appearance of some groups in the political arena in Gaza was artificially stimulated and certainly part of an Israeli strategy to pursue a policy of divide and rule aimed at eradicating an already weakened national movement.

3. Islam was a response to the effects of the secularisation of Palestinian lifestyles and a general move away from the mosque to the cinema. As such the ideology of the new Islamic groups was not always apparent or expressed in terms of a political agenda. It was based on a notion of encouraging a religio-cultural revival of Islam typified by a return to Islamic dress and Islamic social codes of behaviour. The revival depended on a sense of Islamic tradition invented and purveyed by Islamists. The invented tradition, however, allowed the nascent Islamists to adapt their agenda and modify it in a manner that was not always consistently Islamic.

4. New Islamic groups were created, but not as a result of a crisis of identity in the Palestinian community. New groups were encouraged to grow by Israel, and breakaway organisations were created as a result of internal disputes over the primacy of the Palestine question as part of the Islamic revival.

5. The resurgence of Islam did not take place because Palestinians had lost faith in the alternative articulated through organisations like Fatah.

6. The Islamic revival in Palestine was influenced in part by the region-wide phenomenon of Islam and political events including

the Iranian revolution and the struggle of the Mujahidin in Afghanistan; but it was influenced equally by the moderate Islamic tendencies exhibited by the Jordanian Islamic movement during this period.

Most importantly, however, it was the outbreak of the Palestinian uprising known as the Intifada in December 1987 that accounted for the change in the nature of Palestine's Islamic groups into a highly politicised anti-occupation force. The mass nature of the uprising and the symbolism initially apparent in its message of discontent and protest contributed to the sense that political Islam had reached a decisive point in its attempts to achieve its goals. While the Intifada was never an Islamic revolution, it did permit Islamists to organise and achieve levels of political power within society that they had never previously enjoyed. Thus, by the early 1990s, the Hamas organisation had emerged as the main opponent of the PLO, able to mount a serious challenge to nationalist hegemony in the Gaza Strip and West Bank. This challenge has been directed also at the state of Israel.

In the period since the signing of the Oslo Accords between the government of Israel and the leadership of the PLO, Hamas and other Islamic groups have emerged as the largest opposition force to the peace agreement and the prospect of essentially secular rule in Gaza and Jericho. The Islamists are not happy with the notion of the Palestinian National Authority (PNA) paying no more than lip-service to the notion of the re-generation of Palestinian rule according to Islamic rule and practice. They remain intransigent in their rejection of the current peace deal. Capitulation in this matter is unthinkable as it would contradict everything that the movement stands for. As Hamas activist Ahmad Sa'ati notes:

> The Islamic movement would not accept what Arafat accepted ... as long as there is occupation the people have a right to struggle, to practise jihad ... people must be prepared.[8]

1

The Roots of Struggle in Palestine

The emergence of political Islam in Palestine occurred during a period of considerable upheaval. The period addressed by this chapter witnessed the British mandate (1917–48), the growth of Zionist immigration with the stated intention of creating a state for the Jews, and the subsequent partition of Palestine by the United Nations in 1947 into two states. The growth of political Islam in response to many of these changes was part of a region-wide trend towards rethinking the role of Islam in the modern age and the challenge that Western domination and its secularising influences posed for it. But in Palestine in particular the conflict between Palestinian interests and Zionist encroachment meant that it was imperative that the Arab community and its leadership formulate a response. That response came in a number of guises. It came through the emergence of Palestinian–Arab nationalism, with its demands for self-determination, as well as political and physical control over the land. The challenge was also met through the emergence of a radical modernist Islamic movement championed by Sheikh Izz ad-Din al-Qassam.[1] Finally, a marriage of convenience took place between the forces of *ulama*-based institutional Islam and the emerging nationalism of the region's traditional notable families.

The growth of secular Arab nationalism, reflecting regional influence at this stage, occurred largely among the notable class, Christian and Muslim. Ideas of nationalism were a relatively un-developed feature of mass-based demands. Even during the Palestinian revolt (1936–39) the Palestinian leadership was unable to harness the idea of the nation-state to the demands of the rural masses and channel it into an effective demand for rights from the British authorities. This inability was ultimately reflected in the deterioration of the revolt into internecine disputes, with attacks on the notables and the abandonment of any meaningful political demands.

These events were nevertheless important. The failure of the notables to achieve legitimacy opened the path for ideological interlopers like Sheikh Izz ad-Din al-Qassam to encourage the empowerment of peasants through political Islam. While loyalty to the notables did not disappear entirely, Sheikh Izz ad-Din al-Qassam was able to capture the popular imagination and generate support with his own brand of Salafiyya modernist Islam. Although institutional Islam also offered hope to Palestinians during this period, it was unable adequately to meet the challenge posed by colonialism (in the form of the British mandate), the Zionist intrusion into the country and the accompanying modernisation, societal upheaval and dispossession of the peasant population.

By focusing on two individuals, Sheikh Izz ad-Din al-Qassam and Haj Amin al-Husseini, a picture can be built of the emergence of political Islam in Palestine. The history of this period was still largely formed by individuals rather than a politicised mass. The majority of the Arab population was rural, illiterate, poor and dependent on a system of deferential power relations at the heart of which lay the two most important notable families of Palestine, the al-Husseinis and the Nashashibis. Leadership of the community at that time was individualistic and often based on family or clan interests. Personality and politics were, therefore, extremely important in this context.

Past and Present: Invented Tradition

Our People, on the 19 November 1935, a fighter of the jihad, a scholar, a professor and al-Azharite, Sheikh Izz ad-Din al-Qassam wrote a new page in the history of heroism when he fell as a martyr while fighting the British ... al-Qassam is a symbol of sacrifice ... al-Qassam was the spark for the revolution of 1936. [Hamas leaflet, 'The Martyr al-Qassam: No to the Balfour Promise, Yes to the Uprising', 27 October 1988]

Contemporary political Islam in Palestine has constructed for itself a history that is full of brave figures and heroic deeds. For Islamists today, the legacy of the luminaries of the 1930s is an ever-present inspiration for their own activities. It is thus no coincidence that the armed wing of Hamas is named after Sheikh Izz ad-Din al-Qassam (1882–1935), the first radical Islamic leader in Palestinian politics. Sheikh Izz ad-Din al-Qassam was killed by the British mandate authorities in the village of Sheikh Zeid near Jenin in November 1935 and has since become a powerful symbol to many of those involved in the struggle for Palestinian liberation. His legend has grown as a result of his own struggle against the British mandate and the Zionist movement in the 1920s and 1930s. Some writers even claim that it was Sheikh Izz ad-Din's death that sparked what came to be known as the Great Revolt (1936–39) which included the Palestinian general strike of 1936.

The themes of protest inspired by individuals such as the sheikh and Haj Amin al-Husseini, the Mufti of Jerusalem (1895–1974), are echoed in the Palestinian national and Islamic movement of the late 1980s and 1990s. There are certain parallels also between the patterns of Islamic politics in this period and those of the contemporary era, and in the responses to them. In the 1930s, a great deal of protest was organised around the notion that Palestinians should reassert their Islamic identity and transform it into a struggle against the occupation of their land; today the same arguments are just as potent. Similarly, the fledgling political Islam of the 1930s was, like the political Islam of today, diverse and not the product of one voice or one individual. The British authorities in the 1930s reacted to the challenge posed by the resurgence of Islam as a political force through the detention, imprisonment without trial and deportation of Islamic activists, as do the Israelis in the 1990s, often employing the same British emergency regulations, and commonly resorting to the same or similar means.

The Brigand Sheikh Izz ad-Din al-Qassam

Sheikh Mohammad Izz ad-Din bin Abdul Qadar bin Mustafa al-Qassam (1882–1935)[2] was Palestine's first Salafiyya modernist Islamic leader. He has been credited with introducing the idea of armed struggle to modern Palestinian politics and with raising the consciousness of Palestinian peasants, many of whom were illiterate and dispossessed of their land. It was his appeal to a very neglected sector of society and newly-emerging urbanised Palestinian class that won him so much support. His impact on the peasant and working-class communities of Palestine is summed up in a eulogy written after his death in 1935:

> They Killed You!!! ... You fought for good and your memory will live on from the good you did ... None has served the homeland but you with loyalty and where is the valour of the sons of the homeland? ... Those working for it with all their strength rebel against the enemy ... Those who were unrequited in their love of its independence with honesty ...

since you are Izz ad-Din and the only one who is true of faith … They killed you and they were not rightfully appointed to rule you.[3]

Sheikh Izz ad-Din al-Qassam established a political and military organisation that was unique. He encouraged the participation in politics of the illiterate, the poor, the dispossessed, those who had lost the most during the years of the British mandate and Zionist colonisation, and his movement thus reflected the changes taking place in the power structure of the community. He expressed political ideas in a vocabulary with which large numbers were familiar, namely that if Islam. And he stood for principles that many Palestinians were forced to admit were absent from their self-appointed leadership of notables and institutional Islam. As one newspaper noted after his death at the hands of British police:

'Although we differ from the dead martyr as to the means, we are partners with him in the attainment of the ultimate objective. If Arabs despair of justice then every soul and family will become an Izz ad-Din al-Qassam.'[4]

The 'brigand sheikh', as the British authorities called him, was in fact a highly intelligent and articulate man with first-hand experience of fighting not just the British in Palestine but also the French in Syria. Born and educated in the Syrian town of Jebla of a leading Sufi family, in his early twenties he went to study at the famous al-Azhar university in Cairo. Although he followed the traditional curriculum at al-Azhar his years in Cairo coincided with the time when the ideas of Islamic modernists like Jamal al-Din al-Afghani (1838–97), Mohammad Abduh (1849–1905) and Rashid Rida (1865–1935)[5] about how Islam might meet the challenges and changes triggered by increasing Western hegemony in the Middle East were hotly discussed.

Al-Afghani, Abduh and Rashid Rida played a leading role in what was known as the reformist or salafiyya movement.[6] They sought to acquaint Islam with the modern world while still advocating the primacy of belief, arguing that an irrelevant and outdated interpretation of Islam, promoted by a backward and old-fashioned *ulama*, was at the dawn of the twentieth century undermining an entire system of belief. According to Esposito, they believed that 'the strength and survival of the *umma* (Muslim community) was dependent on the reasserting of Islamic identity and solidarity.'[7] Instead of fearing the development of the West they argued that Islam should rise and respond to its challenge. With its own history of civilisation, science and economics, Islam was capable, as a political as well as religious force, of finding solutions to the problems posed by modernity. This response, together with a new Muslim identity, would empower people to govern themselves and oust foreign or infidel rule. The notion of a revived Muslim community encouraged pan-Islamism amongst the modernists and throughout the Muslim world. And in its turn, the pan-Islamist idea, with its emphasis on unity and reform, inspired the rise of the Arab nationalist movement.

The modernist approach first developed by al-Afghani and Abduh was elaborated by Rashid Rida who imbued it with his own *salafi* precepts. Following Abduh's death, Rashid Rida became the publisher of the modernist journal *al-Manar*, and was involved with a religious school close to al-Azhar University. Yet Rida became increasingly conservative as foreign influence over the Middle East became more evident in the first three decades of the twentieth century. Witnessing the rise of secularism among the Egyptian intelligentsia he eschewed the modernising influences of the West, instead drawing closer to the roots of Islam and becoming the first advocate in the Arab world of a modernised Islamic state. His rationale was based on the defence of Islam and its need to respond through inner rejuvenation to these modern pressures before it was too late. Rida became an influential figure throughout the Muslim world. By actively encouraging the young men who read his work and that of his intellectual predecessors, he planted the seed which encouraged the reform and defence of Islam from within.

The extent to which al-Qassam's thinking was moulded by the Salafiyya influence is the subject of debate. Both his contemporaries and his biographers offer contradictory evidence on the question. However, even if Izz ad-Din al-Qassam did not, while he was in Cairo, actually meet or study under either Mohammad Abduh or Rashid Rida, the approach he later adopted to political issues indicates a familiarity with the type of ideas they disseminated. Like the Salafiyya reformers, Izz ad-Din al-Qassam was deeply critical of the *ulama* of institutional Islam, and like them he was aware of the dangers to Islam inherent in the spread of folk-practices and rituals. His anti-colonial stance and defence of Islam through jihad were surely a result of Salafiyya influences. Izz ad-Din al-Qassam was not an intellectual and there is no record of any systematic theological or ideological writing by him. Yet the message he so actively promoted among the Palestinian peasant community was clearly derived from Salafiyya teaching. As one biographer notes, he was sensitive to what he perceived as the backwardness and moral debasement of the Muslims of his day and he believed that the only way they could liberate themselves from foreign occupation and progress would be through the revival of Islam.[8]

Sacred Soil: The Battle in Palestine

In 1921 Sheikh Izz ad-Din al-Qassam left Syria where the French authorities had sentenced him to death for participating in armed opposition, to settle in the northern Palestinian city of Haifa. A steeply-terraced port city, Haifa was in the throes of industrialisation. The port area, home to thousands of poor and working-class stevedores and dock-hands, was where the newly arrived sheikh would find his most receptive audience.

A self-declared enemy of colonialism, and by extension of Zionism, al-Qassam had a huge impact on the Palestinian political scene. The situation at this time was increasingly tense as Palestinian resentment against the excesses of Jewish immigration and land settlement grew turning eventually into a cycle of violence and disturbance that would dog the British mandate authorities throughout their time in the country. The Palestinian national movement was increasingly worried both by the spiralling rate of Zionist immigration and its own inability to prevent the dispossession of Palestinian peasants from land sold to the Zionists by absentee landowners. Yet at the same time its ability to mount an effective protest was undermined by the increasing conflict and competition for power between the rival notable families based in Jerusalem. In addition, the religious leaders of the Muslim community, in particular the mufti and ulama, were engaged in their own power struggles which were linked to emerging secular-nationalist aspirations. They were thus failing to provide the religious response needed to make sense of the momentous changes in all aspects of Palestinian society.

Following his arrival in Palestine, Sheikh Izz ad-Din al-Qassam sought a post in Haifa's prominent Islamic school. The school was funded by the Palestinian Waqf (religious endowment) authorities which by 1922 were headed by the British-appointed Mufti of Jerusalem, Haj Amin al-Husseini. The principal of the school was himself a famous Syrian exile and religious figure named Sheikh Kamal al-Qasab. Sheikh al-Qasab was also a close friend of Rashid Rida, and there is no doubt that during the friendship that followed between al-Qasab and al-Qassam, Rashid Rida's influence would have been discussed and felt. In addition, many of al-Qassam's new colleagues had studied in Cairo and were aware of the modernist debate. The school provided al-Qassam with a strong base, but not his only one.

Besides his job as a teacher, Izz ad-Din held other religious posts. He was appointed preacher in the Jerena mosque in the heart of Haifa's dockland, where his modernist approach to Islam met with a receptive audience. In 1928 the Waqf authorities in Jerusalem appointed him marriage registrar for the Haifa Shari'a court, a function that entailed much travel in the Haifa district. It is said that this afforded the sheikh the opportunity to get to know the rural north Palestine and to befriend villagers in the area. The job involved officiating on festive or joyous occasions in which the whole village or community would normally participate and al-Qassam became well-known and well-liked.

Touring the rural areas gave al-Qassam ample opportunity to preach his message: a call to Palestinians to return to the funda-mentals of the faith, the reform of Islam, and the eschewing of folk-practices that had obscured the real nature of the religion for so long. The influence of Salafiyya thinking on the area of folk-practice advocated by Rashid Rida was never far from the surface of al-Qassam's actions. He tackled the question in an article for a local newspaper in 1925, where he stated:

> As for holding funeral processions with wailing and praying loudly and making noise and visiting graves of prophets and leading men in the known procedure of touching and rubbing the tombs and committing sins and the blatant mingling of men and women and spending money in not the right and proper manner ... it is a device not performed by the Prophet ... .[9]

Al-Qassam's impact in the rural areas he visited was significant, as a report from the collection of the British Police Commissioner remarks:

> During his tours he would bring together the more religiously minded of the villagers and preach to them the doctrines of Islam, cleverly inter-polating such passages from the Qur'an as were calculated to stimulate a spirit of religious fanaticism.[10]

This support would stand the sheikh in good stead in later years when he would rely on the villagers to shelter or aid him and his fighters.

In addition to his official Waqf appointments al-Qassam became closely involved with the Muslim Youth Association (MYA) in Haifa the members of which were young men eager to play a part in current political events. These newly urbanised workers were increasingly politicised yet often alienated from the traditional and institutional politics of the notable families and the religious institutions based in Jerusalem. Sheikh Izz ad-Din opened their eyes to Islamic modernism. He preached to them about the dangers of a stagnant Islam and Islam's need to respond to the challenge of colonialism which, he contended, demanded radical measures, including the defence of Islam through jihad or holy war. This strategy appealed to members of his audience, resonating as it did with the increasing cycle of political violence that was dominating their lives and their society. As his popularity as a preacher grew, the sheikh was also asked to give sermons at the newly-built Istiqlal (Independence) mosque near the Haifa railway works, another mosque with a predominantly working-class congregation.

By the late 1920s and early 1930s al-Qassam spent more and more of his time with the stevedores and vendors of Haifa's dockyards. He set out to teach those who were illiterate to read, using, of course, the Qur'an. A small number of men formed a circle around him, learning and discussing his ideas. It was through these discussions and debates that al-Qassam became increasingly convinced of the need to end colonial domination in Palestine and initiate a return to the primacy of Islam in society. As Police Commissioner Tegart notes, this policy paid off:

> His interpretation of the parts of the Qur'an which sanction the use of physical violence, was unorthodox ... but by his policy of selecting from amongst the poor, ignorant and the more violently disposed of the pious, he was able ... to obtain a small following ... .[11]

One member of the circle who was later captured and tried by the British was reported to have described in his confession why he had joined:

> He joined the gang voluntarily, in order to escape from his miserable existence and he spent about a week with them [al-Qassam and his men] in the caves of the Jenin hills. The Jews and English eat meat with rice, but we poor people have to be satisfied with a few olives, declared the prisoner at the end of his statement.[12]

The prisoner's confession illustrates clearly the difference between the message expounded by Sheikh Izz ad-Din al-Qassam and that of the leaders of institutional Islam and the predominantly bourgeois national movement. Al-Qassam was trying to appeal to the dispossessed to take some control over their own lives. He made them aware of the disparity between their own situation and that of the British authorities and the new Jewish immigrants to Palestine. He also offered a means of expression for protest: armed struggle through jihad. He advocated jihad because the Islamic strategy of *fatwas* and appeals raised by the leaders of the *ulama* and institutional Islam were completely ineffective methods of dealing with the challenge that faced Palestinians at the time. Radical times required radical changes entailing huge risks; unlike the *ulama*, Sheikh Izz ad-Din al-Qassam was prepared to push for the end of colonialism and Zionism and the establishment of an Islamic state.

By 1930 al-Qassam had procured a *fatwa* from Damascus, recognised by Sheikh Badr ad-Din Taji al-Husseini, which declared the struggle against the British and the Jews permissible. This he would read in the mosques and at secret and private meetings with his compatriots, mostly from Haifa, Acre and the villages surrounding Jenin. At this time his message also fell on the receptive ears of young preachers working in the area who were far enough removed from the influence of the institutional Islamic elite of Jerusalem to fear for their jobs, including Sheikh Khalil Eissa, Sheikh Farhan Sa'adi, Sheikh Hussein Hamadi and Sheikh Attiyeh Ahmad.

The sheikh organised small, secret groups of supporters who in turn recruited others, many of whom undertook weapons-training. Members were drawn from the ranks of both the working and peasant classes. Strict secrecy and religious piety were prerequisites of membership. Commitment to armed struggle was explained through the doctrine of jihad – a holy war that takes up the sword against those who have forcefully occupied land holy to the Islamic faith – so that each member knew the worth of his devotion and sacrifice. Each member of the cell gave what he could. Some contributed financially to help with the purchase of arms and ammunition.[13] Estimates of the number of men involved in al-Qassam's secret organisation vary, one being as high as 200.[14]

Glory in Death for the Brigand Sheikh

The events surrounding the death of al-Qassam and three others in the village of Sheikh Zeid provide a chilling insight into the lengths to which he and his followers were willing to go in order to resist the British and Zionist settlers. Al-Qassam was engaged in a real jihad, the British, having failed to recognise the importance of the religious debate introduced by the 'brigand' al-Qassam, were astounded by the reaction of Palestinians following his death. They had seen him simply as one of many troublemakers involved in localised extortion for financial gain, not as a committed activist directed by a strong sense of religious and political duty.

It was believed that the Qassamites (as they became known) were responsible for attacks on Jewish settlements or individual colonists. By early November 1935 it was clear that al-Qassam and a small band of men were planning to strike against the Zionists or the British. On 8 November 1935 it was reported that the body of missing Jewish policeman, Sergeant Moshe Rosenfeld, had been found in a cave near the village of Ain Harod in the north of the country. Al-Qassam's group was thought to be responsible and the police immediately set up search parties. They moved in on the group's hide-out in the village of Sheikh Zeid on 20 November. After a long gunfight, four Qassamites, including Sheikh Izz-ad-Din himself, were killed. Five others were captured.[15]

News of al-Qassam's death spread throughout Palestine. In Haifa, his supporters among the city's labourers, together with peasants from the north, flocked to his funeral. The size of the crowd surprised the police. At least 3,000 gathered at the Jerena mosque where his body and two others had been laid to rest.

While thousands of working-class and peasant Palestinians paid their last respects, the majority of the bourgeois secular-nationalist leaders and those of institutional Islam were absent. The message on both sides was clear: a symbol of martyrdom and self-sacrifice, embodying for the people the selflessness conspicuously absent among their leaders, Sheikh Izz-ad-Din also highlighted the futile tactics of more prominent politicians.[16] Despite public protest at the prevailing political situation, the traditional Palestinian leadership (including the forces of institutional Islam) had privately sold land disinheriting the peasant mass. Al-Qassam, the peasant's friend, had established relations with a group in society that was powerless, increasingly landless and indebted and taught them a powerful political and religious message. The rage of the peasant and lower classes was nevertheless quickly picked up by the nationalist leadership. Within days of the funeral Palestinian newspapers were canonising the brigand martyrs and calling on the British to alter their policy towards Palestinians.

The leaders of the secular-nationalist movement were alarmed by the growing hostility towards both them and the traditional Islamic leadership. Within days of Sheikh Izz ad-Din al-Qassam's death, notable secular leaders such as Raghib Nashashibi, Jamal al-Husseini and Abd al-Latif Salah requested a meeting with British High Commissioner Arthur Wauchope at Government House. At the meeting they discussed the prevailing conditions in the country and the associated tensions resulting from al-Qassam's martyrdom, expressing the fear that their own influence over the Palestinian population might be waning in the light of the recent events.

Qassamite Quest Continues

If the British authorities had hoped that the death of Sheikh Izz ad-Din would put an end to Islamic activism in the country they were wrong. Although no one could really replace this charismatic man, his message and a number of his dedicated supporters lived on and before long there was news of renewed Qassamite attacks in northern Palestine. Sheikh Hussein Hamadi and Abdullah Abu Yunis were largely responsible for taking over from Sheikh Izz ad-Din. Sheikh Hamadi was particularly active in Haifa where, until the British intervened, he attempted to organise in both the Fityan al-Jezireh League and the MYA. The police persisted in their attempts to track down and capture the brigand Qassamites, arresting and remanding another sixteen over the following few months. Despite this and the flight of a number of prominent figures to Syria, Sheikh Farhan Sa'adi and Sheikh Yousef Abu Doreh remained in Palestine to lead the group. They were joined by Sheikh Hamadi, Sheikh Ghazal Hasan Yunis, Sheikh Mohammad al-Mughrabi, Sheikh Mohammad al-Atrees and Sheikh Mustafa ad-Dinassi. Police intelligence reports were able eventually to name over fifty religious activists involved after al-Qassam's death.

The memorial meetings in Haifa in early January 1936 bore testimony to al-Qassam's posthumous power. By this time the various Arab factions including the Istiqlalists, the MYA and the Arab party had come together to discuss al-Qassam's message. The Palestinian leadership had woken up to the power of the sheikh's philosophy and the support that it attracted. His death was now being linked to the political demands made by the representatives of these groups. Thus his martyrdom was, as described by the newspapers, a 'defence of his country against the British' by 'a great nationalist who fell in the cause'. The transformation of al-Qassam's modernist Salafiyya message was rapid and underscored the pragmatic nature of the political leadership at this time. The burgeoning secular–nationalist movement in particular hijacked al-Qassam's death to press for nationalist rather than Islamic demands.

Thus, while the secular-national leadership had been noticeably absent from the sheikh's funeral they were all there at ceremonies to commemorate his death. Three separate meetings, attended by thousands of Palestinians, were held in Haifa on the same day.[17] Haj Rashid Ibrahim, president of the MYA, municipal councillor and member of the secular Istiqlal party, Jaffa newspaper editor Sheikh Salmon Farouqi, Akram Zuaitar from Nablus, Dr Rushdi Tammimi, Sheikh Ibrahim Shanti, Fakri Nashashibi and Jamal al-Husseini all gave speeches. The meetings were not just to mourn the sheikh but to press for political concessions from the British. The party met with their representatives and passed a resolution to protest against the proposed legislative council. Only Sheikh Ibrahim Shanti, owner of *al-Diffa* newspaper, echoed al-Qassam's philosophy when he called on the crowd to prepare a holy war against the British and their Zionist allies.

Throughout early 1936, the Qassamites remained absent from the political arena, hiding in the hills and conducting armed attacks against British and Zionist targets. It was an alleged Qassamite attack which led to the chain of events that culminated in the Arab general strike of 1936 and the subsequent Palestinian revolt which lasted until 1939. During the 1936 rebellion the Qassamites conducted a campaign of assassination against mandate police officers and other Palestinians accused of land sales, arms trading and helping the Zionist cause. Although the British continued to portray Qassamite violence as wanton and Qassamites as ignorant pious followers of Sheikh Izz ad-Din, their role in the 1936 rebellion contradicts this. Unlike many of the rebel peasant bands that roved the country at this time, the Qassamites were dedicated to waging a political struggle. Indeed many believe that it was the example of Sheikh Izz ad-Din al-Qassam's death that ignited both the flame of the strike and the revolt. But although there is no doubt that al-Qassam's martyrdom set an example for the Palestinian people, it was not the sole reason for them to embrace such desperate measures. British intransigence was equally responsible for the turn of events. The British throughout 1935 and early 1936 had consistently stalled on the issue of dealing with the two most fundamental of Palestinian demands: Jewish immigration and the proposal for a legislative council. The secular–nationalist leadership had tried to wrest concessions from them, at the same time calling for restraint among more radical elements in society. By April 1936, however, it was clear that nothing truly meaningful had been achieved.

On 13 April 1936 Israel Khazan, a Jewish immigrant, was killed by Qassamites. Following Khazan's funeral in Tel Aviv, fighting broke out between Jews and Arabs. On 20 April, Arab leaders in Jaffa called for a general strike to be observed by all Palestinians to protest against British policy. Over the next few days the strike spread spontaneously through the country.

The role of the Qassamites in the peasant-based general strike of 1936, which lasted for six months, was significant in its intent rather than its size. Al-Qassam's followers were still living as fugitives in the rural areas and were now led by Sheikh Farhan Sa'adi, a retired Palestine police corporal. By the time the revolt had broken out in late 1936 there was plenty of evidence that Qassamites were involved in the protest and that their members were leading attacks by rebel peasant bands. Qassamites were:

> prominent in the propaganda meetings in which the peasants were called to join the revolt ... and also in acts of terror against those Arabs who were not considered nationalistic enough or disregarded the strike.[18]

Their religious conviction, and activist background, in the nascent Palestinian labour movement provided them with the credentials to convince many in the peasant class to subscribe to their strategy. They were never strong enough logistically, however, to transform the revolt into a total jihad with the goal of creating an Islamic state. They were, though, ascribed a role in the internecine killing that destroyed the Palestinian revolt from within. In this respect, by meting out punishment to Palestinian collaborators, they 'contributed heavily to the rebellious disintegration from within and caused the accumulation of a terrible blood debt in the Arab community'.[19]

The subsequent decline of Qassamite influence in the revolt was preceded by the infamous capture, and later trial, of Sheikh Farhan Sa'adi on 22 November 1937. Sheikh Farhan was the first Palestinian to be tried under new British defence regulations that allowed for defendants to be tried in a military court with the possibility of the death sentence being passed. On 24 November, just two days after his capture, the military court was convened in Haifa. A day later he was found guilty of carrying arms and sentenced to death by hanging.

The execution took place on the morning of 27 November at Acre prison, seventy-two hours after the sentence had been passed. Palestinians throughout the country, particularly in the north, protested against the execution. Strikes were called in Nablus and other towns and demonstrations organised at which eulogies to Sheikh Farhan were read.

The experiences of Sheikh Izz ad-Din al-Qassam in Palestine, his philosophy and the community he worked in, all provide a powerful contrast to Palestine's most prominent Islamic leader of the time, the mufti of Jerusalem, Haj Amin al-Husseini. The two men's approach to the practice of politics under the rubric of Islam and to the developing theology and ideology of Islamic modernism was often diametrically opposed. Their constituency was broadly the same but, as the mufti of Jerusalem, al-Husseini was officially responsible for the welfare of the whole of Palestine's Muslim population. The complexity of the task facing al-Husseini was overwhelming and his role was often the target of criticism. Sheikh Izz ad-Din al-Qassam's popularity among the rural and newly urbanised classes of Palestine undermined the mufti's legitimacy and highlighted the growing disparities between institutional Islam, tied as it was to notable families and landowning interests, and the Palestinian mass whose traditional bonds of fealty wilted under British and Zionist incursion.

Haj Amin al-Husseini:
Mufti of Jerusalem

Amin al-Husseini was born into one of Palestine's most important and noble families. Part of the provincial aristocracy, the al-Husseini family had enjoyed a special relationship with the Ottoman authorities. Through their trading business the family had representatives throughout Palestine. They had benefited from their position as agents for the Ottomans through the appointments bestowed on various male family members. Haj Amin al-Husseini's father and half-brother had also occupied the office of Mufti of Jerusalem, a powerful position which, besides its religious significance, had important political dimensions.

From his birth Amin was destined to assume the mantle of mufti. In preparation for this onerous task his early years were given over to religious training and military service. Like Sheikh Izz ad-Din, al-Husseini received his religious training in Cairo and the period he spent there was important for the young man. Like al-Qassam, Amin al-Husseini fell under the influence of Rashid Rida. As well as studying under Rida, Amin forged a close friendship with his mentor that would last for many years. Rashid Rida often visited the al-Husseini household 'where he took a special interest in Amin and frequently invited him to his home in Cairo'.[20] Rida also went as far as supporting Amin al-Husseini's policies in his journal, *al-Manar*. Amin was obviously influenced by Rida. As a young and impressionable Muslim student he could not have failed to have imbibed Rida's *salafi* approach.

While it is true that both al-Qassam and al-Husseini were affected by the modernist reformist trend sweeping Islamic politics and helping to inspire the formation of groups such as the Muslim Brotherhood in Egypt, both men often expressed completely different approaches to the issue of the need to reform Islam, namely a return to the fundamentals of faith. Theory might be common to them but strategy was not. One explanation for these differing approaches can be found in the changes within Rida's own thinking that occurred in the latter stages of his life and career. While it has been noted that Rida was critical of the traditional institutional forces of Islam such as the ulama and advocated a modernist approach, in later life, particularly following the increasing secularisation of Egyptian society and the pan-Islamic modernist movement, Rida was attracted increasingly to the conservative establishment he had formerly berated. As Esposito notes:

> Rida's primary commitment to an Islamic state and society increasingly made him less amenable to more secular-oriented modernists than to the religious establishment whose backwardness he had earlier criticised.[21]

Here one finds an explanation for the seemingly contradictory influences of Rida in the policies and philosophies of both al-Qassam and al-Husseini. Yet al-Husseini's commitment to modernist Islam did not always coincide with his pragmatic political nature. Al-Husseini was also the subject of considerable pressure from within the ruling elite and his powerful extended family. He was not an unadulterated follower of Rida's philosophy, and there were times in his political career as an Islamic leader when he appeared to represent everything about Islam and its increasing secularisation and decline under Western influence that Rida abhorred.

Britain's Mufti?

Haj Amin al-Husseini was a relatively young man when he was appointed to the office of Mufti of Jerusalem on 10 May 1921 by the British administration. At twenty-six years old he succeeded to the office earlier than anyone expected, following the sudden death of his half-brother Kamal who had previously held the post. The office of mufti gave Haj Amin al-Husseini 'control over Muslim courts, schools, religious endowments (waqfs), mosques, and an annual revenue of Palestine pounds 50,000'.[22] Haj Amin became the most powerful man in Palestine. This power, however, was ultimately controlled by the British, who bestowed religious and therefore political authority on the al-Husseini family as part of their continuing strategy of building up alliances among the indigenous landowning elite. As Migdal notes, this policy 'reinforced the elite that was already entrenched on the strength of its social and economic characteristics'.[23] Britain's paternalistic control over the appointment process could be used either to appoint or replace candidates of their choosing. Palestinian control was in this way circumscribed by British interests and policies.

Through his position Haj Amin, with the blessing of the British, was able to play a pivotal role in the course of Palestinian nationalist politics. He sought eventually to combine his religious role with his political position in the burgeoning arena of Palestinian nationalist agitation. From 1921 to 1929 he concentrated on building up a base of support in the country. The al-Husseini family was determined to maintain its powerful position, secure the loyalty of its tenants on the large tracts of land that it owned and head off political competition posed by the Nashashibi family and the Arab Executive Committee. Al-Husseini achieved his ends in a number of ways, but principally by using his religious status to pursue his own and his family's political agenda. There is no doubt that Haj Amin capitalised on his religious position.

In 1921 the British also created a new institution, the Supreme Muslim Council (SMC), and a year later they appointed Haj Amin its president. The appointment gave him complete control over Muslim affairs in the country and left the British with none. Kupferschmidt notes that the appointment was not because 'of his erudition in Muslim jurisprudence but because of political reasons'.[24] The SMC became an important political as well as religious forum for the Palestinians, thus it also came to be dominated by the conflict between the notable families and their incessant power struggles. In this environment it was virtually impossible for the forces of either secular nationalism or political Islam to respond to the political changes in society demanded by the colonial situation and the creation of a Zionist homeland. Through the SMC the mufti was able to appoint his supporters throughout the country to posts associated with the council, as Kupferschmidt remarks, the Nasha-shibis, 'had directed fierce criticism at Haj Amin and the al-Husseinis in general for having turned the SMC into a partisan instrument'.[25] The Nashashibis, for their part, had concentrated their efforts on securing power in the newly-founded secular national movement. Through political parties like the Arab Democratic party and the Istiqlal party, the Nashashibis along with other notable families set out to undermine the al-Husseinis' influence. This competition for power led to disunity in the face of the real challenge mounted by the Zionist incursion and the increasingly authoritarian nature of the mandate authorities. The lack of faith in the Palestinian leadership engendered by this conflict is reflected in a 1930 newspaper report which stated, 'an Arab village shall tomorrow be a Jewish one. Where is the [Supreme] Muslim Council? Where is the Arab executive?'.[26]

Nevertheless, through his large family system and his power over institutional Islam in the Waqf, Shari'a courts and SMC, Haj Amin built up a base of support, albeit a flawed one (dependent as it was on traditional ties of clan, religion and family rather than the new realities of a rapidly changing society). His relations with the British were of particular importance to him in this enterprise. Haj Amin enjoyed a close relationship with Sir Herbert Samuel and his successor Arthur Wauchope. The British felt that the mufti was a diplomatic character who could be depended upon to represent the Palestinian case with moderation. He was a man with whom they felt comfortable.

By 1929, however, the foundations of this relationship had already been shaken by rioting that broke out between Jewish and Muslim worshippers near the Haram al-Sharif compound and the Western Wall in Jerusalem. In the troubles that followed in Jerusalem, Hebron and Safad, a number of Jews were killed by Muslim rioters. The Zionists blamed the mufti for the outbreak of violence, claiming that he had encouraged the riots. It was not until the Shaw Commission, sent to investigate the cause of the disturbances, found 'no solid evidence to implicate al-Husseini in organising the outbreaks of 23 August 1929' that he was cleared of any involvement in inciting the rioters.[27]

By 1931 Haj Amin had decided on a policy of publicising the increasingly bleak plight of the Palestinians to the rest of the Muslim community. With the support of a number of other Muslim leaders, including the Lebanese Druze, Sheikh Shawqat Ali, he organised the first General Islamic Congress which was held in Jerusalem in December. The motive behind this step was highly ambitious. To the mufti's own way of thinking the congress would tend to strengthen the hands of the Palestinians *vis-à-vis* Zionism and the mandate and at the same time consolidate his own political over-lordship in the country and his prestige in the Islamic world.[28] The congress was well attended and did highlight the Palestinian cause as a religious issue; but its long-term effects were less palpable. As Kayyali notes: 'The euphoria created by the Congress was somewhat deceptive as no great material advantage was reaped by the Palestinians later on.'[29]

Throughout the early 1930s, as peasants were increasingly confronted with dispossession, the mufti was faced with dealing with the demands of a growing and politicised popular movement that wanted strong Palestinian leadership in response to British and Zionist claims. His dilemma was how to respond to popular discontent and yet satisfy the British authorities that he was still intent on preserving the peace and maintaining control. His response reflected his own illusions about the power of institutional Islam and his failure to understand the changes taking place in Palestinian society and their effects on the configuration of power in it.

Institutional Islam

In January 1935 Haj Amin organised an unprecedented meeting of 500 religious notables in Jerusalem to discuss the most pressing issues of the moment: the continued sale of land to Jewish immigrants, the problem of Jewish immigration itself and the inability or unwillingness of the British authorities to halt the process. The meeting, bringing together the many appointees of the al-Husseini family and connected clans, was the first and last attempt by institutional Islam to respond politically to the situation in Palestine. The ulama and clerics of the vast institutionalised network built up under the mandate authorities were, however, increasingly without legitimacy within the community, and this became all too apparent in the events that followed this momentous occasion.

The meeting was a milestone in terms of religious protest against the political situation, and delegates travelled from all over Palestine to attend. In his role as president of the SMC and Mufti of Jerusalem, Haj Amin presided over the proceedings and delivered an important speech. The transcript of this lengthy oration was published widely in the Arabic press. It addressed a number of important themes, including the abandonment by Palestinians of Islam, their consequent weakness in the face of opposition, and the obligations of religious leaders to set an example and guide Muslims along the straight path. Here the resonance of modernist thinking finally surfaced. Haj Amin's public appeals, however, were undermined by the fact that they should have been directed to the members of his own class, namely the ulama and notable families who were engaged in the very land sales contributing to the dispossession of the peasant population. In conclusion, Haj Amin called on the assembled clergy to stop the sale of Palestinian land to the Zionists by threatening religious sanctions against the vendors. The following excerpts from the speech highlight these points:

> If morals remain, morals make nations, But if morals die, nations die ... There is a terrible spirit of nihilism and apostasy attacking the country ... some of our youths are not paying attention to religion and morals. They decorate themselves and behave like women ... Gentlemen, if you do not prevent the treacherous brokers and sellers, who is to prevent them? If you are not the leaders, who are they?[30]

The impact of the speech on the assembled clergy was apparent almost immediately. Within days a *fatwa* was issued against brokers, mediators and sellers of land to Jews. The *fatwa* declared that the brokers of land were enemies of Islam and the Prophet Mohammad, that they would not be accorded religious rights of burial in Muslim cemeteries and that they should be 'neglected, boycotted and humiliated; they should not be made friends with or approached ... Believers, do not take your parents and brothers as guardians if they prefer heresy to faith. He who supports them is an oppressor.'[31] The *fatwa*, however, proved worthless and went unheeded. The political power of the institutional ulama proved ineffective in the face of the political realities on the ground.

By the spring of 1935, popular opinion, particularly as expressed in the pro-nationalist Palestinian press, had began to turn against the mufti. He was criticised for his pro-British stance and his inability to effect meaningful political change. This campaign was orchestrated by the growing secular–nationalist movement still under the influence of notable families like the Nashashibis and Abdel-Hadis. It is difficult, therefore, to make a distinction between real frustration at the political situation, combined with the failure of institutional Islam to respond to political change, and the highly personalised nature of politics in Palestine at this time. The campaign resulted in a period of change. High Commissioner Wauchope alerted the Foreign and Colonial Office in London to the gathering storm clouds but continued to affirm blind faith in Haj Amin's loyalty to the British:

> The press campaign against Haj Amin grows in noise, volume and violence ... I have noticed no change in Haj Amin's attitude towards this government ... But, there are of course plenty of extremists on both sides very hostile and always ready to embarrass the government.[32]

The British were nevertheless alarmed by the hostile atmosphere. Even dignitaries like Sheikh Shakid Arslan complained that Haj Amin was soft with the British and berated him for not taking a more opposition stand. Wauchope even noted in his reports to London that during one of his frequent meetings with Haj Amin the latter advised him to start wearing a bullet-proof jacket!

The Palestinian Revolt and the Failure of Institutional Islam

Haj Amin al-Husseini played no part in the events preceding the outbreak of the Palestinian revolt and general strike in 1936. He would not easily be persuaded to give up his policy of moderation and diplomacy with the British. He had invested much of his political credit with his people in his ability to persuade them that he had the ear of the British and could obtain concessions regarding Jewish immigration, land sales and Palestinian legislative representation. Even when it was clear that the strike would be long-term and that the revolt, largely rural in nature, would continue, the mufti tried to hang on to the last vestiges of prestige which he had attained, before eventually being forced to side with the leaders of the revolt. This policy is hard to understand. By siding with the British Haj Amin risked alienating the peasant mass which both he and his large family network depended on for their immense political power. The al-Husseinis had built power on land ownership and now Haj Amin seemed willing to risk it all in a gamble for continued personal influence.

The notables and the representatives of institutional Islam did not take the lead in the strike. Eventually the strike committee leaders came to Jerusalem to ask the Palestinian political parties to supervise their efforts. They suggested also that Haj Amin form and preside over a national committee.[33] But the reluctance of the established leadership persisted even in the face of these requests: 'Arab leaders knew that the strike and disturbances were highly destructive to the national movement and at times wished they could be stopped.'[34]

Indeed the mufti's part in encouraging or helping to initiate the events of early April 1936 was marginal. Even after he assumed a public role in the events, Haj Amin acted as a moderate Islamic influence rather than a radical one, yet, like King Canute, he could not turn back the tide that was working against him. He capitulated on 26 April 1936 when, following a meeting in Jerusalem attended by representatives of the strike committee, it was announced that the strike would continue and that Haj Amin would be president of the strike council of the Higher Arab Committee (HAC). The HAC would act as an umbrella organisation for all political factions and would encourage internal political disputes to be put aside for the greater goal of the strike.

Haj Amin was forced by circumstance rather than political conviction to go along with majority sentiment. In siding with his people the mufti forfeited his relationship with the British. In May 1936, at a meeting of the HAC, he proposed that Palestinians undertake acts of civil disobedience, such as refusing to pay taxes, to protest against government suppression of the strike. He gave his full support to this aspect of the campaign. 'The Jews are trying to expel us from the country, they are murdering our sons and burning our houses,' he argued. He called upon people to give the strike their fullest support, and to continue until it proved successful.[35] Subsequently he travelled the country speaking at rallies and meetings in support of the strike, praising the people's determination and the sacrifices they were making. He made it clear that he would remain steadfast until their demands were satisfied.

Popular opinion, however, was not satisfied that the mufti was leading in the best way. While scores of strike leaders were being arrested, placed in detention camps, exiled or even deported, the mufti remained in office as the symbol of all Islamic power in Palestine and the accompanying institutions continued to work as normal. In June 1936 youths from Nablus, a strike stronghold, sent a telegram to the mufti urging him to 'suspend all activities' and reminding him that his duty as a religious leader was to place himself at the head of those sacrificing their lives. Messages and deputations, reiterating this call, resulted in the mufti capitulating to popular opinion. By the end of June 1936 'the Mufti finally asked the sheikhs and preachers to arouse Muslim feeling in the name of Islam to support and join the mujahidin.'[36]

At this point the mufti began to emphasise a religious message, claiming that religious issues were at the heart of strike demands. He subsequently submitted a statement to the British High Commissioner for transmission to the Colonial Office, outlining his position as leader of the Muslim community:

> In the continuance of the present policy the SMC sees a danger both to the existence of the Arabs in Palestine and Muslim holy places including al-Aqsa. The idea of establishing a Jewish national home is primarily a religious idea ... Arabs will not accept in any form a Jewish national home in this Muslim Arab country, nor will they consent to the immigration of Jews, which endangers the Arabs existence.[37]

The mufti also complained to the government that the sanctity of mosques was being disregarded by the British troops sent to quell the disturbances and that the Shari'a courts in Nablus had been converted into military barracks. There is no doubt that by this point the mufti was using his religious position to claim leadership of the strike. He used the religious notion of Jewish usurpation and the spectre of the raising of a 'third temple' at the al-Aqsa site to rally the Muslim masses and communicate to the British government the need speedily to resolve the issue.

The British, for their part, had promised (in July 1936) that a commission would be sent to investigate Arab complaints. The full terms of reference were not yet specified and no announcement was made regarding the suspension of Jewish immigration. The commission would be headed by Earl Peel. It was also decided that the time had come to dispose of Haj Amin al-Husseini. He had served his purpose and in turning against the British had signed his own inevitable warrant for arrest.

Left in Exile: the Mufti Banished

By the end of September 1937 the game was up for the Mufti of Jerusalem. The British, in their desperate attempts to quell the revolt, moved against existing Palestinian institutions including the SMC, the HAC and the national strike committees. The British authorities, commenting in their colonial reports, had decided that the most influential Muslim in Palestine, Haj Amin al-Husseini, was working against British interests. Haj Amin was summoned to Government House and dismissed from the presidency of the SMC and other religious committees including that of the Waqf. It was inevitable that he would be arrested as part of the British crackdown, but before the British could lay their hands on him, Haj Amin and some of his colleagues escaped from Palestine, settling eventually in Lebanon.

Had the British overestimated the influence and power wielded by Haj Amin al-Husseini during this period? A case may certainly be made for this argument. After all the mufti had already proved himself hopelessly out of touch with the Palestinian community and had subscribed to the revolt only after considerable pressure had been exerted on him. The legitimacy of his leadership had already been tarnished by his inability to marshal the Muslim community through the *fatwa* to stop land sales to the Jews. His control over the institutions of Islam was used predominantly to maintain traditional lines of power based on the rule of the notable families. The same was true of the power of other notable families, which by 1939 had mostly left the country (either voluntarily or through deportation), leaving the Palestinian community virtually leaderless.

The revolt in Palestine continued but by 1938 had degenerated into increasingly internecine conflict, destroying previous gains made against the British and the Zionists. By 1939 and the eve of the Second World War the Palestinian revolt had all but fizzled out, its internal momentum lost, the will to struggle sapped. Haj Amin was publicly both lauded and reviled for his contribution to the cause. As Stein points out: 'embedded in the ... revolt were a variety of disparate components, including racial, religious, anti-colonial, anti-Zionist and familial factors.'[38]

Political Islam: a New Trend?

The final decade of British rule in Palestine witnessed further decline in Palestinian fortunes. The Second World War ended in victory for Britain but undermined its position as a colonial power in the post-war order. Palestinian calls for independence were futile in the face of Western guilt over the Holocaust.

For its part, political Islam in Palestine had offered both hope and bitter disappointment. By 1948 the leadership of both institutional and modernist Islam was in exile and the Muslim community was leaderless. The mufti remained in exile, having forged dangerous and disastrous alliances with Nazi Germany. Institutional Islam, through the Waqf and Shari'a courts, schools and other religious foundations, was weak and ineffective. The majority of Qassamites had either fled the country or been imprisoned. The Qassamite movement died out and with it the modernist Salafiyya attempt to make sense of the Palestinian question.

There were, however, some grounds for hope. Through the Muslim Brotherhood movement, political Islam had created new if rather tender roots in Palestine. The Muslim Brotherhood, founded in Egypt in 1928 by Hassan al-Banna, was a movement of political Islam committed to a reformist approach. The leadership of the brotherhood in Egypt, alert to the gathering crisis in Palestine, pledged its support to the Palestinians. The brotherhood regarded Palestine an as important issue because the third most holy site in Islam was located in Jerusalem. An attempt by the Zionists to create a state on land which the brotherhood considered holy in the most literal sense would never be acceptable. However, according to the reformist perspective of the organisation the situation in Palestine had been brought about largely because Palestinian Muslims had abandoned their faith. The brotherhood argued that a process of Islamic revival was imperative for the land to be saved from infidel intruders. Thus, jihad would follow the revival of Islamic life in the country. The objective of the jihad would be the establishment of an Islamic state, and a resurrected caliphate. The brotherhood's strategy included the staging of rallies and meetings in Egypt to discuss the Palestine issue, a commitment to provide troops to wage jihad against the Zionists, fund-raising projects and the publication of books and leaflets on the subject. In October 1945 the Muslim Brotherhood sent emissaries to establish new branches in the towns of Jerusalem, Nablus, Gaza and Haifa.

The establishment of new branches attracted members from the local Muslim community and in particular appealed to the leaderless ulama of institutional Islam. In particular, clergy from the notable families were among the first to join the Jerusalem branch of the brotherhood when it was opened in 1946. Jamal al-Husseini, Mohammad Ali Ja'abri, Nimr al-Hatib and Zafir al-Dajani, all appeared on the membership rolls. According to Mayer, by 1947 there were twenty-five branches of the brotherhood in Palestine, with membership estimated at 'between 12,000 and 20,000'.[39] The local branches in Palestine acted as a conduit for the mother organisation in Cairo. Local branches at this stage were charged with disseminating the message of the brotherhood as widely as possible. This message was simple yet powerful:

> to spread and teach the values of the Qur'an, endeavour to achieve higher standards of living, to fight against poverty and illiteracy, and participate in the construction of human civilisation according to the spirit of Islam'.[40]

The branches in Palestine, however, held no real power. Decision-making still took place in Cairo, policy was formulated there and strategy transmitted to the satellite branches. This centralisation of power ultimately left the Palestinian branches of the brotherhood weak in the face of the upheaval wrought by the United Nations partition of Palestine and subsequent Arab–Israeli war of 1948–49.

An example of this centralised decision-making can be found in the issue of organising mujahidin for the inevitable conflict between Arab and Zionist in Palestine. Instead of encouraging and supporting local branches in an attempt to marshal a fighting force within Palestine in the autumn of 1947 Hassan al-Banna 'ordered the branches of the Society to start preparing for jihad'.[41] By October the first fighting forces appeared in Cairo and were subsequently sent to the Egyptian border with Palestine. The brotherhood did wage a limited jihad against the Zionists but the armed campaign was not organised from within. Its volunteer ranks were predominately Egyptian and the Palestine-based branch do not even appear to have been encouraged in intelligence-gathering operations or forms of logistical support. This left the organisation in Palestine isolated and weak in the face of Israel's first military victory against the Arabs.

The ensuing Arabisation of the conflict hastened the decline of political Islam in Palestine which had been harnessed during the mandate period by figures like Sheikh Izz ad-Din al-Qassam and Haj Amin al-Husseini. Yet even by this early period it was already clear that the Palestinian–Islamic political trend would always interact with the dynamic of nationalism, in both its pan-Arab and Palestinian form. This interaction would not always be characterised by harmony but it would highlight the unique relationship between the political forces of Islam and nationalism in the Palestinian context.

Conclusion

There is no doubt that political Islam under the British mandate represented a diverse force. Its heterogeneous nature was reflected in both institutional and modernist salafi Islamic responses apparent through the examination of individual leaders and movements such as Sheikh Izz ad-Din al-Qassam, the Qassamites, Haj Amin al-Husseini and the al-Husseini family.

Institutional Islam represented by Haj Amin al-Husseini and his supporters denotes the most enduring example of political Islam in Palestine. It reflected largely the current ordinance of power, as it continued to do through the subsequent Jordanian rule of the West Bank (1948–67). In terms of translating Islamic political ideas into a mobilising force among the Muslim community institutional Islam failed. It was, and remains, weak and symbolic. It is a legitimator of ruling interests; the *ulama* are largely apolitical and occupied chiefly with maintaining the influence of Islam and the notable families in a society undergoing fragmentation, upheaval and disintegration.

Al-Qassam's impact was an example for future generations. His brand of political Islam appealed to the popular mass, its radical message finding a receptive audience among Palestine's new social and political classes. Following his death, his philosophy, sustained by memories of his charismatic personality, became submerged in the general disintegration of society during the years of Palestinian revolt. Nevertheless, the impact of his ideas made the message of new organisations like the Muslim Brotherhood and the Islamic Liberation Party easier to represent to the Palestinians. In addition, Izz ad-Din's example, his courage, call to jihad and work among the Palestinian peasant and working classes has inspired the present-day Islamist organisations such as Islamic Jihad. It is even claimed that Islamic Jihad was founded as a present-day response to Sheikh Izz ad-Din al-Qassam's jihad to protect the holy land of Palestine and its Muslim inhabitants from the forces of colonialism. The message of al-Qassam lives on in the refugee camps of the Gaza Strip and the West Bank. It has galvanised the Islamic movement, encouraging Palestinians, in the name of jihad, down a path of political violence to liberate Palestine from Israeli rule and establish an Islamic state.

Turbulent Times: 1948–67 in the West Bank and Gaza Strip

The Division of Palestine

The war of 1948 resulted in a humiliating defeat for the Arab armies at the hands of the Zionists. The territory that had not been lost to the new state of Israel came under the control of either the Jordanian government who formally annexed the West Bank, or Egypt, which placed the Gaza Strip under military administration. The Palestinians living in captured areas became refugees, and over 300,000 fled their homes and lands for Jordan, Lebanon, Syria, Iraq and Egypt.[1] The war had also compounded the virtual dissolution of the Palestinian political community. The Palestinians who remained in what became known as the West Bank and the Gaza Strip, faced the huge task of rebuilding their society.

The political framework of both the Jordanian and Egyptian administrations was each a reflection, not of the needs of the Palestinian community, but of the respective political orientations and agendas of King Farouq and Gamal Abdel Nasser of Egypt, and King Abdullah and later King Hussein of Jordan. These agendas were often in competition with one another. If Nasser's rule over the Gaza Strip was characterised by the increasing secularisation of society and the rise of both Arab nationalism and Nasserism in politics, then the opposite was true in the West Bank. Both Jordan and Egypt had fought in the 1948 war, but this did not necessarily make them allies over the Palestinian issue. Rather this period saw the subjugation of the Palestinian cause under the wing of Arab nationalism and inter–Arab state competition for hegemony over the area.

For political Islam the control of the very different Egyptian and Jordanian regimes meant that this period would become one of mixed and diverse fortunes with new organisations and activities apparent in the Gaza Strip and West Bank. While the Muslim Brotherhood in the West Bank flourished and new groups, in particular the Liberation Party (Hizb Tahrir), were established, in the Gaza Strip the revival of the Muslim Brotherhood was decimated as a result of Nasser's hostility to political Islam.

The period after the 1948 débâcle was crucial in forging a Palestinian concept of nationalism. Palestinian nationalist ideology bound the community together and played a major part in determining its collective decision to remain in those parts of Palestine that had not fallen to Israel. The concept of nationalism, as it had developed by this stage, was instrumental in keeping a sense of Palestinian nationhood alive, shaping the identity of the Palestinian people through their culture, historical heritage and common roots.

With military defeat, Islamic politics in Palestine entered a period of considerable change. The leadership of institutional Islam was still largely absent. The existing offices of Islam, such as the Waqf and Muslim councils, which the Palestinians had controlled under the mandate, were placed under the authority of either the Jordanian or Egyptian state structure.[2] Even the custodianship of the Muslim holy places was placed under the control of the Jordanian Ministry for Religious Affairs. In addition the SMC created in Palestine by the British was formally abolished by Jordan in 1951. The *waqf* system was riven asunder by the geographical break-up of the country.

The political message of Islam was also severely dissipated in the face of the Zionist victory. The forces of Islam had already been weakened before the war and during it they were unable, despite promises of a jihad, to mount an internal challenge. The Muslim Brotherhood, with the exception of a few battalions from Egypt, never produced the army of men it claimed was ready to wage jihad and die as martyrs. After so much rhetoric a sense of disillusion must have set in among the remaining, leaderless members of the brotherhood which had proffered a military solution against Zionism but failed on the battlefield.

The Islamic movement, the system of Islamic politics that had built up so rapidly during the final two decades of the British mandate, had not prepared its members and supporters for the possibility that the holy soil of Palestine would be wrested from their hands by the infidels. The movement had thus to face new realities. How had the Holy Land, the land visited by the Prophet and captured by Abu Bakr and Saladin, fallen into the hands of non-Muslims? What was the nature of Palestinian Islamic society under the Arab rule of Egypt and Jordan, and what would be the future of the Islamic movement?

The Gaza Strip on the Eve of War

Life in Gaza before the War: Family Factions and Frictions

Before the 1948 war the Gaza district, which included the towns of Gaza, Khan Yunis, Beersheba and a large number of villages,[3] was relatively neglected by the British mandate government. The district of Gaza was 'one of the poorest areas in the country'.[4] Although the port provided an important outlet for local trade it was limited in its use. The economy was primarily based on agriculture, supplying in particular the burgeoning trade in citrus products that had sprung up during the mandate. Industry was very small-scale and based on a few artisan skills such as Gaza black pottery, the manufacture of cloth and carpet-weaving. Unemployment was always a major feature of this region, leaving many families impoverished. Traditional and conservative mores and values dominated the lives of Gaza's inhabitants. Religion was not politicised to the extent that it had been, for example, in the north of Palestine, particularly in Haifa. Religious practice was mostly a personal affair with the community celebrating feast days and engaged in Islamic folk-practices.

A few important and notable Palestinian families had laid roots in Gaza, mainly as a result of the trading links that the location afforded. These links were important during the Ottoman period when some of these families acquired status in return for administering the collection of tithes and taxes on behalf of the Ottoman rulers. The names most frequently associated with political and economic power were Husseini and Shawwa but there were others whose influence was more localised. In Khan Yunis, the al-Agha and Farrah families had long vied with each other for positions of importance in the municipal council, while the Sha'ban family was closely associated with the *waqf* system and so was engaged in the upkeep of mosques and Islamic sites as well as the administration of alms to the poor. Directives regarding holy places and the appointment of preachers or teachers for Islamic institutions were issued from the SMC in Jerusalem which under the mandate was dominated by the Husseini family and its supporters.

Local politics in the Gaza area centred on a seemingly eternal, often bitter competition between the notable families for power in local institutions like the municipality. This struggle continued even through the years of the general strike and the revolt (1936–39). As one British official noted during the last year of the revolt: 'There is endless friction between the families of Khan Yunis. It centres particularly in the competition between the al-Agha and Farrah for the post of mayor.'[5]

Institutional Islamic politics in Gaza were, as in the rest of Palestine, centred on the support of or opposition to the mufti and his Husseini faction. The pro-Husseini faction included Mousa Sourani, Rageb Abu Ramadan, Abdel Haq Abu Sha'ban, Ahmad al-Agha, Abdel Rahman al-Farrah from Khan Yunis and Sheikh Mohammad Awwad from Faluja, all of whom served on the Islamic Council (Majlis al-Islami) and helped promote the mufti's Arab party.[6] Through this support, local patronage of these landed families was preserved and power remained in their hands.

Of the six political parties active in Gaza at this time the mufti's party 'had more effect'. It was popular and gained much of its support through the promotion of its message in local mosques.[7] The mufti's supporters also played a leading role on the Gaza national strike committee in 1936. The strike committee thus included figures like Mousa Sourani, Fahmi al-Husseini, Hussein Kheil, Asim Basisou and Yousef Sayeh. Mousa Sourani, along with Fahmi al-Husseini and others, was imprisoned by the British and sent into exile in the village of al-Arish in the northern Sinai desert. Other members of the strike committee, including Adel Shawwa and his brother Rushdi, were supporters of the Nashashibis and the Defence party and maintained a close allegiance with the Jerusalem base.

Many of the Gaza notables were arrested or exiled by the British authorities during the revolt but were all released during the latter half of 1939 and early 1940 when the revolt was in its death throes. Gaza, like the rest of Palestine, remained relatively trouble-free throughout the 1940s and the notable families remained politically marginalised from the decision-making process. In Gaza, however, the full impact of the 1948 war was felt immediately, changing forever the social, political and economic fabric of the entire area.

The Muslim Brotherhood Gets a Foothold

Before the war of 1948 the Islamic movement was a relative newcomer to the political scene in Gaza, existing primarily in the form of local branches of the Muslim Brotherhood (Ikhwan al-Muslimin) established in 1946 by visiting emissaries from Egypt. The chief of these figures was Sheikh Abdel Muiz Abdel Sattar, the assistant instructor-general of the brotherhood in Cairo. The emissaries spent a considerable time in Palestine and played an important role in establishing the future direction of the brotherhood there, raising funds and directing policy after branches were founded in local districts. The organisation and ideology of the brotherhood in Gaza largely reflected those of the mother organisation in Cairo. The brotherhood adhered to its broadly reformist message, encouraging the community to maintain Islam as a primary focus of daily life and urging an interpretation of Islam as a modernising force. Revival was concentrated on the individual, through worship, education and study. The organisation in Gaza was as rigidly hierarchical as it was in Egypt with decision-making centralised in the hands of the spiritual elite; as a force for political Islam, its lack of independence, and the localised response to political change, left it weak and often powerless.

The brotherhood in Gaza quickly attracted members, estimated at around 500 by 1947. Among them were some of the area's most important political and economic figures. The Gaza branch, whose offices were located in the Rimal area of the town, figured as one of the more important brotherhood centres in Palestine, ranking alongside those of Jerusalem, Haifa, Jaffa, Nablus and Jenin. The movement's spiritual mentor, Hassan al-Banna even paid a visit to Gaza in 1947. Two Gaza representatives, Mohammad al-Taha and Abd al-Fatah Dukhan, were appointed, in December 1946 and January 1947 respectively, to regional committees that maintained the close links with Cairo. Their work involved frequent trips to Cairo and meetings with brotherhood representatives there.

The partition of Palestine and the internationalisation of Jerusalem by the UN in November 1947 meant that the Gaza branch soon became involved in Palestinian resistance to the plan, an active role in politics that it had not envisaged playing. Indeed, a localised role was the only one that the brotherhood could play as it became increasingly apparent that the Palestinian national leadership was unco-ordinated, disorganised and poorly prepared for what lay ahead. Muslim Brotherhood committees had, therefore, to act in the context of a splintered national community and in Gaza as well as a few other locations they worked alongside other Palestinian political groupings in an attempt to prepare the people for conflict. Their contribution did not go unrecognised. As one former member noted:

Before the Arab armies arrived on the scene the Muslim Brothers had created a presence for themselves. So from 1947 to 1948 the Ikhwan helped in the organisation of national committees, the Jihad Maqadas ... the Ikhwan came and helped in the Palestinian struggle.[8]

Dr Haider Abdel Shaffi, the prominent Palestinian leader and Gaza resident, noted the symbolism of the brotherhood's local contribution and even the appearance of mujahidin from Egypt during this period, remarking that:

As early as 1948 the Ikhwan supporters came to fight with the Palestinians in the war as a serious attempt to support the Palestinian issue, and many died on this soil.[9]

However, the co-ordination between the various Muslim Brotherhood branches that were active seems to have been limited, which is understandable given the relative infancy of the movement. The brotherhood joined forces with other groups because it was unable organisationally to take an independent stance – its membership was in the hundreds rather than the thousands – and it did not have the capacity to strike out on its own. The ties with Cairo had created a dependency that paradoxically both guided and shackled it once the time came for decisive and strong policy. Despite its popularity, the organisation could not compensate for a lack of infrastructure to support its grand schemes; in two years there was no time to build the mosques that might have sheltered refugees, nor the health services or welfare facilities to ameliorate the effects of war. Instead the Muslim Brotherhood in Palestine had a collection of leaflets, books and pamphlets and the promises of the brotherhood in Cairo to provide the mujahidin army waiting to wage a holy war against the Zionists. The Palestinian Muslim Brotherhood looked to its centre, its heart, in Cairo for direction and found it wanting.

When the war between the Arabs and the newly-founded state of Israel did break out the Muslim Brotherhood was able to make only a limited contribution to the battle. The massed ranks of the mujahidin never materialised, although a token force of Egyptian brothers, supported by Palestinians in Gaza and the southern area, did participate in early battles. In Palestine, the existing branches and members of the brotherhood were caught in the flight of the Palestinian community from towns and cities like Haifa, Jaffa and Majdal. The disintegration of society affected every political group leaving branches abandoned, leaders in exile and membership numbers depleted. No political organisation, even Islamic, remained untouched by the disaster that befell the Palestinian people in 1948.

The Gaza Strip after the 1948 War:
from Jihad to Jaw-Jaw

Following the 1948 war the indigenous population of Gaza, estimated at 60–80,000,[10] found itself coming to terms with an influx of 200,000 dispossessed Palestinians who had fled from towns and hundreds of villages. The land was barely large enough to provide a basic living for its original inhabitants let alone this new refugee population which instantly turned the Gaza Strip into one of the most densely populated regions in the world. Refugee camps were set up to provide basic shelter and amenities to thousands of homeless and penniless families, but the sand dunes and citrus groves could not sustain everyone.[11]

Both the indigenous and refugee populations had also to adjust to a change in the political administration of the area. The British were gone, the new state of Israel was on their doorstep and the Egyptians were now in charge. The Egyptians did not harbour any territorial ambitions *vis-à-vis* the Gaza area. With desert regions already making up thousands of square miles of Egypt, politicians in Cairo did not want to acquire yet more poor land, let alone land that housed a large refugee population. Yet rather than place political control directly in the hands of the Palestinian population, a military administration was established to bring order to the chaos in Gaza and the smaller towns of Rafah and Khan Yunis and to promote Egyptian rule over the area. Egyptian army personnel were placed in key civilian posts and took charge of maintaining security. Decisions were made in Cairo, and the Palestinians of the Gaza Strip were subject to the same laws as Egyptian citizens. The Egyptians did see a time in the future when the Palestinians would recapture their lands from the Israeli usurpers and control would be restored to them. But this was a long-term goal and it ignored the short-term realities of a population living under the control of a political administration not of its own making.

Under the Egyptians it was inevitable that internal Palestinian politics would change. A political distinction was very rapidly made between the refugee and indigenous populations. Tension between the two groups soon became apparent and was exacerbated by the co-option of leaders from the notable families by the Egyptian authorities. The Muslim Brotherhood also played its part, advertently or inadvertently, in widening the gap between the politicised refugee community and the ruling families and their supporters. By stepping into the breach left by Waqf authorities when the latter were unable to support the refugee community and provide welfare, it highlighted the weakness of institutional Islam in the face of new changes.[12]

Reaching the Refugees:
the Muslim Brotherhood in Gaza

The fortunes of the Muslim Brotherhood under the Egyptian administration were now inextricably tied to the centre in Egypt and became a reflection of the larger more established organisation. The brotherhood's fate was also tied to the fortunes of the prevailing political regime. This is not to say, however, that the Muslim Brotherhood in Gaza had no part in the development and articulation of local political issues affecting, in particular, the refugee community.

From 1948 to the early 1950s the brotherhood continued its pre-war activities and expanded, becoming popular in particular among the male youth as a result both of the part it had played in the 1948 war and of its vehemently anti-Israeli, anti-compromise stance. The movement represented something to which the dispossessed population could relate because it not only offered political slogans but also practised what it preached. The brotherhood thus became a political training-ground for many figures who would in later years rise to the apex of the Palestinian national resistance movement:

> After the state of Israel was formed in 1948, some of those who were to become Arafat's senior colleagues did join the Brotherhood for a while. Arafat did not, though he did make use of it.[13]

The new refugee camps were particularly fertile ground for the brotherhood. As one former member recalls: 'Every camp had a branch, plus the branches in Gaza and other places.'[14] By 1949–50 there were between ten and twelve branches in the Gaza Strip alone. The young boys, some as young as six and men who joined were recruited in the refugee schools by teachers who were already members or sympathisers. The membership rolls swelled quickly. In Nussierat camp alone there were more than 100 members by 1950. Joining the movement entailed participating in a ceremony wherein the would-be-member pledged an oath to the brotherhood and, placing his hand on the Qur'an, stated, 'I promise to be a good

Muslim defending Islam and the lost land of Palestine. I promise to be a good example to the community and others.'[15] There were no membership cards, no uniforms. 'We wore the same clothes that we wore to school or anywhere else for that matter, we were very poor, many were barefooted,' commented one former member. The increase in membership, however, appears to have been short-lived and, according to one former member, for very specific and pragmatic reasons:

> The poorest people are traditional people and conservative by nature and the defeat of 1948 was a great shock. There was a turning inwards. I myself joined the Muslim Brotherhood in 1949 (for a short period of time) but I joined not for deeply religious reasons but because of the political message offered by the brotherhood.[16]

By concentrating its activities in the refugee camps in the post-1948 period the brotherhood built a strong base of local and popular support, harnessing the energy of the young refugees and directing it to an Islamic agenda. The activities of the movement at this time took two directions: first religious study and some sports; and second a pseudo paramilitary programme where the rudiments of guerrilla training were passed on to the young recruits. Small study groups would meet on a regular basis at the homes of leaders or teachers. There the group would hear stories about the *hadith* (Islamic traditions) or the Qur'an or lectures on particular themes, including the recovery of Palestine. Young members were encouraged to attend festivals organised by the Muslim Brotherhood to celebrate particular Islamic events such as Eid al-Fitr at the end of Ramadan. Programmes of lectures were arranged, with speakers travelling from Egypt. Young refugees were also encouraged to join summer camps organised by the brotherhood locally where they would engage in 'sporting activities, like football, and treks around the country'.[17] The military training they received was basic, involving night marches and camping expeditions. The leaders of these units sometimes had arms acquired during the war but ammunition was very scarce. It was the sentiment that lay behind the military training that was important. The recruits were told that they were being prepared to be the soldiers of the future. As one member remarked:

> We were looking forward to the military struggle that would be waged to get our homeland back. The brotherhood believe in God and when they enter the war they are not afraid because they are armed by God's power,

understanding that if they died they would go to paradise and not hell. Alive or dead, then, it didn't matter.[18]

The leading lights of the Muslim Brotherhood by this time included Fathi Balawi, Riad Zanoun, Ismail al-Khalidi, Hani Basisou, Mohammad Taha, Abd al-Fatah Dukhan, Aziz ad-Din Taha, Salah Khalaf (Abu Iyad) and Khalil al-Wazir (Abu Jihad). Most of these new leaders were teachers in the schools that had been set up in the refugee camps, Fathi Balawi and Salah Khalaf, for example, taught in the Khalid Ibn Walid secondary school in Nussierat camp. They were popular with the boys they taught and were respected in the community. Their place in the school system was very important, giving them direct access to a young, enthusiastic and receptive audience. As one member, who was in his teens in the 1950s, pointed out: 'A great many (boys) were illiterate or ignorant and therefore the teachers played a very important educational role. They used the schools to recruit.'[19]

The leader of the ever-expanding brotherhood, Riad Zanoun, soon delegated power and devolved the organisation in Gaza into small units or groups which were referred to as families (*usra*). The heads of each group, usually a teacher or school student with secondary education, were called princes (*emirs*). These leaders were charged with imparting the religious message to members. The role of the families was paramount. As Abu Mohammad notes: 'All the activities of these families were religious in nature and religion was the principal reason for our being.'[20]

By the early 1950s it was increasingly clear that the brotherhood was seeking a dominant role in the politics of the Gaza Strip. Nevertheless, co-ordination between members of local branches was limited by the constraints imposed by the Egyptian military authorities and the leadership of the brotherhood in Cairo. Frequent communication between Gaza and Cairo was apparent and despite the activities of the young leaders was directed to the single goal outlined by the leadership: the retrieval of Palestine.

The brotherhood functioned during this period as an important and primary stepping stone for many politically active young men who saw the organisation as the only one representing shared values and ideals. Through its programme of involvement in the refugee community, its religious philosophy of encouraging the practice of Islam and its revival in a modern age, and the ideological call to liberate Palestine and establish an Islamic state, the brotherhood was the only political organisation of any substance. Its message, did, however, despite the rhetoric about liberation, remain broadly reformist, focusing on social regeneration and education.

The Muslim Brotherhood in Gaza was particularly affected by the coup of the Free Officer Movement in Egypt in July 1952. The coup, ultimately led by Gamal Abdel Nasser, brought down the monarchy in Egypt and led to the installation of the military in the highest posts of political power. From 1952 to 1967 the fortunes of the brotherhood in Gaza were entirely dependent on the policies formulated by Nasser to deal with the perceived threat the Muslim Brotherhood organisation posed to his nationalist–secularist regime. Nasser's relentless promotion of secular Arab nationalism as a vehicle for power, not just domestically but regionally, was formidable to any political opposition. In addition his unadulterated success at promoting Arab nationalism in the region resulted in a concurrent move away from alternative ideologies with Islamic foundations. Nasserism had a tremendous impact on the development of an ideological response to the establishment of the state of Israel in Palestine, to Zionism and also to the forces of conservative rule active in the region. The Palestinian community was enamoured of Nasser's rhetoric, believing that the united forces of the Arab world would deliver their land back to them. In the face of this sweeping phenomenon the Muslim Brotherhood in Gaza was ill-equipped to rise to Nasser's challenge.

Nasser and the Muslim Brotherhood

Following the coup in Egypt the Muslim Brotherhood went through a brief honeymoon period when it was allowed to operate more freely than it had done under the previous government of Prime Minister Nokrashky. Many prominent figures in the Free Officer Movement had been involved with it and formed close attachments to its organisation, which was one of the strongest political groups in Egypt. The brotherhood had in its turn supported Nasser and his comrades, believing that they would install a government sensitive to the needs of Islam. Right from the start of the revolution it 'reiterated pronouncements, publicly and also privately to the government, about the need for established government on the basis of Islam.'[21]

Rather than immediately antagonise the Muslim Brotherhood, Nasser led its members to believe that the same vision for Egypt was shared by the Free Officer Movement. He even offered the organisation three cabinet posts. The relationship, however, was a front and, combined with the underlying tension and conflict within the brotherhood itself following the assassination of Hassan al-Banna in 1949, the facade of cordiality was dropped within a year of the coup. In the summer of 1953 the brotherhood criticised the regime for its ties with the British. It was no surprise, therefore, when, in January 1954 the following notice was published in *al-Ahram* newspaper:

> The Revolution will not permit that a reactionary drama should be repeated in Egypt in the name of religion, and will not permit anyone to play with the fate of this country in order to satisfy private passions under whatever pretext. It will not permit the exploitation of religion in the service of vested interests.[22]

The proclamation ended by announcing that the Muslim Brotherhood should be dissolved by order of the revolution led by the Free Officers Movement. Throughout 1954 arrests of members of the organisation were carried out.

In September the Revolutionary Command Council (RCC) announced that prominent members of the Muslim Brotherhood would be stripped of their nationality and forced to leave the country. Among this number was one of the most significant figures the organisation's branches in Palestine and Jordan, Said Ramadan. The son-in-law of Hassan al-Banna, Said Ramadan had acted as an (goodwill) ambassador to the brotherhood in Palestine and from 1945 had helped to set up many of its branches. By the time he was stripped of his citizenship he was comptroller-general of the organisation in Egypt. Along with many other exiled brothers, Ramadan fled to Damascus, Jerusalem and then Jordan where they were all to play a significant role in the movement.[23]

The Attempt on Nasser's Life

On 8 October 1954 the Egyptian government announced the arrest of the Muslim Brotherhood's spiritual guide, Hassan Ismail al-Hudaiby. The move outraged and galvanised the movement's supporters, whose ranks had by this time swelled to thousands. The brotherhood's attempted retaliation came at the end of the month when, on 26 October 1954, an activist tried and failed to assassinate the president while he was on a visit to Alexandria. As Stephens notes, 'This attack gave Nasser an opportunity to strike a crippling blow at the Muslim Brotherhood, who had emerged as his most determined and dangerous opponents.'[24] The reaction of the authorities to the assassination attempt was swift, brutal and wholesale:

> Execution by hanging of five activists of the Muslim Brotherhood, was a culmination point in the present crisis of the Brotherhood, highlighted by its dissolution by government, the jailing of its leaders, detention of [thousands] of its members, the discovery of its large arms caches and prosecution on charge of attempted violent revolution.[25]

Around 18,000 members were arrested and imprisoned in the crackdown and the organisation was severely weakened as a result. The ideals of Nasserist secularism had triumphed temporarily, through the sheer use of force. The repression struck at the heart of Egyptian society, for the appeal of the Muslim Brotherhood had been widespread and the organisation popular with ordinary Egyptians. Nasser's repression could not, however, eradicate the movement. It simply forced it underground where it was to become a militant, radical and more potent force.

The impact of political change in Egypt was felt inevitably in Gaza. At a general level the influence of the military over the administration of the Gaza Strip was translated into a political monopoly with Gazans excluded completely from decision-making. For members of the Muslim Brotherhood the effects of Nasser's policy were severe. The clamp-down following the assassination attempt on the president was just as brutal in Gaza as in Egypt and from 1952–54 Gazan activists came under the scrutiny of the Egyptian military authorities. Leaders such as Riad Zanoun and Fathi Balawi were called in for questioning and sometimes detained. As one veteran Islamist from Gaza noted, 'The crackdown on the Brotherhood in Egypt meant that the Egyptian security forces in Gaza persecuted leaders and members alike and this resulted in large numbers of the movement being imprisoned or forced to leave.'[26]

At the time of the crackdown it was estimated that there were eleven branches of the brotherhood throughout the Gaza Strip with a total of approximately 1,000 members.[27] It was the policy of the Egyptian authorities to eradicate these branches and as in Egypt, the brotherhood was forced underground. In such circumstances the organisation's contacts with Cairo were difficult to maintain and its activities took on a very localised complexion. By 1955 the brotherhood in Gaza, as in Egypt, found itself in alignment with the communists who were also being persecuted by the Nasser regime.

Palestinian Protest

The political climate in Gaza changed under the rule of the Free Officers. It was noted of Gaza town that: 'Inevitably [it] has become more Egyptian in aspect than it used to be … pictures of Egyptian leaders hang in many of its shops and offices.'[28] Under the Egyptians, membership of the municipal and local councils was by appointment rather than free election. Any semblance of power placed in Palestinian hands was nothing more than a facade: 'Egyptian judges share the duties of jurisdiction with local jurists [but] the controlling administrative body has a majority of Egyptian members.'[29]

In the period following the crackdown on independent political life in the Gaza Strip the Egyptian authorities steadily disarmed the Palestinian population. The logic behind this policy was to stop the increasing number of border incidents between the Gaza area and Israel, which were a source of growing tension between the Israelis and Egyptians. Some attributed these incidents to the Fedayeen forces newly organised by the Egyptian army, others to dispossessed refugees who crept across the border to their former homes, gardens and fields. As one author wrote: 'The Gaza peasant cuts the barbed wire and returns to his fields to sow the wheat. He cuts the barbed wire again at harvest time. He returns with a bundle of wheat stalks and is shot dead on the wire. The next day it is proclaimed that an infiltrator has been killed.'[30]

The border incidents eventually provoked a sharp reaction from the Israelis who, in November 1954, bombed Breijj refugee camp. The attack left at least fifty dead and brought home to Palestinians the disastrous consequences of the disarming and just how defenceless they were. The militants in the Muslim Brotherhood were provoked into action and in co-operation with the communists played a part in organising the protests and demonstrations that followed throughout 1954–55. It is alleged that the communists made the initial overtures to individual leaders of the brotherhood, notably Fathi Balawi. According to another activist, 'Sheikh Izz ad-Din, a Muslim Brother who had been excited by a demonstration, gathered the elementary schoolchildren and led them in a march from Nussierat beach to Gaza beach. He was arrested.'[31] The demonstrations of 1954–55 were not so much against the Israeli attacks as an expression of anger at the Egyptian authorities for leaving the local Palestinian population without any arms to defend itself.

Tensions in Gaza intensified in the first months of 1955. Locally animosity towards the Egyptian authorities increased when a previously secret report concerning a plan to resettle refugees in the Sinai desert fell into the hands of the communists. The United Nations Relief and Works Agency-approved plan forwarded by the Egyptian authorities met with considerable resistance when the news was leaked locally. Through the framework of the Teachers Union, the communists, with support from the Muslim Brothers, organised refugee resistance to Nasser's resettlement plan. The brotherhood provided electoral support to the communists, allowing them to assume a majority in the union, while the communists printed secret pamphlets voicing their opposition to the rehabilitation scheme. The involvement of the Muslim Brotherhood in this issue led some to speculate that its protest was less a reflection of genuine concern about the resettlement plan than an opportunity to attack Nasserist policy: 'The Muslim Brotherhood took advantage of the demonstrations to reflect its opposition to Nasser *per se*, rather than the political issue at hand. It wasn't against the scheme, just against Nasser.'[32]

The protest against the resettlement plan coincided with an Israeli raid on 28 February 1955 against an Egyptian army camp near the Gaza city railway station. Forty Egyptians were killed and another thirty-one injured while thirteen Jews were wounded. The attack highlighted once again the vulnerability of the Palestinian population under Egyptian military protection. The motives for the Israeli attack appeared mixed:

> Some professed to believe that Israel hoped to provoke an Arab counterattack which would give it an excuse to fill out its borders, at least to the old frontiers of Palestine, before the Arabs could re-establish unity of action.[33]

Following the attack Israel was condemned by the UN and widespread demonstrations were reported throughout the Gaza Strip. The Egyptian authorities, unable to control the situation, imposed a curfew on the area. Colonel Salah Gohar, the director of Palestinian affairs for the Egyptian army, was reported to have remarked in an interview at the time that 'he could not blame the mood of the rioters but that the authorities were tracking "subversive elements" who infiltrated into the ranks of the refugees to exploit the situation and cause disorders.'[34] The Egyptians were, in other words, convinced that the 'infiltrators' were the communists and the brotherhood.

Despite the curfew, refugee leaders organised further protests and presented the Egyptian military governor, Abdullah Rafaat, with an ultimatum requesting arms and military training. In addition they demanded that the Egyptian authorities cancel the resettlement plan for the Sinai. The role of the communists and the Muslim Brotherhood in formalising these general feelings into specific and channelled political action indicated their strength of will in the face of severe political repression. The Egyptian authorities tried to enlist the help and support of local traditional leaders, notables and religious figures but the refugees' demand for action continued. After a week the authorities drew up a proclamation which stated that 'The Sinai project was no longer of substance and that the camps would be armed and general military conscription would be declared soon.'[35] The demonstrations had proved successful in eliciting a change of policy from Nasser: 'The demonstrations disturbed Nasser … To us it was clear cut, the only move we would make was back to our homes. Nasser realised that he had to consult us, work with us …'[36]

At the end of the protests the Egyptian authorities announced that no arrests would be made, but Nasser did not intend to allow the dangerous alliance between the Muslim Brothers and the communists to continue. The promises that were made to pacify the people of Gaza were easily broken. The refugee camps were never armed. Instead, Nasser allowed the establishment of Egyptian-supervised fedayeen camps and late in 1955 got the permission of King Hussein of Jordan to transfer 500 fedayeen from Gaza to the Hashemite kingdom. The Palestine Division, as it was called was commanded mostly by Egyptian officers and was insignificant militarily. The issue of general military conscription was never raised again.

Nasser was not prepared to let political stability in Gaza be threatened by the Muslim Brotherhood and the communists. On 9 March 1955 'the police raided the homes of communists, patriotic Muslims and even the independents'. According to one former local activist:

> No distinction was made between the arrests of Muslim Brothers or communists. The authorities sent us to prison in Egypt, they didn't care whether we were Muslim Brother or communist. I was in the same prison as Sayyid Qutb the famous Egyptian Muslim Brother.[37]

The Gaza Muslim Brotherhood was severely weakened as the Egyptian authorities took out the members one by one. Those who had evaded capture in the crackdown of 1954 were apprehended after the Israeli bombing incident. The few pockets of underground resistance to Nasser's secular vision for the Arab world were nearly annihilated along with the communists. The Muslim Brothers were still languishing in Egyptian prisons when the Israelis occupied the Gaza Strip for the first time, following the Suez campaign of 1956.

The First Israeli Occupation of Gaza

The first Israeli occupation of the Gaza Strip lasted four and a half months, from 31 October 1956 to 17 March 1957. The Israelis, acting in support of France and Britain during the Suez crisis, invaded Gaza and the Sinai and only withdrew as a result of American threats to withhold financial support.

In the first days of the occupation the people of Gaza were ordered by the Israelis to stay inside their homes: 'Citizens and refugees of the Gaza strip, do not go outside, the danger of bombing awaits you on the roads. Everyone should remain in his house or tent ... Do not use or keep any arms.'[38] The entire area was cut off from the rest of the Arab world. The Palestinians nevertheless sought ways to agitate for an end to Israeli rule:

> Active resistance was supported and backed by the passive resistance and civil disobedience of the population. Strikes, mass demonstrations, close-downs – until shopkeepers were forced to open under armed threat; children stayed away from school; women and girls marched through the streets demanding the withdrawal of the Israelis, the return of the Egyptians and the release of prisoners ... .[39]

The occupation provoked continued protest from the local population: 'The communist party led demonstrations with the nationalists but there was no Muslim Brother activity during this period.'[40] Some in Gaza, however, remember that there was limited resistance to Israeli occupation from the remnants of the brotherhood and like-minded religious activists:

> Only during the brief period of the Israeli occupation did they [the Muslim Brotherhood] become visible again. There was a degree of Islamic resistance and agitation through leaflets and the such but no armed resistance.[41]

However, brotherhood resistance against Israeli occupation, forged in the small remaining underground cells, was no more than token. Weakened and depleted under Nasser, the organisation no longer had the ability to mobilise activity among the refugee and local populations. At the same time, however, the prospect for the brotherhood of a return to Egyptian rule was frightening. The organisation could not survive the embrace of Nasser whereas under the Israelis it saw at least a chance to regroup and regain some organisational strength.

Return to Nasser's Egypt

The return of the Gaza Strip to Egyptian authority was 'viewed as a victory in 1957 by Gazans and ushered in a period of much warmer relations between Palestinians and Egypt.'[42] This view, however, was not necessarily one held by the remnants of the Muslim Brotherhood. The last decade of (1957–67) the Egyptian administration witnessed changes aimed at developing the area both economically and, at least in a cosmetic sense, politically. Palestinians were appointed to higher positions in the network of institutions governing the area. A new municipal council was appointed and in 1959 the Egyptians announced plans for the formation of a national union and legislative council for the Palestinians. In 1961 and 1962 elections were held, first for the committees and central committees and then for the legislative council. Although it was designed to deliberate over all local issues (except security) in reality the legislative council was little more than a talking-shop. The prominent Gazan and a key figure in the council, Dr Haider Abdel Shaffi, notes that 'The legislative council wasn't very effective but it indicated our presence.'[43]

The membership of the legislative council represented a spectrum of opinion, from left to right, from refugee to town-dweller. But it is noteworthy that there is no evidence of any member of the Muslim Brotherhood standing for election to it or of the brotherhood being given any role in council activities. The tide of Arab nationalism and secularism, combined with Nasser's brutal repression in 1955, had turned against the religious-political activists. Nasserists and Ba'thists now totally eclipsed the Muslim Brotherhood in Gaza among all segments of the population. Gaza city became an entertainment centre to which Egyptians would flock at weekends to enjoy the privilege of tax-free shopping and spend their evenings at the countless night-clubs, casinos, restaurants, cinemas and hotels. More and more young Gazans were open to the secularising influence of Egypt. Dress codes changed in favour of a more relaxed and Western approach, young men wore trousers and shirts rather than traditional *galabaya* while young Gazan women grew up wearing miniskirts and short dresses. Furthermore, the younger generation of refugees was increasingly well-educated with more and more young Gazans going to university in Egypt and other Arab nationalist countries. Religion still figured in peoples' lives; after all, more than 95 per cent of the population of the Gaza Strip was Muslim and traditional Islamic feasts were still observed. But the realm in which Islam impinged was narrowing increasingly to the domain of personal practice.

For the Muslim Brotherhood, the political situation during this period grew progressively worse. By 1958 it was severely depleted; thousands of its members had fled to the Gulf or to Jordan. One of the present-day leaders of the Hamas movement notes that during this period 'they [the brotherhood] were always attacked by Nasser, and the Arab nationalists had started misleading the people in their social, economic and political quest – a quest that would lead to the failure of 1967.'[44] Eventually only a handful of cells remained and all had ceased to operate in a manner likely to promote their cause. In 1966 a meeting of the brotherhood was held in Kuwait to review the situation in Gaza. At the meeting, attended by regional represent-atives of the brotherhood, it was decided the Gaza brotherhood would be led by Hani Basisou. Basisou was put in charge of a politically powerless and insignificant organisation. The brotherhood was by this time unable to play even a small role in the political life of the community or in its relations with the Egyptian authorities. Following the execution of the Islamic radical Sayyid Qutb in 1966, Nasser ordered the final suppression of the brotherhood in Gaza. This comprehensive sweep of Islamic activists resulted in the arrest of any figure associated with the organisation. Hani Basisou and Ismail al-Khalidi were arrested along with surviving members and subsequently exiled. Among those arrested was the young Ahmad Yassin who would in later years lead the organisation's revival.

New political groups now cut into the potential of support among the traditional and conservative males who might formerly have been attracted to the ideology of the brotherhood. One group in particular, many of whose leaders had been active previously in the brotherhood, attracted this segment of the population. This organ-isation was called Fatah and, as Mustafa Hala remarks:

> The formation of the Fatah movement [in 1959] struck hard at the heart of the Islamic movement and contributed to its weakness. Many of its well-known figures moved to join in the new movement. Fatah became

the main and principal challenge to the Islamic movement in occupied Palestine.[45]

The establishment in 1964, by Nasser, of the Palestine Liberation Organisation (PLO) was the final nail in the coffin for the brotherhood during this period. Nasser had eclipsed the organisation, repressed them and ensured that political Islam in Gaza, as in the rest of Egypt, would take second place to the aspirations of the secular Nasserist ideal. From 1966–67 there was a distinct rise in anti-brotherhood feeling in Gaza, encouraged by hostile Egyptian policies. According to Idwan, 'The Brotherhood was portrayed as collaborators, hostile to the regime. This made it virtually impossible for any work in the name of the Brotherhood to be carried out in Gaza.'[46] By the time of the Six Day War in 1967 the Muslim Brotherhood played no role in the politics of Gaza and the structures it had attempted to create in the late 1940s were almost non-existent.

The West Bank under Hashemite Rule

Life in the West Bank Region Before the 1948 War

Before the 1948 war the kidney-shaped area of the West Bank which includes the towns and cities of Ramallah, Nablus, Jerusalem, Bethlehem, Hebron, Tulkaram and Jenin was a part of the geographical entity known as Palestine. The area had witnessed increasing urbanisation and the decline of rural life. Jerusalem was increasingly marginalised both as a religious and a political centre while cities like Haifa grew in importance. Aspects of religion had, as was illustrated in Chapter One, become politicised through the internal politics of the notable families and their supporters in the religious elite.

Local politics, particularly in Jerusalem, remained dominated by the notable families, whether expressed through an emerging nationalist or Islamic agenda. The power struggle between the al-Husseinis and the Nashashibis endured the most profound changes in Palestinian society during this period. The battle for power extended to Muslim institutions with the emergence of a religious elite largely loyal to and in the pay of the al-Husseini faction. This obsession with the politics of the notable families, their power and prestige, coupled with their economic influence, ultimately weakened the Palestinian community at this most crucial point in its history.

Any notion of national unity in the face of the twin threats of colonialism and Zionism were undermined by this perpetual internal struggle.

Under Jordanian rule Islamic politics in the West Bank diverged along two paths – one, the Waqf and other official Islamic bodies, guided by the Jordanian government in Amman, and the other represented by the Muslim Brotherhood and the Liberation Party (LP) in opposition (nominally or actively) to the government and the monarchy. The activities of these groupings seldom converged or became a source of irritation. Traditional and Hashemite-sanctioned Islam occupied a realm whose boundaries were strictly delimited by the authorities and sanctioned by the government in Amman. The politics of the Friday sermons delivered by preachers in the pay of the Waqf were symbolic of the legitimating role traditionally associated with Sunni politics and religious functionaries employed by the state.

Institutional Islam

Following the 1948 war the traditional seats of religious authority in Palestine – the Waqf, the SMC, the post of mufti of Jerusalem and the heads of the Shari'a courts – underwent a debilitating trans-formation.[47] The Jordanian government placed all these institutions and the power of appointment to all posts in them in the care of its own Ministry of Religious Affairs. The Waqf lost the political independence it had obtained through the period of the British mandate and, like the SMC, its financial independence. All religious functionaries became salaried members of the Jordanian civil service and their activities were effectively curtailed by the power of the authorities. The Jordanians also appointed a new mufti to Jerusalem, a Hashemite loyalist Sheikh Husam ad-Din Jarallah, thus preventing the return of the exiled Haj Amin al-Husseini (al-Husseini went instead to Egypt, where he established the All Palestine Government,[48] and allied himself with the Egyptian regime). The Waqf in Gaza was severed from its Jerusalem base, ending the long tradition of co-operation and appointment that had always flowed between the two areas. The Muslim and Waqf authorities in Palestine were no longer unified but under the authority of three different powers: Israeli in Israel, Jordanian in Jerusalem and the West Bank, and Egyptian in Gaza.

Islam as institutionalised in the Waqf and other religious bodies was effectively curtailed as a channel through which the population's frustrations and desires could be communicated following the refugee upheaval. Funds from endowments were enough to cover the salaries of preachers and other religious functionaries, but with the loss of many properties to the new state of Israel, mosque-building and welfare work could not expand to meet the changed circumstances of a large proportion of the population. For a long time, the new refugee camps in the West Bank were without a place of worship and the building of welfare clinics and hospitals was severely constricted by lack of funds.

For others the pernicious power of the Jordanian authorities was felt at all levels. Preachers were forced to work within the system and therefore place a seal of approval on its legitimacy. The Ministry of Religious Affairs in Amman maintained a vigilant watch over their activities in the West Bank, and preaching activity was further circumscribed when the Jordanian Parliament approved legislation under the title of the Sermonising and Instruction Law in 1955 permitting the censorship of sermons written for the Friday prayers. A separate body, the Council for Preaching, was founded in 1962 to control even further sermons and other activities in Waqf-run mosques.

The Sword and the Qur'an:
the Muslim Brotherhood in the West Bank

While their Egyptian and Gazan counterparts were crushed during the 1950s and 1960s the West Bank branches of the Muslim Brotherhood survived the period of turmoil. Following its amalgamation with the Jordanian movement the West Bank brotherhood emerged as one of Jordan's most significant political groupings. It endured peaks and troughs in its relationship with the ruling regime but essentially it came to represent the face of a loyal opposition in the kingdom. Loyalty to the monarchy was legitimated through direct linkage between the Hashemite ruling-house and the Prophet Mohammad, shored up by Hashemite custodianship of the holy places in Jerusalem.

The amalgamation of the Jordanian and West Bank branches of the brotherhood contributed to the growth of the organisation throughout the 1950s. Existing branches in the West Bank were enlarged and assumed important roles and new branches were opened. The new branches were established in conservative and traditional towns and villages such as Hebron, Jenin, Tulkaram, Salt, Karak, Ma'an and Irbid. The decline of the natural centre of the organisation in Egypt also gave the Jordanian leadership greater significance, particularly when it was declared that the Muslim Brotherhood's headquarters would be moved from Cairo to Jerusalem, following Nasser's crackdown in 1954. Once in Jerusalem, the brotherhood established the World Muslim Congress, printed a newspaper entitled *al-Jihad* and actively began to recruit more Palestinian members.[49]

The brotherhood filled a political vacuum in the Palestinian community after its defeat in the 1948 war. According to Smith: 'The defeat of the Brotherhood's forces and the repression of political activity fostered the growth of support for the Muslim Brothers, the one movement that was allowed to operate in the West Bank.'[50] The message of the brotherhood struck a chord in both the Jordanian and Palestinian refugee communities at a time when, Abidi argues, there was a 'perceptible clash between the forces of conservatism and modernism manifested in religio-political extremism'.[51]

For the brotherhood in the West Bank this was a significant period of growth. By contrast to the brotherhood in the Gaza Strip, during this period it was tolerated, albeit grudgingly, by the ruler. It was also the only political group to survive the turmoil of 1957 when the king outlawed all political parties. It was very active politically throughout this period and in the 1950s and 1960s participated successfully in elections to the Jordanian national legislature.

The fortunes of the Muslim Brotherhood were strongly linked to its political policies. Its reformist political programme was almost identical to that of the brotherhood in Egypt and was clearly influenced by Egyptian ideologues, particularly Hassan al-Banna. The role of the Egyptian Brothers in the Jordanian movement after 1954 was also very significant in setting the movement's direction. The organisation concentrated on promoting the revival of Islam in modern society. As Abidi remarks, 'This was not just a statement of a general truth, the movement in the West Bank constantly attacked what it saw as specific deviations from this principle in everyday life'.[52] However, unlike its Egyptian counterpart which found itself at odds with the state, the brotherhood in Jordan never actively opposed the ruling regime or its claim to legitimacy.

The survival of the Muslim Brotherhood, when all other political parties and groups were declared illegal, was due to its general conservative/ traditional orientation, in keeping with the regime itself. The brotherhood never sought to overthrow the Hashemite monarchy or change the regime through a revolution but instead sought change through the channels erected by the state. It was careful not to incur the wrath of the regime even when it opposed particular policies or acts. Even in the West Bank it placed the Palestinian nationalist agenda on the back-burner, pursuing instead its anti-imperialist pro-*shari'a* agenda and distancing itself from the national movement. In 1962, for example, the brotherhood defied a call by the nationalists in the West Bank to boycott the Jordanian elections and thus 'maintained close ties with the king and his court and came out in support of the regime when it clashed with its nationalistic internal opponents'.[53] For the most part, brotherhood criticism of the regime revolved around particular religious issues of the day or concentrated on anti-imperialist, particularly anti-British, sentiment.[54]

Leadership and Organisation

From 1948–67 the leadership of the Jordanian brotherhood underwent a number of changes which stemmed from the arrest and subsequent exile of prominent figures from Egypt. Originally the movement was headed by a Jordanian, Abd al-Latif Abu Qura, who was its spiritual guide. He was replaced in 1953 by a young Jordanian lawyer named Abd al-Rahman al-Khalifa. With the arrival in 1954, however, of the famous Egyptian brother, Said Ramadan, Khalifa stepped down temporarily in favour of the more senior and experienced man. But Said Ramadan remained in Jordan for only a brief time. In 1955, having been stripped of his Egyptian passport, he was expelled by the Jordanian authorities. Khalifa took over the leadership once again and until 1963, when he was temporarily replaced by Dr Yousef al-Athm, helped direct the movement throughout Jordan and the West Bank. Al-Khalifa oversaw the expansion of the organisation's activities in the East Bank and maintained the amalgamation of the West Bank with headquarters in Amman. Al-Khalifa and al-Athm were both from provincial Jordanian towns, educated yet deeply pious men. To this day they have remained loyal to the Hashemite monarchy and intent on preserving the Islamic nature of society.

Politics of the Periphery

The nineteen years of Jordanian control over the West Bank transformed the Muslim Brotherhood's role there. This change should be viewed in the context of the political transformation that took place in Jordan following the assassination of King Abdullah in 1951 and the succession of his grandson, Hussein, to the throne in 1952. Under King Hussein, Jordan experienced rapid political change: the introduction of constitutional government, the challenge and opposition of an array of radical nationalist forces and the subsequent repression of the majority of political parties.[55] Most political forces were critical of the continuing British influence over Jordan and hostile to the policies of the young king.

The branches of the brotherhood in the West Bank went from being the principal, catalytic mover of the movement outside Egypt to the poor relation of the organisation in Amman and the East Bank. In 1948 and shortly after there was an initial expansion, with new branches and increasing membership rolls but after 1954 branches shrank or disappeared and membership dropped. The urban nature of the brotherhood in Palestine before 1948 was undermined by the new prominence of Jordan's capital city, Amman, assuming importance over Jerusalem in the post-1948 era. The sixteen branches in the West Bank, including Jerusalem, Hebron, Nablus, Jenin, Qalqilya, Jericho, Anabta, Dura, Surif, Sur Bahir, Aqabat Jaber camp and Tulkaram, now operated as part of the organisation in Amman. Any sense of independence was lost, and no Palestinian Muslim brother based in the West Bank assumed any high-ranking role. The post of spiritual guide stayed firmly in Jordanian hands. Even famous West Bank figures like Sheikh Nashhur ad-Damin from Nablus, who led his branch from 1946 to the 1960s, had to travel to the East Bank to consult with the leadership there. There is no evidence of independent decision-making within the organisation in the West Bank during this period. Muslim Brotherhood leaders in the West Bank identified themselves strongly with the Jordanian branch, more so than with the Egyptian centre. According to one, 'We were all part of the Ikhwan movement in Jordan rather than the movement in Egypt, all our organisational links were with the Ikhwan in Amman and as far as I remember we were always part of the Jordanian movement.'[56]

At the local level, however, individual branches continued along the same lines as before 1948. The general guidelines for the organisation in the West Bank were set down in Amman. Branches focused on local activities while issues pertaining to the Palestinian question, although occasionally addressed, were for the most part ignored.[57] In some towns and villages the Muslim Brotherhood was able to present an active and cohesive front, leading one of its figures from Nablus to conclude that it was 'the strongest group in the land of Palestine – in terms of both support and membership'.[58] Membership records, however, were never properly maintained and files compiled by the Jordanian Intelligence Service at the time reflect a low membership during this period, noting that it never reached more than 700 at any one time.[59]

In many ways the activities of the branches in the West Bank during this period reflected the original intentions of the movement's founder, Hassan al-Banna, when he established the Muslim Brotherhood in Isma'iliyya in 1928. Hassan al-Banna had not intended the organisation to undertake a radical revolutionary role. His vision encompassed a movement that first liberated the Muslim mind, through education, and then encouraged the Muslim to play his role in an Islamic society. The seven-point programme of the brotherhood at this time had been: the interpretation of the Qur'an in the spirit of the age; the unity of Islamic nations; raising standards of living, realising social justice and security; the struggle against illiteracy and poverty; the emancipation of Islamic lands from foreign domination and, finally; the promotion of universal peace and fraternity according to the precepts of Islam.[60]

The Muslim Brotherhood in the West Bank embraced these principles on all but one count. Members of every branch, from Hebron to Tulkaram and Nablus, organised their activities as Muslim Brothers around the Islamic notion of *tabligh wa da'wa* (education and preaching). Thus, for example, in June 1960 the branch in Jerusalem, which owned a building in the Old City near St. Stephen's Gate, 'opened a three-class school for adults in Jerusalem to take part in the government's campaign against illiteracy. The Qur'an was also to be taught in this school in an attempt to regulate the behaviour of the pupils in accordance with Islam.'[61] Education was highly valued and a central core of brotherhood activities during this time.

Only on the issue of the emancipation of Islamic lands from foreign domination did the Muslim Brotherhood in the West Bank appear less than zealous. Eclipsed by the rising appeal of the political parties of the pan-Arab trend, the Muslim Brotherhood concentrated on the task of internal Islamic renewal of Palestinian society. The issue of national liberation through the revolutionary Arab nationalist vanguard did not concern it. There was no call to arms, just a call on Muslims to return to the mosque and pray. The Gazan and

Egyptian wings of the movement had, in contrast, established small paramilitary wings with the specific aim of conducting jihad against Israel. Indeed, the brotherhood in the West Bank was further limited by the directive from Amman that armed struggle was not part of their programme.

Portrait of a Branch: Nablus

A profile of an individual branch in the West Bank will afford a deeper insight into the brotherhood during this period although it reflects a likeness rather than an exact microcosm of the movement as a whole. On the level of organisation it illustrates the importance of the relationship with Amman rather than Egypt, and a pattern of internal political control which was neither democratic nor broad-based. In addition, the social composition of the branch gives some idea of the type of people who were attracted to the ideology of the brotherhood and whether they shared a particular socio-economic base.

Nablus, Palestine's most important commercial centre, is 60 kilometres north of Jerusalem. Its citizens have always played an important role in politics. Its notable families, including the Masris, Nablusis, Tuqans and Anabtawis have always involved themselves in the political life of the city and the surrounding area as an extension of their considerable economic interests. In the late nineteenth-century Nablus became an important manufacturing centre, famous for its soap and its goldsmiths. Its agricultural hinterland also encouraged its growth as a trading centre and it had a thriving market.

The Muslim Brotherhood in Nablus was established as part of the 1946 drive by the Egyptian movement to create a network in Palestine. With the support of Egyptian leader Sheikh Sattar and Sheikh Nashhur ad-Damin, the branch was established at around the same time as branches in Jerusalem and Jaffa. The chairman of the Nablus outpost was Sheikh Nashhur ad-Damin. The membership roll included male members of the leading Masri, Nablusi, Tuqan and Anabtawi families, young men in their early twenties or thirties who were attracted to the brotherhood's new message and perspective on Islam. The leadership came from the educated urban elite and professions, with a particular link to teaching. The members came from the educated urban middle classes, from the refugee community and also included farmers and skilled workers.

The pyramidal organisational structure of the Nablus branch was typical of other areas. At its head was the leader, in this case Sheikh ad-Damin, and under him an administrative assistant and then an administrative committee which included the branch secretary and treasurer. The membership of this committee, despite regular elections, remained unchanged for decades. On joining the Muslim Brotherhood in Nablus all new members swore an oath of allegiance to the organisation and agreed to observe Islamic values. The oath included the following statement: 'I promise to be a good Muslim, to be an example to the community and spread the word of God.'[62] In many respects, membership was about the affirmation of faith and its public practice in the name of the Muslim Brotherhood. Public identification with the organisation consisted of religious obligation, education and charity work on behalf of the brotherhood in the local community.

The Nablus branch headquarters were in the old municipal building. This location at the heart of the city and on the fringes of the market area was convenient for all its members. For the more prosperous a visit to the headquarters simply entailed a short walk from their hill-top villas in the (Rafidiyah) neighbourhood; for members from the casbah and surrounding refugee camps attendance could be combined with business or shopping in town. The old municipal building is large, containing a library as well as meeting halls and small rooms where tutorial size Qur'an classes could be held. The centre was always popular and many activities were hosted by the branch throughout this period. Subhi Anabtawi who was a leading member in both the branch in Nablus and in his family village of Anabta recalls the types of activities that went on: 'We had group study, organised with school teachers, and free summer schools'.[63]

Other activities included literacy classes, lessons in the study of the Qur'an, the collection of *zakat* (Islamic tax) and the creation of *zakat*-funded projects, as well as meetings to discuss particular Islamic or political issues and a large range of sporting activities. The links of official Islam with the branch in Nablus were non-existent: 'The Waqf and Imams had no influence over us and sometimes we were considered by them to be extremist in our views ... They felt that their leadership ... might be eroded by us and our activities', commented Mr Anabtawi.[64]

Although the branch was not large its members were keen adherents to the philosophy of the Muslim Brotherhood and were thus able to make an impact on locally-held perspectives on religion and politics. The works of figures like Hassan al-Banna, Said Ramadan, Rashid Rida and Mohammad al-Ghazali were studied by the brotherhood and disseminated at meetings held throughout the city. In addition, the Nablus branch was able to distinguish itself from other branches through its appointment of its own Muslim Brother preacher, Sheikh Nashhur ad-Damin, who was paid to preach on the branch's behalf and who was a particularly influential figure during this period.

The Nablus branch, then, was the largest and most important in the West Bank and many of the links that were forged with or by individual members during this period turned into lifetime allegiances withstanding the upheaval of the 1967 war, the Israeli occupation and subsequent further dispersal of members, many of whom went and worked in the Gulf states. The activities of the movement in Nablus and elsewhere laid firm foundations, allowing the brotherhood to withstand the change of political direction, following the Israeli occupation of the West Bank in 1967. These foundations were also firm enough to encourage a new generation of leaders in later years.

The Liberation Party (Hizb Tahrir)

The Muslim Brotherhood was not the only politically active Islamic group in the West Bank. There were others, Islamic in ideology but with political orientations different from that of the brotherhood. Their development reflected the continuing trend of diversity within Palestine's Islamic movement, apparent from the time of Sheikh Izz ad-Din al-Qassam and Haj Amin al-Husseini. This heterogeneity was the product of an approach to political Islam that strove to break from a monolithic and static relationship with religious ideology to form a radical approach to Islam and politics.

The Liberation Party (LP)[65] was founded in 1952 by Sheikh Taqi ad-Din an-Nabahani, a West Bank Palestinian. Sheikh Nabahani, a school teacher, was from the northern West Bank town of Tulkaram. He had been involved with the Muslim Brotherhood but broke away from the group in 1950–51 as a result of ideological differences.

The appearance of the LP added a new dimension to Islamic politics in Palestine and affected the development of Islamic political movements throughout the region. Although it was the first indigenous Palestinian Islamic party, its philosophy was decidedly pan-Islamic and anti-colonialist in orientation. Sheikh Nabahani did address the

Arab–Israeli conflict but his priority was the need to overthrow corrupt Arab regimes whose leaders had departed from the Islamic path. Nabahani's approach represented a new departure, presenting a world-view radically at odds with prevailing trends in the Islamic movement at the time.

The philosophy of the LP, formulated in copious writings by Nabahani, was a departure from that of the Muslim Brotherhood. If the Muslim Brotherhood was a conservative reform movement, the LP was its opposite: radical and dedicated to the resurrection of the caliphate by overthrowing corrupt Arab states. If the Muslim Brotherhood could be described as a member of the loyal opposition in Jordan and supporter of the institution of monarchy based on lineage to the Prophet Mohammad, the LP was outspoken in its criticism of the Jordanian regime and the monarchy. This resulted in the absence of any real relationship between the LP and the Muslim Brotherhood (although there were attempts at co-operation throughout the 1950s) or the LP and the Hashemite regime.

Sheikh Nabahani had earlier in his life been involved with the brotherhood whose philosophy had helped to shape his politicised Islamic perspective. But a number of irreconcilable differences between his own and the brotherhood's outlook led to his decision to undertake and promote a new and different Islamic agenda in the West Bank. Sheikh Nabahani surrounded himself with a number of close associates, Islamic intellectuals and religious functionaries, to form this powerful Islamic movement. Among this number were religious figures and preachers like As'ad and Rajab Bayyud al-Tammimi and Abd al-Qadim al-Zullum.[66]

Throughout the early to mid-1950s the LP concentrated both on disseminating its message and on recruitment. Liberation Party members would distribute Nabahani's pamphlets and booklets at mosques and meetings throughout the area. All sectors of society were identified as potential recruits although teachers and educational professionals were targeted specifically. Members of the LP would travel to towns, refugee camps and villages and hold lectures in mosques or other locations. They would inform their audience of the foundation of the new party and outline its principal goal, namely the establishment of an Islamic state. After this large meeting a smaller, interested group was encouraged to join a further meeting. At the second meeting a further presentation would be given and then the lecturer would encourage a discussion. At the end of this second meeting new members were encouraged to join.

The LP, however, was never a mass movement and remained small, notwithstanding its own high estimates of membership. Any success in recruiting new members was always undermined by fierce repression from the Jordanian authorities. Thus, while the LP did organise large meetings or capitalise on Islamic festivals to promote its message, it concentrated on the creation of small groups or cells throughout the West Bank. It had members in small cells in towns like Jerusalem, Nablus, Qalqilya, Hebron, refugee camps like Aqabat Jaber in Jericho and villages like Azzun and Bourqa. Its headquarters were initially in Jerusalem rather than Amman but were soon closed by the police on orders from the Jordanian government. Hebron then became the strongest base of the party, with supporters drafted in from other areas. The most prominent figure in Hebron was As'ad Bayyud Tammimi, a preacher by profession, who later led the movement in Kuwait and then supported the Islamic Jihad movement in Jordan in the 1970s.

Party activities concentrated on the elaboration, articulation, dissemination and discussion of Nabahani's Islamic philosophy. The fundamental role of Islam in the lives of all Muslims was the essential message of the party. Meetings were essentially study groups *(halaqa)* and were the backbone and most distinctive feature of the party. As Abu Ali a former member, noted, 'I joined a *halaqa* of five members. We would meet regularly and discuss Nabahani's ideas.'[67] *Halaqas* would meet on a weekly and sometimes daily basis playing an important role in the lives of new recruits. The indoctrination of as many supporters as possible became the principal activity in these sessions.

The study-group dynamics were a reflection of power flows within the group as well as within the wider arena of the party as a whole. At the head of the study group was a learned religious functionary who had devoted his life to Islam. The leader of the group would in turn be a member of a *halaqa* group consisting of his intellectual peers and led by a more experienced man who in turn would attend another *halaqa* group. This system permeated the entire movement with Nabahani at the top. In the case of the group in the village of Bourqa, for example, the leader was a man called Farouq Habayeb, a student of Nabahani. Around him were his disciples those members of group who were recruits to LP philosophy, who had come to listen to the leader and examine Nabahani's ideas as disseminated through the group leader. The themes explored in the *halaqa* meetings were selected by the leadership and ranged from examinations of imperialism to economics to processes of government. According to Abu Ali, selected texts were examined by the *halaqa*, 'The teacher used Nabahani's books, one would read a chapter and then there would be a discussion'.[68] The spiritual nature of the group, which may have met at a mosque or a member's house, was always emphasised and worship was often part of the meeting.

Ideology and the Party

> We believed that the Arab governments must be overthrown, this was our goal … We want liberation for the whole Islamic world, we weren't Palestinian nationalists. [Abu Ali, Bourqa Village, 18 August 1993]

Ideologically the LP offered an alternative to the mainstream philosophy of the Muslim Brotherhood, although some authors acknowledge that the philosophical roots of the two organisations were much the same.[69] The LP described its aim as the revival of an Islamic way of life requiring 'the return of Muslims to an Islamic society in the *dar al-Islam*'.[70] The radical approach in Nabahani's writing reflected a complex world-view in which issues such as imperialism, economic policy, state structure and political systems were analysed rigorously. Nabahani went as far as prescribing the immediate destruction of current state systems in the Middle East through jihad. He called for the resurrection of an Islamic state system respecting the five pillars of the Qur'an. According to Nabahani the Islamic state is the utopian goal of the LP, a state system where Islam relates to five spheres: the system of rule, economic system, social system, educational system and foreign policy. In Nabahani's philosophy the Islamic state can be created anywhere.[71] This pan-Islamic approach helped widen the party's appeal to other groups in the Middle East which was accelerated further by the dispersal of members following a Jordanian crackdown throughout the 1950s.

One active member of the party and leader of the cell in the village of Azzun, Fathi Mohammad Salim, stated his understanding of the principles of the party at his trial in 1960. He declared:

> I am a member of the Liberation Party and I work for the dismemberment of the existing entities in the Muslim world in order to replace them by the principles of my party. I have conducted propaganda for these principles and the publications which are before the court were in my possession.[72]

A principal theme explored in party publications and leaflets and discussed at meetings was imperialism. The LP was opposed to any manifestation of imperialism (Western or Eastern) and its effects in the Middle East. Nabahani's writings, which explored the theme of imperialism at great length, blame Western imperialist machinations for the rise of Arab nationalism. To the LP, Arab nationalism was the antithesis of the pan-Islamic ideal of a utopian state where all are in the abode of Islam (*dar al-Islam*) and where Western-constructed barriers are eradicated.

The consequences of this particular stance were apparent in LP strategy. In the post-1948 era the concept of Arab nationalism was deeply entrenched in the political order of many regimes throughout the region. In the case of Palestine a nationalist movement had formed under the British mandate in response to the nationalist ideology of Zionism and this remained significant under the rule of the Jordanians, often leading the movement into conflict with the Hashemite authorities. The LP, however, remained completely opposed to the adoption of any nationalist (whether Arab or Palestinian) stance. Its self-prescribed role was to issue the call of Islam by replacing the existing infidel and un-Islamic systems of government with the 'concepts and ideas of Islam, to the extent that these Islamic concepts form the general public opinion of the society'.[73] The party viewed itself as playing a vanguard role, taking the message out into the population and ensuring a wide audience.

Shackled Fortunes

The LP was doomed to failure in the arena of local politics. Its anti-monarchical philosophy did not endear it to the regime which regarded its aims as inimical to the Hashemite kingdom. The party initially sought official registration under the Parties Law but permission was denied by the Ministry of the Interior in March 1953. The reasons for denial were stated clearly: 'The applicants were told that the basic tenets of the proposed platform were contrary not only to the spirit but to the very terms of the Jordanian constitution.'[74] The proposed party was perceived as especially threatening to the stability of the regime at a time when a new era of authority was being established under the newly-crowned King Hussein. Confidence in the monarchy had been weakened following the assassination of King Abdullah in July 1951 and the subsequent crowning and abdication of Abdullah's son and Hussein's father, Talal. The 1953–56 period witnessed an internal tug-of-war between the new monarch's supporters and the radical nationalist/socialist opposition which was encouraged by pro-Nasser forces. The proposal to form a pan-Islamic party such as the LP on a platform that envisaged the dismantling of the monarchy in Jordan was, in such circumstances, inevitably rejected.

The LP, however, was not deterred. It remained a political association and for as long as it was tolerated it played an active role in Jordanian politics. In the West Bank, too, it continued to carve a political niche for itself. Supporters still organised meetings locally to promote Nabahani's philosophy, and publications and pamphlets authored by Nabahani were promoted. In October 1954 the LP fielded four candidates, under the guise of independents, in Jordanian parliamentary elections. Sheikh Ahmad ad-Daur from the northern West Bank town of Qalqilya and running for the Tulkaram sub-district was the only one of the four who was successful; he was even re-elected in the next parliamentary poll in 1956. As the sole member of the LP in parliament, Sheikh ad-Daur became a well-known figure, particularly for his opposition role in debates. Ad-Daur's work within parliament struck many as at odds with a party ideology which portrayed the Jordanian political system as a negation of the Islamic state. It can only be supposed that ad-Daur's position in parliament was viewed as an opportunity for the LP to have a representative within the system, someone who might be able to lobby on its behalf.

Political tensions increased in Jordan throughout 1956, resulting in the fall of the leftist Nablusi government, the appointment of a new cabinet, its subsequent fall and the imposition of martial law. In the face of increasing leftist and nationalist opposition encouraged by the governments of Egypt and Syria, King Hussein ordered a crackdown on radical political elements. It was inevitable that the LP would be one of the first casualties and Sheikh ad-Daur compounded matters by voting in favour of a no-confidence motion against the new government, selected by the king, in the House of Representatives. This act immediately identified ad-Daur as an opponent not to be tolerated.

The decision to outlaw the activities of all political partisans following an attempted coup and demonstrations in 1957 extended to the Liberation Party. Despite the imminent threat of prosecution, repression, heavy penalties and exile, the LP continued with its activities, but was forced underground. Sheikh ad-Daur was arrested by the Jordanian authorities in 1958 and sentenced to two years imprisonment for illegal membership of a prohibited political party. After his release he was placed under house arrest in Qalqilya. The arrest also meant the forfeit of his seat in parliament. Yet despite the wave of arrests and the members who were forced into exile (including the party's founder Sheikh Nabahani) LP activity continued in the West Bank. Illicit leaflets were published by remaining activists and for three years the party attempted to organise throughout the area. Meeting in secret, the *halaqa* groups were the only means through which ideas, policy and strategies could be communicated by the clandestine leadership. The Jordanian security services, however, kept the party under surveillance, determined to prevent it from playing any further role in the political life of the regime.

In 1960 and 1961 the authorities cracked down on the LP once again. Fifty alleged members from the West Bank, particularly Nablus and Azzun, were brought to trial by Jordanian military courts sitting in Nablus and Amman – in highly publicised cases. This number was significant, considering the relatively small size of the party at this time. The sentences meted out ranged from imprisonment to house arrest. This time the trials effectively silenced the movement in the West Bank. The autocratic leadership style which characterised the LP did not provide an adequate support system during a period of crisis and in the few years between the establishment of the party and the crackdown of 1957 there was not enough time for an organisational infrastructure to be created that could endure political upheaval.

With Nabahani and many other high-ranking LP officials like Ali Fakr ad-Din, Abd al-Qadim al-Zullum, Harith Katibah and Salih Abu as-Salam al-Muhtasib, having fled to the Gulf states or Lebanon, party communication lines were severely weakened. The Jordanian authorities sent a very clear message to the LP during this period and played a major role, along with internal dissension and accusations that the party was backed by the United States Central Intelligence Agency (CIA), in weakening the overall impact of its philosophy.

Impact in the Palestinian Community?

There are many aspects of the LP which point to strong feelings of loyalty and especially duty among its members and to a real sense of vision from its founders. The organic nature of Nabahani's philosophy demanded a complete commitment from his followers. Yet the LP vision jarred with the reality of the Palestinian community and most Palestinians were not attracted to it.

The LP philosophy was comprehensive and at times highly

complex and littered with contradictory perspectives on the same issue. While the prolific Nabahani analysed and philosophised, his ideas were rarely put into practice. The pan-Islamic and essentially anti-nationalist message of the party was unattractive to many. Nabahani's pan-Islamic ideas were seen as a reflection of an earlier age, of the time when philosophers like al-Afghani, Abduh and Rashid Rida were influencing Palestinian Islamists like Sheikh Izz ad-Din al-Qassam and Haj Amin al-Husseini.

The LP took an uncompromising stance in its dealings with all other Palestinian and Jordanian political actors. Thus, in the context of the Palestinian community, it was never able to support the goals of the nationalist movement and other national organisations in the West Bank. Party leaflets published in the late 1950s and early 1960s are testimony to this intransigence. towards a Palestinian national entity, echoed by present-day Islamic movements in Palestine: 'Hence, for the Liberation Party the creation of a Palestinian entity and a state in the West Bank is a great crime and is absolutely forbidden.'[75]

Despite the harsh repression and the arrest and imprisonment of members, the LP in the West Bank and Jordan survived and remained active throughout the 1960s. The organisation was covert and anonymous, becoming increasingly introspective and no longer responding to the political circumstances of the day. The *halaqa* meetings held at secret locations throughout the West Bank maintained the practice of discussing Nabahani's philosophy. The party's principal activity, in terms of the outside world, was to publish leaflets that were always critical of the Jordanian regime and its Palestinian policy. During the war against Israel in 1967 the LP was reported to have distributed leaflets which, 'called on Iraqi troops in Jordan to overthrow the regime'.[76]

Despite all these negative factors, the LP did appeal to a certain, predominantly male sector of Palestinian society, namely disgruntled Muslim Brotherhood members or those religiously-observant Muslims who sought closer ties to political Islam. Nabahani's work required great commitment from his supporters, yet there were enough Palestinians around who were willing to adhere to his strictures and who agreed with his world-view. He appealed to conservatives, which is why there was a concentration of LP members in traditionalist towns or villages like Hebron and Tulkaram. The interpretation of Islam found in his writings also appealed a number of male religious functionaries.

The Eve of Conflict

By 1967 and the second Arab–Israeli war the forces of political Islam had undergone dramatic change in both the West Bank and Gaza Strip. In Gaza they had been decimated by Nasser's crackdown against the Muslim Brotherhood and a societal swing towards secularism and nationalist politics. In the West Bank the Muslim Brotherhood had been incorporated into the Jordanian structure and transformed into a moderate Islamic force for change. Only the Liberation Party propounded a radical Islamic agenda. While ultimately working towards the same goal – the creation of an Islamic state – the constituent organisations of political Islam nevertheless advocated political strategies that were radically different from each other. Some strategies reflected a reformist approach to Islam emphasising the need to work within the system to effect change in policy; others advocated the overthrow of existing political systems, whether conservative monarchies or Arab socialist republics.

The Islamic movement during this period was also subject to the varying responses, for the most part hostile, of the governing authorities. The regimes of Jordan and Egypt recognised the potency of political Islam and the strength of the message it sought to disseminate among the masses. Whether represented by the Muslim Brotherhood or the LP, political Islam offered a serious challenge to the ruling forces of the state and to the stability of political systems that were vulnerable to change from active social forces of opposition. The response of these more vulnerable regimes was heavy–handed repression of any manifestation of political Islam, which was not permitted a separate existence. For these regimes, the only acceptable manifestation of Islam was that sanctioned by the state through its structures.

Whether the forces of political Islam could withstand the impact of the forthcoming conflict seemed highly dubious given their weakened state and the rise of secular nationalism. Nasser's vision of Arab nationalism had found a receptive audience among Palestinians and his support for the newly-founded PLO added impetus to the nationalist trend. Neither the Muslim Brotherhood nor the Liberation Party was able philosophically or logistically to match the support for nationalism as the vehicle for Palestinian liberation.

The Six Day War and the First Decade of Israeli Occupation (1967–76)

Introduction

The Six Day War in which the armies of Egypt, Jordan and Syria lost to Israel had a profound effect on the Islamic movement in the Middle East. For the movement the war was a watershed, marking the decline and bankruptcy of pan-Arab nationalism and other Western-secular ideologies. The defeat by the Zionist state and symbol of the West was a confirmation of Arab weakness which catalysed a crisis and reassessment of the secular values and ideologies proffered by the radical Arab elites of states like Egypt and Syria. The year 1967 became 'the most vivid confirmation, in Muslim eyes and before the world, of political and military impotence'.[1]

Throughout the Middle East a phase of political soul-searching began. The crisis of identity, the search for something new, an alternative to defeat, occupied the intellectuals of the region. Explanations were sought, new approaches advocated. The debate focused on the Palestinian issue which, for a time, was seized upon and transformed to mean many things. As Kepel remarks, 'People began to transfer their allegiance from their own heads of state to the Palestine resistance, in other words, to militant revolutionary organisations'.[2] For a brief period, then, from the late 1960s to the early 1970s the Palestinian cause became a symbol for the Arab world, 'transcending', as Ajami notes, 'localised and parochial concerns ... a vehicle for bringing about social and political change ... confrontation between the larger force of imperialism and anti-imperialism ... '.[3]

Islam played its part in this debate. Along with socialists and communists, Islamic thinkers and activists sought an answer. As Donohue argues: 'Some would date the new vitality of Islamic actors from the defeat of the Arabs in their war with Israel in 1967'.[4] Certainly there was a marked rise from this point onwards in both the activities of Islamic movements and the symbols of Islam in debates about the political future of the region. 'The solution', cried Islamist advocates, 'is Islam'. Islam, or rather its absence from the political milieu before 1967, explained the defeat. The Arabs had abandoned their religion in favour of Western notions and political ideologies. Modernity had been largely a Western-influenced response to change, but had, argued the Islamists, proved ineffective. A return to Islam, incorporating sincere devotion to the practice of the faith rather than the lip-service of state elites, would guarantee the resurrection of the Arab nation to its rightful place in the international arena.

In the Palestinian arena itself, however, the notion of self-identity and pride which was the response to the defeat of 1967 was rooted in nationalism rather than Islam. The Palestine Liberation Organisation (PLO), which had been founded by Nasser in 1964, was transformed during this period. The organisation was restructured and in 1969 Yasser Arafat the leader of the Palestinian nationalist group, Fatah, became president. From 1967 the strategy of the PLO, as an umbrella structure for more than ten nationalist groups, was dedicated to liberation through armed struggle and the support for fedayeen (guerrilla) forces. The PLO National Charter (1968) highlighted a commitment to the liberation of the whole of Palestine and the creation of a Palestinian state in which Jews, Muslims and Christians would coexist. By this time the PLO was based in Jordan where its strength in the community led to the accusation that it was a state within a state. King Hussein, alert to the potential threat to his rule, moved against it in September 1970 eventually ousting Arafat's forces to Lebanon. From Jordan the PLO and its constituent organisations, including George Habash's Popular Front for the Liberation of Palestine (PFLP) and Nayef Hawatmeh's Democratic Front for the Liberation of Palestine (DFLP) continued their armed campaign and encouraged the communities of the West Bank and Gaza Strip to remain steadfast in their resistance to Israeli occupation. Within the movement an ideological change was apparent by the mid-1970s when the PLO announced that it would settle for a Palestinian state in the West Bank and Gaza Strip. This decision coincided with a period when the PLO's increasing prominence in Lebanese politics led to its disastrous involvement at the outbreak of the civil war in 1975.

By this time the struggle for self-determination had diverged along two tracks, first in relation to the state of Israel and its military occupation and second in relation to the Arab states which had failed to deliver statehood for the Palestinians and had betrayed their cause in the process. It is no coincidence that the Palestinians mounted a serious challenge both to the legitimacy of the Hashemite kingdom as well as to the Lebanese state during this period. The Palestinian cause thus provided Arab leftists and radicals with a source of inspiration. Inter-state politics in the Arab world throughout this period were increasingly influenced by the Palestinian issue and the challenge set down by the PLO; the latter's radical approach threatened conservative regimes like that of Jordan. The Arab states responded by seeking to champion the Palestinian cause for two reasons: as a way of achieving legitimacy in the region; and as a way of controlling the PLO's strategy and potential threat. The solution offered by Palestinian nationalism at this point was the subject of manipulation by every Arab regime in the area.

For this reason, the resurgence of Islam in Palestine cannot be dated from the defeat of 1967. While this approach is applicable to other cases, for example in Egypt where the crisis of identity and socio-economic decline following 1967 permitted Islam to flourish and contribute at a political level, it is not strictly relevant to the case of Palestine. A revival of secular-nationalist sentiment was more than apparent as Palestinians pledged their support to the constituent organisations of the PLO and these organisations' strategy of armed struggle. Here the political impact of Islam would not be felt at the mass level for at least another decade and then under historically specific circumstances.

The War and the Palestinian Issue

It was apparent by the beginning of 1967 that a lack of unity, exacerbated by the political experiences of the Islamic movement as a whole, permeated the Islamic groups of the West Bank and Gaza Strip. The movement had developed in an uneven manner, with no co-ordination between the two geographical areas. In the West Bank the Muslim Brotherhood had reached a peak of political power and legitimacy under the Hashemite regime although its branches were effectively subsumed under the Jordanian movement. At this time the Muslim Brotherhood in Jordan was operating through an organisation called the Islamic Centre Society. The society had been formed in 1964 as a means of further circumventing the 1957 law prohibiting the formation of political parties and was registered as a charity operating within the charitable societies law. Under this law the society was free to operate and organise activities, including the dissemination of its political agenda. As tension rose during the months preceding the war in 1967 the Jordanian section of the brotherhood decided, to the taunts of Nasserists and Ba'thists, on a policy that supported King Hussein. The brotherhood in the West Bank followed its lead and likewise remained staunchly pro-Hashemite. The stirrings of Palestinian nationalism were again ignored and the mosque became a refuge from the debate surrounding the true value of nineteen years of Jordanian rule.

In the Gaza Strip, on the other hand, the Muslim Brotherhood was virtually inactive. Nasserism had gripped the collective imagination of Gazans and was further strengthened by a new educated élite which had studied in Egyptian universities. Even some of the current leaders of the Hamas movement, like Dr Mahmoud Zahar, admit their support for Nasser during this time:

> At that time [1967] I fully supported Nasser's system – just as everyone else did. He taught us how to dismiss Israel and work towards the creation of one Arab state. Although I must admit I had already noticed the contamination, disruption and poverty in Egyptian society by this point. Yet we were amazed by the personality of Abdel Nasser.[5]

It should not be forgotten that Nasser was not adverse to portraying himself as a friend of Islam within the framework of his nationalist ideal. Despite his hostility to the Muslim Brotherhood, his regime did not hesitate to call for a jihad in 1967.[6] In direct contrast to 1948, in 1967 the remnants of the Muslim Brotherhood in Egypt and Gaza were unable to play any military role. Nasser had encouraged the development of a Palestinian nationalist organisation and under his direction the Palestine Liberation Army (PLA), the military wing of the PLO, had established training units in the Gaza Strip. Military training was extended to large sectors of the population.[7] Nearly all political activity revolved around the nationalist movement which in turn was under Nasser's control.

The Palestinian position during the 1967 war was often overshadowed by the political competition and disputes between Arab states. Both Nasser and the Syrians had gained political mileage and support for their respective claims that they were campaigning on behalf of the Palestinians. Even King Hussein was compelled to make a stand on the Palestinians' behalf. Yet the role of the Palestinians in the events leading up to and during the war can only be described as minimal:

> During this period we weren't even Palestinians, we were Jordanians and we had the passports to prove it. We played no part in the war. We just kept our heads down when the fighting began and hoped for the best.[8]

The Six Day War (5–11 June 1967), the third conflict between Israel and the Arabs, served to highlight the Arab aspect of the Palestinian cause rather than the Palestinian essence of the conflict with Israel. The reasons for the war were based on an increasing belief within the military communities of Egypt and Syria that Israel was preparing for confrontation. Within Israel it was argued that hostile Arab acts, including pacts between Egypt and Syria and the closing of the Tiran Straits, were the provocation for further regional conflagration. The Israelis took the first action with air strikes which incapacitated Egypt's air force. As Gresh and Vidal note: 'once the Arab air force had been annihilated, Israeli troops took only six days to secure the Egyptian Sinai, the Jordanian West Bank … .'[9]

Waging Holy Jihad?

During the conflict with Israel in 1967 Islamic leaders from other Muslim countries called for support from outside Palestine. In Egypt, the sheikh of al-Azhar University, Hassan Ma'moun, issued a fatwa at the outbreak of the war in which he called for a jihad to be waged to save Palestine: 'Muslims and Arabs all over the world … Attack these evil doers and kill them … in order to liberate usurped Palestine.'[10]

Even King Faisal of Saudi Arabia called out, on the eve of the war: 'To jihad citizens! To jihad citizens! Nation of Mohammed and Islamic peoples.'[11] At the end of the war when Jerusalem had fallen it was said that King Faisal 'was more pained than any other Arab leader except the gallant little Hashemite [King Hussein] about the Zionist occupation of East Jerusalem and the al-Aqsa mosque.'[12] Faisal's call probably had more to do with the competing claim of the al-Sa'ud and Hashemite families to custodianship of the Holy Places than with a real desire to see jihad waged for the Palestinians.

In the immediate aftermath of the war, however, the response of these external Islamic actors was severely muted, especially as Jerusalem had been not only occupied but annexed *de facto* by the government of Israel. It was not until September 1967 that the World Islamic Conference (WIC) met in Amman to discuss Jerusalem's holy sites and offer its proposals to recover them from Israeli occupation. Islamic leaders from all over the world were called to attend. The meeting, however, ended in procrastination with a decision to hold a future meeting or 'Islamic summit conference' to 'raise the Islamic world and peoples for the rescue of Islamic holy places from Zionism's desecration.'[13] The Muslim world clearly lacked a unified commitment on the issue of another conflict with Israel. While the call to jihad was made from Arab capitals no one rushed to volunteer for the approaching confrontation with the Zionists. There were no contingency plans for a possible Israeli victory and the impact this would have on Islam. Perhaps more importantly, the whole Islamic debate failed even to address the question of the Palestinian Muslim population that would now live under the rule of infidels.

The Israeli Occupation of the West Bank, Jerusalem and the Gaza Strip

The impact of the war and the imposition of Israeli occupation in the West Bank and Gaza Strip had profound consequences for Palestine's Islamic movement. The whole rubric of politics was deeply affected by the Arab defeat. Yet the defeat threw up new ways of addressing the issue of Palestinian struggle for self-determination: the option of armed struggle (fedayeen fighting) assumed a high level of legitimacy and there was a rapid rise in the status of the Palestinian national movement and its constituent parts. The Palestinian struggle became increasingly secularised and avoided any hint of a sectarian debate. The PLO now declared itself a secular, non-sectarian liberation movement dedicated to the establishment of an independent Palestinian state.

Throughout all this, religion, whether Islam or Christianity, continued to play a role in the lives of individual Palestinians. While it is true that the Marxist ideologies of the Palestinian left became more popular and while the idea of organised political Islam may have been eclipsed temporarily by the sheer appeal of figures like Yasser Arafat, Khalil al-Wazir (Abu Jihad) and George Habash who were leading the national movement, Islam did not of course disappear altogether from people's lives.

Following the Israeli occupation, Palestinians began to draw a distinction between their political and religious lives. Irrespective of whether an individual was Christian or Muslim, this presented an interesting cultural dilemma. In Palestinian society the identity of an individual was very closely bound to a religion, whether it was practised by worshipping at the mosque or the church. Such affiliations fulfilled more than a religious function; they acted as a familiar signpost for Palestinians and were an organic part of most people's identities.

Yet Islam played almost no role in politics in the West Bank and Gaza Strip. The occupation did more than change the political order; it changed the economic, social and cultural nature of Palestinian society. Initial changes in the Palestinian economy caused by the shift of employment away from agriculture and into the Israeli labour market brought temporary prosperity. This, combined with the flow of Palestinian remittances from the Gulf states, affected the prevailing social structures and allegiances in Palestinian society.[14] The positive effects of this economic and social change were far outweighed by the continuing Israeli occupation, expropriation of Palestinian land and the repressive political rule of the military authorities. Nevertheless, economic change resulting in the further secularisation of society weakened the appeal of the Islamists.

The Islamic Response to Israeli Occupation: West Bank and Gaza Strip

The groups representing political Islam had to contend with the effect of the Israeli occupation on their organisations. In addition, the Muslim Brotherhood, the Liberation Party (LP) and the traditional Islamic institutions all had to face the ideological repercussions of an Israeli (Jewish) occupation of the Holy Land as opposed to an Arab (Muslim) one. Their responses were muted. However, the Islamic perspective on the impact of Israeli occupation was unexpected and certainly did not always reflect the views of nationalist Palestinians and the fedayeen movement. As one leader declared, 'It was the good fortune of the Ikhwan al-Muslimin in the Gaza Strip to have Nasser defeated by the Israeli army. After all, he had been the most significant enemy for our movement and now he had been defeated by Israel – the number one enemy of all the Arabs.'[15]

With the war over and the impact of Israeli occupation daily apparent, the Islamic movement had to come to terms with the new reality and develop a response to it. The response, however, was not always forthcoming; while institutional leaders of Islam played a marginal role in the community, the brotherhood was partially paralysed. As society faced repeated trauma, alien occupation, the effect of war, a loss of identity and the threat of permanent annexation, the once vibrant and vociferous Islamic alternative was unable to respond. However, many individual Muslims were outraged at the thought of a Jewish occupation of Islamic soil. One Islamic activist from Hebron announced:

> The Israelis intruded on our holy places, they created a burning feeling in our souls by these acts and abuses. In the past, before the creation of the Israeli state, Jews and Moslems had lived peacefully side by side in Jerusalem and Jews were allowed to freely [sic] practise their faith. But when the situation was reversed and the came to rule we were not allowed to practise our faith [a reference to the closure of the Ibrahimi mosque in Hebron] as we had always done.[16]

On the whole, however, the activities and organisation of groups like the Muslim Brotherhood and the LP were curtailed either through decisions within the organisations not to resume their activities or by sheer lack of interest and support from within the community. According to a number of leading Muslim brothers, as soon as the war was over and it became apparent that the Israeli occupation would not be temporary, steps were taken to slow or even halt organisational activity. The links between the sister and mother organisations in Jordan and Egypt were also loosened either as a result of closed borders or of the difficulties involved in travel between the areas. This situation highlighted the deep dependency that had formed between the Palestinian branch and its counterparts in other countries. Without the parent organisation, the Palestinian Islamic movement was bereft of a strong and stable organisational structure. For too long it had acted as a satellite and knew no other role.

Institutional Islam

The catalyst that galvanised the institutional leadership of Islam immediately after the war was the *de facto* annexation of East Jerusalem and the Old City on 28 June 1967 which meant that the Dome of the Rock and al-Aqsa mosque were now under the control of the Israelis. In addition, the decision by the Israeli authorities to disband the Palestinian municipal council finally provoked a response from leaders of the community and other Islamic notables connected to Jerusalem's leading families.

One figure to emerge during this period was Sheikh Hamed as-Sayeh, president of the Shari'a court and Jerusalem's chief religious judge (*qadi*), who mobilised the Palestinian Islamic protest against the Israelis. Sheikh as-Sayeh had fled to Jericho during the war but the Israelis brought him back to the city to conduct the first Friday prayers at al-Aqsa mosque under occupation. As-Sayeh subsequently undertook a dynamic role in organising the Muslim community. He helped orchestrate the resumption of institutional Islam in the West Bank.

A month after the *de facto* annexation of Jerusalem, Sheikh as-Sayeh invited twenty-five Jerusalem notables to discuss and formulate a response to the annexation and the continuing Israeli occupation of the West Bank. The meeting was held also for another, less open objective: many of the participants were there to ensure in some way or other, the continuation and representation of Jordanian interests. The meeting had many interesting aspects, not least because, as Ibrahim Dakkak notes:

> The resolutions taken ... were political in nature, based on a religious fatwa ... [which] stipulated that during the absence of the Moslem sovereign [King Hussein], the Moslems at the place of his jurisdiction should administer their affairs through his representatives.[17]

The decision to issue such a *fatwa* was important and seemed to offer hope that the Muslim establishment would challenge Israeli authority politically. It was also, however, designed to perpetuate Jordanian interests in the area rather than Palestinian national interests under Israeli occupation. The *fatwa* sought to legitimise the continued practice of placing Palestinian Islamic affairs under the authority of the government in Jordan. In addition, the meeting decided upon the formation of a new committee known as the Higher Islamic Committee (al-Ha'i al-Islamiyya al-'Ula) (HIC) which would preside over Palestinian Muslim affairs. What remained unclear was the exact role the committee would play in defending these interests. It was clear, however, that the committee would enjoy close ties with the Jordanian regime.

The Battle for the Waqf

By late 1967 the institutions of Islam in Jerusalem and the West Bank were the subject of a power struggle between Jordan, through the Ministry of Religious Affairs, and Israel, which claimed responsibility for Islamic affairs in Jerusalem and went on to place all the city's holy sites under the supervision of its own Ministry of Religious Affairs. The possibility of an independent Palestinian clerical body which could represent and support the Muslim community shrank between these two powers. Institutional Islam, which in the 1930s had almost had a monopoly on the political representation of Muslim Palestinians, was now increasingly likely to represent the opinions and views of the regime in Amman rather than the refugee Muslims of the West Bank. While it can be argued that these leaders were, ultimately, working in the interests of Palestinian Muslims through the support of a Jordanian option, such an interpretation fails to acknowledge that by this point Muslim Palestinian popular opinion was: (i) increasingly hostile to a Hashemite solution to the Palestinian issue; and (ii) moving towards support for radical secular Palestinian nationalist issues. Here was a classic example of a communication gap between leaders and the population.

For a while, however, the Higher Islamic Committee (HIC) attempted to make an impact on Israeli political and military opinion while at the same time representing Hashemite interests in Jerusalem and the West Bank. In their first declaration (issued on 24 July 1967) the committee members asserted that they would not co-operate with the Israeli authorities or encourage their preachers to submit their Friday sermons for Israeli censorship. This raises a contradiction: the Palestinian clergy had been willing to co-operate with the Jordanian authorities and submit their sermons for censorship. Surely, in this context, authority was authority whether it was Jordanian or Israeli? It was not made clear whether the HIC was essentially a religious or political body. Some members argued that it had the potential to be a nationalist institution,[18] yet others argued that the HIC was not formed to agitate on behalf of the Palestinian national movement. The committee was formed hastily with little serious deliberation over its formal role or objectives other than its part in mounting a protest against Israeli erosion of Jordanian authority over the practise of Islam in Jerusalem and the West Bank. It was clear that the HIC sought to invoke a religious appeal and encourage religious activities in a political attempt to undermine the Israeli authorities. In this it failed.

An HIC memorandum of West Bank Muslim leaders outlined the real lines of power and influence within the country's Islamic institutions. The signatories of the document based their argument for non-recognition of Israeli jurisdiction on the fact that as far as they were concerned 'Arab Jerusalem [was] an integral part of Jordan', with which it had entered into union in 1950 with 'complete freedom of choice'. The memorandum ended by declaring:

> We hereby record that the annexation of Arab Jerusalem is an invalid measure taken unilaterally by the occupation authorities against the will of the inhabitants of the city who reject this annexation and insist on the continued unity of Jordanian territory.[19]

The composition of the HIC was interesting in itself. As well as religious figures, members included those who might have been considered as secular political figures such as Ruhi al-Khatib (Mayor of Jerusalem), Hamed as-Sayeh (Shari'a court), Said Sabri (qadi) and Hassan Tahbub (lawyer). Indeed, of the twenty-five members on the committee only seven were religious dignitaries or administrators. Politically active Islamic sheikhs and qadis from the West Bank were conspicuous by their absence. Instead, these figures, including the Muslim Brother leader Sheikh Nashur Damin and other activists like Sheikh Said Bilal and Sheikh Izz'at al-Ma'ari, became involved in smaller local committees or groups which were linked to the newly-formed and more secular National Guidance Committee.[20]

While the HIC was able to issue memoranda and protests to the Israeli authorities, it failed to appeal to the natural bond that the Muslims of the West Bank felt for their holy sites and their Islamic administration, courts and schooling, and so was unable to gain popular support from within the Palestinian community. The HIC was in fact a symbol of continuing Jordanian interests in the West Bank. Its control over the Islamic administration of the area was its only direct link to the Palestinian population and it exploited this link, not through the popular leaders who were rising from the ranks of the refugee and urban Palestinian communities, but through the old framework of politics conducted through Palestinian notables.

Throughout this period, then, the power of the Waqf and other Islamic institutions declined under Jordanian control. Its autonomy was minimal with localised committees addressing particular administrative tasks. Institutionally, however, the administrative structure of Islam became closely entwined in the Hashemite system and, therefore, bound to Hashemite claims to legitimacy derived from Islamic links to the Prophet Mohammad. As Dumper remarks though, 'In the main the Jordanian government did not alienate the religious establishment and was able to offer it sufficient inducements in terms of salaries and status to procure its support.'[21]

The West Bank:
Nationalist Ascendancy and Islamic Demise

The experiences of the Islamic movement on the West Bank during the first decade of Israeli occupation were unique. Political conditions were radically different from those in the Gaza Strip and socio-economic factors under Israeli occupation altered the way in which the movement operated. The West Bank through the first decade of occupation was the centre of a power struggle between pro-Jordanian conservative elites and the emergent nationalist movement. The relationship between East Bank and West Bank after the occupation of the latter was not completely severed. The Israelis 'open bridge'[22] policy not only allowed a flow of people and goods but also permitted the politicians and supporters of the regime in Amman to maintain power among the Palestinians. The Israelis were not adverse to this development hoping that Jordanian influence would overwhelm support for the nationalist ascendancy. Thus during this, more than any other decade, the Islamic movement's activities and objectives reflected developments outside the Islamic community.

While initially it looked as though the Islamic movement might have a role to play in the struggle against Israeli occupation, it soon became apparent that its leaders were unable to sustain an Islamic response to the occupation and its authorities and policies, including the settlement of Palestinian land. As Nissim notes, 'Few religious leaders seemed adequately equipped to guide today's Muslims through the spiritual crisis arising from the need to harmonise the conflicting values of the old and the new way of life.'[23] By the end of 1967 the attempts by the leadership of institutional Islam to influence the political policies of the occupation authorities were exhausted. The leader of the HIC, Sheikh as-Sayeh, was deported. His replacement, Sheikh Izz ad-Din al-Alami, maintained a low profile, obviously wishing to avoid the same fate as his newly-departed colleague. Irrespective of the political status accorded to these figures under the Jordanian administration, the Israeli authorities refused to recognise their influence; in this way they were increasingly marginalised and excluded.

The Muslim Brotherhood: Weak Link in the Chain of Jihad

The most important change for the Muslim Brotherhood in the West Bank after the Israeli occupation was the severe disruption of its link with headquarters in the East Bank. The leaders in Amman ordered a 'cessation of day-to-day contact with the West Bank' leaving the branches there, already struggling, to come to terms with the immediate impact of occupation, without the direction that had always come from Amman.[24] Branch leaders and activists in the towns of Jerusalem, Hebron and Nablus, increasingly aware of the problems of trying to sponsor an Islamic message in a politically secular climate, decided reluctantly, therefore, to close branch offices and cease overt ties with the movement in Jordan. As one leader noted:

> Immediately after the war the Muslim Brotherhood closed all of its offices in the West Bank. Some members went to the movement in Amman and made a life for themselves there. Others stayed but they did not do anything. They felt that the market for ideas and the importance of Islamic ideology was closed for the time being.[25]

Another member from Hebron remarked:

> In the case of the Ikhwan all the offices in Hebron were closed after the war and activities ceased under this organisation's name. Thus the name went away but some people continued with their work. Some in the leadership went underground and many leaders left.[26]

A further reason given by leaders and members of the brotherhood for the decision to close their offices and cut down activity was fear of arrest by the Israeli authorities. There were rumours that the Israelis would use information on the brotherhood from captured Jordanian intelligence files to eradicate completely the organisation in the West Bank. Although in the event there were no arrest campaigns against the organisation during this period, the fear of arrest was enough to cause an exodus of members from the West Bank to neighbouring Jordan.

The Muslim Brotherhood had also recognised the force behind the rise of the Palestinian national resistance movement and that Palestinian political identity now revolved around the notion of nationalism, not political Islam. The brotherhood was thus forced to reconsider the manner in which it presented its public image and the appropriateness of its message. The passivity of the leadership and the consequences of this were felt acutely. The occupation proved that the movement had not been able to provide capable theologians who could mobilise supporters. One Muslim Brother from Nablus explained how divisions within the remnants of the organisation became increasingly apparent: 'As the years passed a problem arose. The older established leadership grew too old and was unable to follow the new developments around it and the undertones of a society that was changing rapidly in those first years of the occupation.'[27] By the 1970s the brotherhood had reached a crisis point, as Subhi Anabtawi, its leader in Nablus pointed out:

A gap was created. They [the leadership] grew out of touch and they lost some of their appeal, especially to the growing numbers of youth. It was a time in the market where the strength of numbers and the military occupation ruled and it was hard for the Ikhwan to find a place in this atmosphere.[28]

Collectively it was concluded that the time was not right for the Muslim Brotherhood actively to promote its specifically Islamic political agenda and the organisation decided to bow out, for the time being, from the battle to win the hearts and minds of the Palestinian community.

The depleted membership of the organisation was not renewed by a stepped-up recruitment drive. This can be explained by the prevailing political climate as well as the lack of leadership in the West Bank through which to direct such initiatives. Even within the formerly safe circle of family, friends and peer group where the brotherhood might have recruited new members, there was a noticeable decline in this type of activity, and other functions such as the publication of books and pamphlets all but ceased. Finally, the scope of the Muslim Brotherhood's political contribution during this period was circumscribed by financial difficulties brought about by the occupation. Membership dues declined, funders were forced to curtail their contributions as assets in Palestinian bank accounts were frozen by the Israeli authorities and financial support from Amman was hampered by the severance of direct economic links between the East and West banks.

While the organisational side of the brotherhood was wound down, the Israeli occupation did result in a palpable change in the way in which former adherents of Ikhwan ideology viewed their own political situation. Whether the Brotherhood liked it or not, the occupation demanded a response from the Islamic movement. With time this change was reflected in Palestinian brotherhood thinking. In the words of one Muslim Brother, Sheikh Ibrahim: 'After 1967 and the Israeli occupation we knew we would have to change our political priorities as an Islamic organisation. The main theme that we then had to organise around was to bring an immediate end to the occupation,' in this way the Israeli occupation served to immediately 'Palestinianise' the ideological bent of the Muslim Brotherhood. 'The occupation resulted in a great growth of consciousness, especially with the Israeli occupation of the al-Aqsa mosque. This act really hit at our spirit and made us feel the pain of the whole situation for all Islamic peoples,' declared Sheikh Ibrahim.[29]

From this perspective the Israeli occupation of Palestinian land was not just a military or political act by one state against another group of people but a religious act of aggression in a long-standing conflict between the Jewish and Muslim peoples. This conflict, illustrated in the chapters of the Qur'an and the stories of the *hadith* (sayings of the Prophet), took on a fresh perspective in the light of the perceived defeat as the Jews occupied the Islamic holy places. For this reason the Israeli occupation of Jerusalem acted as a catalyst in a process that resulted eventually in the emergence of a more specific Palestinian Islamic trend. While this trend acknowledged its roots in the Muslim Brotherhood in Egypt and Jordan it began also to reflect the prevailing political perspectives of the Palestinian community. As one Islamic theologian from Hebron asserted:

> The war was a point of breakthrough where most Palestinian Muslims were concerned. It signified an end to the slogans, ideologies and an end to the Arab regimes. Also with the 1967 war and the occupation of Jerusalem and al-Aqsa an awakening from this point took place. Eventually a new strategy arose, an understanding which was completely different from the past thoughts and actions ... Muslims realised after 1967 that they could no longer rely on others to provide solutions.[30]

The Muslim Brotherhood still looked to al-Banna's writing for inspiration. It had always regarded the Palestine issue as relevant to it and placed it in the wider context of a debate about the influence of the West and the impact of imperialism in the Arab and Muslim world. Yet the Palestinian brothers found little in such writing to help address and counter with strong mass appeal the dual blow of the Israeli occupation and the rise of the secular radicalised Palestinian national movement.

Throughout its short history Palestine's Muslim Brotherhood had always relied on the writings of members in other countries and other political contexts. The events of 1967 and the first decade of the occupation failed to elicit an internal response In their defence, the leaders of the movement in the West Bank argue that until 1967 there was no need for them to formulate a specific Palestinian perspective because the ideological precepts of the movement as a whole were applicable and workable in the context of that time. In any case, until the war, top-rank decisions over substantive political and religious issues within the movement had been taken by the leadership in Amman. Policies had never emanated from the West Bank and the West Bank branches had made no attempt to build an autonomous leadership.

Brotherhood members also argued that the movement's ideological development was weak because it was periodically repressed by one government or another. In the words of one Islamic radical in Hebron: 'The problem was that all authorities were preventing the development of our ideology ... we could not reach the point of ideological liberation at a time when it was needed.'[31] According to such supporters a specifically Palestinian ideological trend could not be developed because the repression of the movement had deprived it of its intellectuals and thinkers. But this argument is belied by the experience of the brotherhood in Egypt where the leadership, intellectuals and theological thinkers produced a vast body of scholarly work even though most of them had been imprisoned. Indeed the repression of the movement in Egypt served to radicalise certain intellectuals, foremost among them Sayyid Qutb, and provoke them into producing important tracts that today remain relevant to Islamists the world over.

In addition to weakness as a result of the severance of its links with Amman, the Muslim Brotherhood's strong identification with the Hashemite regime was also problematic. While the branches in Nablus, Jerusalem and Hebron prospered under the king's benign patronage, they suffered once the war was over. The brotherhood had bestowed legitimacy on the policies of the regime in Jordan, even when those policies were directed against the Palestinian population. This, quite naturally, affected its standing in the West Bank and the radical change in political orientation after the war among the majority of Palestinians living in the camps and urban areas.

The Six Day War and the immediate effects of the occupation on the Muslim Brotherhood were, then, devastating. The movement wound down its activities while its members left the country or stayed on under a cloud of silent rage against the Jewish occupiers of their holy sites. There is considerable debate about whether or not the call to jihad by the brotherhood in the West Bank resulted in anything tangible – certainly it was not echoed in the mosques. It failed because the nationalist movement had taken over from Islam as a vehicle of protest, and captured its fighting spirit.

Yet Islamists claim that they did undertake a military role in the struggle against Israel – within the framework of Fatah. According to Ziad Abu Ghanemeh, a Jordanian brother:

> After the war the Islamic movement, especially the Ikhwan, were involved in the fedayeen war against Israel. But they did not operate under the guise of their own organisation but in the name of Fatah. Some of the most famous operations were executed by the Muslim Brotherhood.32

Brothers in the West Bank also attested to their involvement as fighters in Fatah's military wing. One explained that they were forced to join Fatah because their own Muslim Brotherhood branches were, by this time, too small and weak. The move was seen in pragmatic terms, and the members were viewed as Islamic fedayeen. Another veteran Islamic radical from Nablus supported the existence of a Fatah–Muslim Brotherhood military link at this time, saying:

> In fact I'd go as far as saying that during this period there was a branch of Fatah which was designed to take care of the Islamic movement and any linked military activity.[33]

The evidence to support such claims is, however, elusive. These statements probably bear some testimony to the receptiveness of Fatah to new members who believed that an Islamic agenda should be pursued alongside the nationalist one, but no more.

The more radical and leftist groups within the Palestinian nationalist camp such as the PFLP or the communists, had nothing to do with the Islamist school of thought promoted by groups like the Muslim Brotherhood. Although there had been previous examples of co-operation as, for example, in Gaza between the brotherhood and the communists, this was the exception rather than the rule. In addition, in the immediate aftermath of the war, the radical groups were themselves undergoing transition. Internal activities superseded the issue of relations with other political actors. The radical groups, fired by revolutionary vigour, were preparing to take up an armed struggle against the Israelis.

The reformist approach embodied in the philosophy of the Muslim Brotherhood was the ideological antithesis of the radical approach. This ideological gulf did not, however, mean that the radicals and leftists in the Palestinian movement were out to make enemies of the Islamists. There was a general policy to avoid internal conflict and antagonism within the Palestinian community. If disputes occurred it was not over the competing beliefs of religious or socialist or Marxist solutions. One leftist leader in Gaza remarked that: 'I talk primarily from personal experience. The leftists in general didn't start any attack on the basis that it was religion involved but other factors. In other words there was never an attack on Islam during this period.'[34]

In sum, the evidence to suggest that the Muslim Brotherhood in the West Bank supported ideologically or logistically the struggle to end the Israeli occupation is scant, except for the indication of brotherhood members fighting in the ranks of Fatah. Most evidence suggested by members of the brotherhood points to a decline in activities and a turn inward, ignoring the popular call for struggle. The organisation largely relinquished its vanguard role to the Palestinian left and stood by and watched the Palestinian masses turn to arms, not in defence of Islam but in defence of nationalist ideals which called for a national secular state in the whole of Palestine.

The Liberation Party:
Radical Islam in Retreat

People here are raised on the *assir al-harb* (juice of war). Yet they can't defend themselves, their land or their family. [Abu Ali, Bourqa, 1 September 1993]

By 1967 the LP's activities in the West Bank had been severely circumscribed. Since its repression in 1956–57 the party had found it increasingly difficult to organise its activities and advertise its cause. The leadership was now permanently based in Lebanon, making communications difficult. Following the Israeli occupation of the West Bank the LP had to formulate a response to circumstances that were anathema to everything the party stood for.

Within a year the leadership in Beirut had reached a decision about the future in the West Bank and called on remaining members there to bring a halt to their activities. Under the conditions of a Zionist occupation, party members were to cease their struggle. The road to victory was temporarily blocked by the Israelis, and the party would have to bide its time. The impact of this decision was not as calamitous as it might have been had the party survived King

Hussein's crackdown in 1967. Most LP supporters had followed their leaders out of the West Bank and settled in Jordan, Lebanon and other Arab states. The depletion of party ranks in the West Bank, therefore, made the call to cease activity pragmatic. A contrary call to step up attacks on the Israelis or widen activity would have been impossible to implement and would have left the party open to ridicule from other Palestinian political parties and repression from the Israeli authorities.

Although the LP did not lose all its support in the West Bank, it became increasingly secretive, its activities confined to a few small *halaqa* groups. These met in secret at particular mosques where Nabahani's works would be discussed. It was not the intention of remaining members to play a part in the political arena; the call to jihad, to resurrect the caliphate and establish an Islamic state was in abeyance.

The Muslim Brotherhood in the Gaza Strip: the 'Conscious Decision'

In the Gaza Strip those few remaining activists or supporters of the Muslim Brotherhood who had survived the repression of Nasser viewed the Israeli occupation ambiguously. Activists' responses to the end of Egyptian rule and the onset of an Israeli occupation varied according to age and experience. Some were positively glad that the Israelis had defeated Nasserism and undermined the credibility of pan-Arabism. After all, the routing of Egyptian forces from Gaza meant a respite in the anti-Muslim Brother campaign. No one actually expressed any regrets over the defeat.

Nonetheless, there was little for the Muslim Brotherhood to hold on to in the direct wake of the war and the Israeli occupation. While logistically speaking, the prospects for its future were no worse under Israel than under Nasser, at all other levels the Gaza movement was weak and disorganised. But although there was no real Muslim Brotherhood organisation in Gaza after 1967, those with an allegiance to the movement argue differently: 'By this point [1967] the seeds of the Ikhwan al-Muslimin had been planted in Gaza, particularly among the new generation of high school students ... the defeat made the Palestinian people here more sympathetic to the Ikhwan and their work after the defeat of Nasser.'[35]

If the seeds of political Islam were sown during this period, the movement nevertheless had a few cold winters and summer droughts to go through before it was able to grow in Gaza. The hopes of the Muslim Brotherhood were pinned on the demise of nationalist and imported ideologies at a time when they were thriving in the overcrowded refugee camps of the Gaza Strip. Such hopes were, for the time being, in vain. It was impossible for a movement like the Muslim Brotherhood to compete against the rise in support for the Palestinian national liberation movement and the active commitment that Gazans gave to it. Even if after 1967, as Dr Mahmoud Zahar, the leader of Hamas, claims, 'the people returned to their religion [and] started to study Islam thoroughly and began to live Islam as a system governing their way of life,'[36] this trend was most definitely not discernible among the majority of the population at the time.

Contact between Egyptian and Gazan branches of the movement ceased in the immediate aftermath of the war. Many brothers from both the Gaza Strip and Egypt had been imprisoned as part of Nasser's continued campaign against them when the war broke out in 1967. According to Assad Saftawi, 'In 1965–66 there was yet another crackdown on the Muslim Brotherhood in Egypt as well as here. This meant that more arrests took place.'[37] The Gaza movement was nothing more than a small band of men who shared the same political and religious views. Now, with the Israeli occupation, all hope of any organisational links between the two branches disappeared.

The Brotherhood's lack of power within the community and a period of almost total political obscurity meant that Israel did not perceive the organisation as either a political or military threat to the establishment of order. Accordingly, the Israeli military forces in Gaza in 1967 took no action against the remnants of the movement; there were no arrests and individuals were not singled out by the authorities as potential troublemakers. For its own part, the small Muslim Brotherhood took a decision not to confront the Israeli occupation authorities. According to a leader of the organisation at that time, 'The Muslim Brotherhood took a conscious decision not to engage with the rest of the Palestinian movement ... in any acts to resist the effects of the Israeli occupation of Gaza.'[38] Part of the brotherhood's logic in choosing such a strategy was that it believed this was not the time to take on the Israelis. Its greatest priority was to reconstitute, build-up and reorganise the movement after years of repression under Nasser.

There was another reason for this decision, as explained by Assad Saftawi:

The Ikhwan al-Muslimin employed a degree of wisdom in their decision not to confront the Israelis at this time. Any confrontation would invite the Israelis to crack down on a newly-revived and infant Islamic trend. Such repression would not help after years of pressure from Nasser and at a time when a large number of neighbouring Arab regimes still regarded us as enemies.[39]

During the first years of Israeli occupation the Muslim Brotherhood in Gaza did not, therefore, play any part in the attempts by the Palestinians to resist occupation or join in the growing trend towards armed struggle. Instead, it stayed in the mosques and prayed for deliverance from both its nationalist counterparts and the Israeli occupation. The brothers did not make any significant inroads in recruiting from among Gazan youth, who now supported the nationalist and radical leftist rejection of Israeli rule and were preparing to join the fedayeen struggle for liberation. 'Reconstitution' for the brotherhood meant little more than a low profile, a strengthening of the old underground network of Muslim believers, encouragement of former members to return to the fold and a resumption of preaching. There were no publications or clandestine printing presses, and the flow of brotherhood literature smuggled from Egypt during Nasser's regime became a trickle. Financial support from Egypt was so reduced that the organisation became dependent on local contributions and the occasional remittance from ex-members working in the Gulf states. This was not enough to finance any immediate programme of activity or to rebuild the organisation's infrastructure.

It is notable that in the post-1967 period, Muslim Brotherhood branches in the West Bank and Gaza Strip were once more under the same political administration. The Israeli occupation of the two areas meant that contacts between these two formerly distinct geographic entities could be resumed. However, there was no immediate attempt to take advantage of the situation. Eventually, it is claimed by the brotherhood, an attempt was made at Sheikh Yassin's initiative, to forge contacts with fellow members in the West Bank. From the early 1970s it is alleged that monthly meetings took place between representatives of the brotherhood from the Gaza Strip and from Hebron and Nablus. Nevertheless, the two organisations remained distinct entities still tied to a history of their respective experiences under Egypt and Jordan. Once again this reflected the inability within the movement to think or behave like a Palestinian–Islamic movement within an explicit arena of Palestinian politics.

The First Decade: Iron Fist Occupation

Coming to terms with and subsequently resisting the occupation was the principal concern of many Palestinians in the first decade of Israeli rule. Among this large group were those who were involved or about to become involved with nascent political Islam, and whose primary aim at this time was to gauge a suitable response to the changing political context. This reaction was slow in coming. For the better part of the decade many argue that the force of political Islam was inactive and that the reason for this was clear: 'The strength of Palestinian nationalism and the widespread backing of its proponents kept the Islamic movement dormant.'[40] The brotherhood for its part argued that its organisation was active in a general social revival of Islam that began in the first decade of occupation. It should be noted, however, that this revival was the result of artificial stimulation given the movement as a result of a benign Israeli policy towards the Islamists in the occupied territories. The political activities and events of the decade truly shaped those of the years to come, particularly in Gaza. Indeed the opportunity, once again, to present a West Bank/Gaza Strip comparison allows the political contrasts between to the two areas to show through.

Gaza: Fedayeen Forces

This is the way to liberation of my homeland. And so, my brothers, I'll fight on. [Fedayeen recruitment poster, 1968]

The Israeli occupation of the Gaza Strip had a catalytic effect on all but institutional Islam and its traditional leaders. 'Although local inhabitants were initially stunned by the occupation, a fierce guerrilla movement sprang up quickly'.[41] When the Egyptian army was forced out of Gaza it left behind arms and ammunition. These stocks were used by remaining forces from the PLA and by individuals wanting to take up the armed struggle against Israel. The mini-war waged by Palestinians in the Gaza Strip lasted for some three years before it was finally crushed in 1971 by the Israeli military, under the orders of Defence Minister Ariel Sharon.

The fedayeen fighters of the Gaza Strip were modern revolution-aries fighting for national liberation, not religious salvation. The fedayeen movement spawned heroic idealised images of male and female commandos attacking the enemy, all against the highest odds.

They symbolised the Palestinian national movement and were always portrayed in a vanguard role, drawing inspiration from the guerrilla movements of Vietnam, China and Latin America. Furthermore, they were portrayed as educated, urban, worldly and sophisticated, not as traditional, conservative or rural figures. A product of the modern age, they were nevertheless willing to make the ultimate sacrifice in the struggle for Palestinian liberation. Such sacrifice, made on behalf of a struggle for nationhood and a nationalist movement, was well-rewarded by the religious establishment. Declared as martyrs (*shahid*) these fallen fighters were promised the rewards in paradise accorded to the fighters of jihad or a holy war.[42] Yet they were always called 'fedayeen' never 'mujahidin' (fighters of the jihad for God). This distinction is important in the symbols that were called into play during this period. The contribution of the leftist movement, particularly in Gaza, reflected a growing political trend within Palestinian politics. To call these leftist fighters 'mujahidin' would have been political as well as religious blasphemy.

The organisation of fedayeen fighters in the Gaza Strip reflected the attitude of the population to the prospect of a prolonged Israeli occupation. Gazans are proud of their role in establishing the fedayeen movement at a time when no such development occurred in the West Bank. Yet the odds stacked against the Gaza fighters were high. This was no Vietnam situation where both the terrain and the numbers involved in combat were an important aid; this was no Algeria where more than 10 million Algerians took on a French fighting force of 400,000. This battle was fought in an overcrowded desert-like strip of land that afforded no natural cover. Nevertheless, within the first year of occupation a number of small fedayeen groups had sprung up. The fighters were housed in the refugee camps or hid in the citrus groves of wealthy Gaza landowners. From these sites they were able to carry out raids against Israeli soldiers while avoiding instant detection. The numbers involved were small and their campaign was never going to defeat an army as sophisticated as the Israel Defence Forces (IDF) a feat the combined armies of Egypt, Jordan, Syria and Iraq had failed to achieve. The fedayeen hoped their tactics would serve as a catalyst, that their actions would encourage a mass Palestinian uprising and provoke Israel to withdraw from the area. Within a year the smaller groups merged and it was noted that while 'a year ago there were twenty-seven separate commando organisations; now there are at most five or six … in response to demands of the Palestinian people for unity.'[43]

The most active of these groups was the newly formed PFLP, an offshoot of the Arab National Movement (ANM). In Gaza the PFLP became instantly popular with the previously secularised socialist population that had grown up under Nasser's administration and played a key role in the Gaza struggle. A PFLP leader from Khan Yunis described the situation in Gaza from 1967 to 1971: 'Following 1967 the PLO, through groups like the PFLP, established the fedayeen domination ... when armed struggle was practised by Gazans the Israelis felt a danger and their feeling grew against those Fedayeen factions.'[44]

This three-year period was notable for the emergence of armed struggle as a strategy for liberation in the Gaza Strip. This approach reflected the larger ideological changes within the Palestinian national movement towards political violence. Faced with Israeli occupation and state violence against their community, the Palestinians armed themselves. The ideology of armed struggle was, by this time, broadly secular in content; Palestinians were asked to take up arms not as part of a jihad against the infidel but to free the oppressed from the Zionist colonial regime. The vocabulary of liberation was distinctly secular.

In the early years of occupation, then, the Palestinian people, unlike most of their Arab comrades, experienced a growth in their nationalist movement and in the discussion of a nationalist solution to the conflict with Israel. They also reversed the view of struggle with their slogan: 'We will liberate Palestine first, then the rest of the Arab world'. Ideology or values representing a resurgence of political Islam was not present in this mode of thinking. The radical left dominated the political scene with only the conservative forces of Fatah balancing the left's promotion of revolution through political violence.

The Islamic movement was unable to offer Gazans a viable alternative to the philosophy of the fedayeen struggle. Even those figures who were later leaders of the movement in the 1980s and 1990s admit their attraction and flirtation with the national movement at this stage:

I felt the feeling deep down of the disaster of 1967 ... After the war I was forced to re-think the situation ... I was forced to re-think and look for the right answer. And at first I discussed and tried to support the nationalist trend and use my support for Palestinians through the nationalist system.[45]

According to Haider Abdel Shaffi, 'After 1967, during the first four years of the occupation accompanied by militant resistance on behalf of the Palestinians here, there was no sign whatsoever of any Islamic re-emergence. The national feeling was represented by the PLO.'[46]

In 1971, however, as a direct result of Israeli policy, the situation in Gaza was irrevocably changed. No longer able to contain or control the fedayeen attacks, the Israeli government ordered a military response. The whole of the Gazan population was targeted by a relentless policy designed to halt fedayeen activity through the razing of homes and, more frighteningly, the transfer of thousands of Gazans. As described by press reports at the time:

> Opposition to the removal of refugees arose when it became apparent that Israel's objectives went beyond mere security ... So far as there is a policy, it is to move out one of five of the 180,000 people who occupy the Gaza camps ... A little over a week ago ... a giant bulldozer nosed its way into the Gaza Strip and methodically began to reduce to rubble houses that Palestinians had lived in for almost twenty years ... 500 people, half of them young children, were homeless ... We went back ... Another twenty houses had vanished; another 200 people were homeless.[47]

The numbers involved in the transfer were shocking. As many as 15,000 suspected fighters were deported to detention camps in Abu Zneima and Abu Rudeis in Sinai. The people transferred had had no opportunity to defend themselves. This security policy successfully instilled terror in the camps and wiped out the fedayeen bases.

Political activity was further restricted. The Gaza municipal council, founded under the Ottomans in 1893, was disbanded and the Israeli authorities took control of municipal services. The nationalist movement at both the level of armed struggle and political leadership was crushed. The political leadership had either been divested of any vestige of official power or transferred out of the camps. The sense of defeat within the Palestinian community, at this time, was palpable.

Phoenix from the Flames: Political Islam in Gaza

> There began a new era, when the movement grew in strength. The reasons for this growth are manifold. The occupiers, in these early days, were ready to encourage the growth of the Muslim Brotherhood to act as an internal contradiction to the nationalist movement, which they had engaged on many fronts. [Assad Saftawi, Gaza city, 21 December 1989]

The defeat of the fedayeen movement in Gaza during the late summer and early autumn of 1971 resulted in a gradual shift in the balance of Gaza's own dynamic of internal politics. A debilitated national movement could not hope, at this stage, to fulfil the comprehensive role formerly assigned to it by the local population and a political vacuum thus emerged. The legitimacy of the national movement remained intact, but the Israelis pursued a policy that frustrated attempts by nationalists to build their own institutions, provide services for the local community or represent them politically. Through this policy, which was to backfire badly in later decades, the Israelis helped promote the eventual resurgence of political Islam in Gaza.

According to Haider Abdel Shaffi, 'As soon as the nationalist armed movement was broken, then we experienced the incipient emergence of the Islamic movement. This began around 1973–74.'[48] It is clear that there was a deliberate decision within the Islamist movement at the time to resume activities in the public realm and to be increasingly vocal.

'The Creator': Sheikh Ahmad Yassin

The revitalised Islamic movement was the product of a unique individual who emerged during this period to lead a generation of young activists into the heart of Gazan society and later into the realm of politics. Sheikh Ahmad Yassin was to prove central to the future role of Islamic politics in the Gaza Strip.

Ahmad Yassin came into the world in turbulent times. The year of his birth, 1936, was the first year of the Palestinian revolt against the British mandate. By the time he was three the revolt had been defeated. Yassin grew up in the small village of Jourah in the Majdal region where his life revolved around rural pursuits. By the time he was twelve the members of the family were refugees in Gaza city. The war of 1948 had disrupted life in the village and everyone had fled south fearing the Israeli advance. They never went back, settling instead like so many others in the despairing Gaza environment. The Yassin family found employment in weaving and fishing and a home outside the refugee camps in the Jawrat ash-Shams district of Gaza. They later settled in the highly populated Zeitoun quarter of the sprawling city. Yassin himself soon found work at a local sea front restaurant, making his contribution to the economy of the extended family (his father had married twice).[49]

During his schooldays in Gaza, Yassin came into contact with the Muslim Brotherhood. He was a pupil at the Palestine Secondary School where a number of Muslim Brothers taught. He worshipped subsequently at the al-Khadra mosque and attended lectures and speeches of religious figures like Sheikh Abaseri and Sheikh Ghazali organised by the brotherhood. His ambitions were similar to those of many of his contemporaries: he wanted to be a teacher. During the early 1950s, he took the opportunity to study in Egypt and gain the qualifications he needed. He went to Ein Shams University in Cairo where he registered for a teacher-training course for a year, specialising in Arabic and English literature. On his return he took a job in one of the local schools. In addition to his teaching activities he organised religious instruction for his pupils, telling them stories of the *hadith*, teaching them to pray and read the Qur'an and taking them on trips to the mosque.[50] As a school teacher Yassin achieved a certain status in society which, combined with his public spirited role as an arbiter of local disputes, meant that the Yassin household was soon known throughout Beach camp where he lived and further afield in the Gaza area.

Although Yassin had no formal religious training his interest in the role of Islam was increasingly apparent and soon he began to preach the message that had always been promoted by the Muslim Brotherhood when he was a young member. Following Nasser's crackdown on the movement in 1966 Yassin tempered his association with the organisation but remained a faithful adherent of its philosophy. He continued his religious activities, concentrating on the task of Islamic education. He took the principles of *tabligh* and *da'wa*,[51] articulated by the Muslim Brotherhood and leaders like Hassan al-Banna, and turned them into his principal obligation. In keeping with the brotherhood's outlook, politically Yassin was a reformist who called for a gradual approach, encouraging a return to Islam within society before addressing wider political issues. His self-appointed role was to bring religion to the secularised youth of Gaza, to encourage them to return to Islam, to read the Qur'an, pray five times a day and observe Ramadan, in other words to be exemplary Muslims. Yassin also preached in the mosque. His efforts to promote religiosity brought him to the attention of the Egyptian authorities who imprisoned him briefly during the crackdown on the brotherhood in 1966.

In the period directly following the Israeli occupation Yassin remained politically inactive. Along with so many other like-minded

Muslims he knew that the popular tide of support in Gaza favoured a Palestinian nationalist solution. Nasser may have been defeated but the nationalist principles he had promoted were now embraced by the PLO which was supported throughout Gaza. By 1969–70, faced with the prospect of continued political marginalisation, the remnant of the brotherhood was galvanised into action. Attempts were made to revitalise the organisation. A new committee was formed to head it, Sheikh Ahmad Yassin was appointed leader on the strength of his record of work among the youth, and older members of the organisation were charged with administrative tasks such as the collection of *zakat*.[52]

By 1972–73 Sheikh Yassin had attracted a small band of followers who made a point of worshipping at his mosque and visiting his home in Shatti camp on a regular basis. Among them was a core of young men who would later fill the highest ranks of the movement: Abd al-Aziz Rantisi, Ibrahim al-Yazouri, Abd al-Fattah Dukhan, Isa al-Ashar, Salah Shahadeh and Mahmoud Zahar. Yassin's role is clearly acknowledged by Zahar: 'No one can deny that the resurgence of Islam depends on such people ... Sheikh Yassin played a remarkable part and no one can deny that he is the creator of the new Islamic movement in Gaza.'[53] Nevertheless, the sheikh was ready to bide his time before entering the political arena. This concentration on social activities, education and learning was summed up by Sheikh Yassin when he declared: 'We have to be patient because Islam will spread sooner or later and will have control all over the world. Patience will shorten the journey of Islam.'[54]

Even at this early stage Yassin had the charismatic appeal which contributed to his later ascent to the apex of Islamic politics in the area. Physically disabled from an early age and plagued by ill-health,[55] he was confined to a wheelchair. But his thin, pinched face, closely-shorn beard and brown eyes challenged any visitor. His life was simple and he had a certain ordinariness which set him apart from many other political leaders in Gaza and which helps to explain his unadulterated relationship with his followers. He lived in a poor deprived neighbourhood where work and other opportunities for advancement were few. His house, like those of his neighbours, was cramped. He had been exposed to the educational experience of Egypt but he was not a great scholar or theologian. Unlike Haj Amin al-Husseini or Sheikh Izz ad-Din al-Qassam who both studied at al-Azhar and came from families with a tradition of religious learning, he had received no formal religious training. Even the title of sheikh was an honorary rather than a theological one. He did not theorise the importance of Islam in politics. Instead, he involved himself with the society he lived in. Rather than communicate his ideas through the pages of books, spending his time elaborating a particular concept on paper, he chose the dynamic of the spoken word in the mosque and in the sermon. He was essentially a teacher who was in his natural element communicating in this fashion and he had instant appeal for those who lived around him or shared his experiences. He was a refugee who had grown up in a small insignificant village where people were conservative and religious.

Yassin's teaching was from a particular and very specific perspective. He continued to preach the call of the Muslim Brotherhood and sought the re-establishment of a flourishing Islam through the cultural revitalisation of the Gaza Strip. Yet while this early period allowed the movement time to regain its strength, establish its leadership and draw up an agenda, it did not see the resurgence of Islam as a mass response to the end of the Nasserist era, the Israeli occupation, the defeat of Palestinian nationalist forces in Gaza or the call for jihad. It was only in the second decade of the occupation (1977–87) that Sheikh Yassin and his colleagues would acquire a large following.

These early years were spent in quiet contemplation of the role that Yassin and like-minded men might play in their own society. He surrounded himself with educators, doctors and others who could offer a service to society and who shared a common background and vision. The importance of playing a political role was not emphasised. This outlook was reflected in Sheikh Yassin's decision in 1973 to form a small welfare and charity-based society called the Mujama (Islamic Congress) which would eventually rise from the ashes of fedayeen defeat to challenge the hegemony of the national movement. The Mujama's decision to operate in an area hitherto neglected by the institutions of the national movement was significant in so far as it reflected the genuine desire of Islamic activists to provide services and support within their own community coupled with a desire to avoid a confrontation with the nationalists over hearts and minds by respecting their sphere of activity, and a close adherence to the principles of the reformist and gradualist approach of the Muslim Brotherhood movement.

The Mujama, supported by Israel, began to organise a network of welfare and education services which in later years would become one of the movement's most important assets. As Gilles Kepel remarks, this was a region-wide phenomenon: 'Islamic welfare networks were coming to play an essential part in assimilating those elements of the population who aspired to taste the fruits of modernity and prosperity but could not get at them.'[56] Sheikh Yassin's supporters focused their activities on the most deprived areas of the Gaza Strip. They established small clinics in the refugee camps, offering the services of a doctor or a dentist, running kindergartens, organising classes in the study of the Qur'an and *hadith* in the mosques. Where there were no mosques the Mujama converted small rooms or buildings, provided copies of the Qur'an and other religious material and set up a public address system for the call to prayer. It also organised a wide range of sporting facilities, concentrating on the martial arts and football. Football stadiums or grounds owned and administered by the Mujama were found throughout the Gaza Strip. The collection of *zakat* was continued in order to finance the Mujama's welfare and education activities and important links were established with small traders and merchants in the camps.

Conclusion

During the first decade of the Israeli occupation of the West Bank and Gaza Strip there is little evidence to support an argument for the revival of Islam as a political force. Changes in the socio-economic patterns of Palestinian society were definitely evident but they did not result in a soul-searching exercise where Palestinians questioned their Muslim identity and criticised the failure of their leaders in the nationalist movement to effect meaningful political change. The evocation of symbols of national unity, solidarity and steadfastness (*sumud*) by the nationalist movement was effective in channelling the political energies of the community to face the increasingly authoritarian nature of the Israeli occupation.

The Muslim Brotherhood used this period to regroup and reassert itself as a religious organisation dedicated to a programme of social reform. The group was influenced by the dynamic of Islamic resurgence regionally but was unable to generate the necessary internal political climate for change. It did not find a politically receptive audience nor would it do so without the catalyst of external actors such as the occupation authorities. Only through Israel's subsequent policy of divide and rule within the Palestinian political community in the West Bank and Gaza Strip would Islam as a political force become significant.

4

The Second Decade of Occupation (1977–86): the Rise of Islam

During the second decade of the Israeli occupation (1977–86) religious revivalism was on the rise in the Gaza Strip and West Bank. Whether at a socio-cultural level this revivalism was imposed or embraced willingly requires examination. Resurgent Islam was still relatively undeveloped politically and the appeal of organisations such as the Muslim Brotherhood was not widespread. Instead, particular geographic areas known for their religious conservatism and traditionalism provided fertile ground for the activities of the nascent Islamic movement. The tension between the Islamic movement and the national movement, particularly in the Gaza Strip, reached new heights during this period.

Confidence building best describes the changes that took place during this period within the organisations of political Islam, with the emergence of a nascent Islamist trend apparent by the end of the decade. The second decade of occupation also saw the rise of a new, highly politicised Islamic organisation which eschewed the programme of leaders like Sheikh Yassin and Ibrahim Yazouri. Known eventually as Islamic Jihad, this new organisation advocated political violence as a means to attain power and change the existing structures of authority.

Internal and external developments were both crucial determinants of the path of political Islam during the 1980s. The Iranian revolution in 1979 was one important influence, although not in the manner most observers predicted. Internally, the deployment of Israeli funds for the promotion of Islam, particularly in the Gaza Strip, also played an influential role in shaping the fortunes of an organisation like the Mujama, but again with unpredictable results. Aspects of Israeli policy towards political organisations in the occupied territories during this period display all the signs of classic divide-and-rule policy. Israel's benign encouragement of the Islamic movement was designed to strengthen Islam in the face of the nationalists in the form of the Palestine Liberation Organisation (PLO). By nurturing a conservative and traditional trend, the Israeli authorities hoped to diminish the progressive and radical appeal of the movement for national liberation. Yet by turning a blind eye to the activities of the Islamic movement Israel helped promote a phenomenon which would, in years to come, turn on its benefactor.

The ten years that preceded the Intifada were full of change. Islam was reasserted in Palestinian society both through the continued provision of a vast range of important social and educational services and also, more disturbingly, through the use of force, beatings, public hate campaigns and acid attacks on individuals who disagreed with Islamic militants. Of course, change was not uniform. The West Bank had in the past been the centre for the Muslim Brotherhood, but this was no longer the case. The epicentre of political Islam moved to the Gaza Strip where the forces of political Islam could make a greater impact on society. Whether or not the majority of Palestinians wanted to return to the straight path of Islam was often not important to the Islamic vanguard that followed the banner raised by Sheikh Yassin and his cadres in the Muslim Brotherhood and later the Mujama.

As in previous phases of its development, again this revitalised movement did not distinguish itself through its anti-occupation activity; its political energies were devoted to defeating the enemy within, namely the Palestine Liberation Organisation. Indeed, the main criticism levelled against it was that by attacking the nationalists it was betraying the struggle against the Zionists. This argument was decisive in determining the levels of support that the Mujama was eventually able to achieve in the second decade of occupation. As a leading Gaza figure noted: 'They emphasised that the only path to liberation was through the realisation of an Islamic state. Even at this stage they were voicing political ideas, they belittled fighting the occupation ... .'[1] This attitude was a barrier to mass support, for the vast majority of Gazans preferred to direct their political energies to ending the Israeli occupation rather than to the re-Islamisation of their own society.

Nascent Islamists: Mujama Makes its Mark

By the second decade of the occupation, the Muslim Brotherhood in the Gaza Strip, led by Sheikh Yassin, had embarked on a period of rapid expansion. While continuing to run education programmes and offer some limited welfare assistance, the brotherhood extended its influence into other areas of Gazan society. It was able to do this in a number of ways, its path smoothed by an Israeli policy of non-interference. The creation of the Mujama was one way in which Sheikh Yassin and a dozen of his colleagues could disseminate their message of revivalist Islam throughout the Gaza Strip. The Mujama would be charitable in nature and in time an important vehicle for the brotherhood, giving a social facade to the organisation's increasingly political, nascent Islamist activities. Through their own mosques, libraries, schools, health clinics and kindergartens the Mujama would help establish an institutional basis to promote its message. This message was still broadly reformist, focusing on the re-Islamisation of society through education and preaching.

The challenge, for the Mujama, lay in encouraging Palestinians to reject the increasing secularisation of their lives and their affiliation to nationalism as a means to liberation from Israeli occupation. Considerable efforts would be made to change the secular nature of Gazan society. The strategies to implement this message, however, increasingly reflected a more activist and violent character. The enemy of Islam was identified as the nationalist movement, in particular Palestinian leftists and communists. Throughout the decade, the nationalist movement was targeted by the nascent Islamists of the Mujama as a major obstacle to the achievement of their goals. Nationalists were regarded as traitors to the Muslim faith, as heretics, who were worse than infidels. The nationalists were blamed for the failure of Palestinians to liberate themselves because they had encouraged the young to abandon Islam.

In 1978 Israel's civil administration in Gaza encouraged Sheikh Yassin and his colleagues to submit an application to register the Mujama as a charitable society. Permission was granted, as such official recognition was frequently denied to other Gazans during this period, the decision was viewed with suspicion by the local political community. Although the Mujama described itself as a charity, the Israelis were well aware of its political aspirations. But as the events of the years following 1978 highlighted, they were willing to turn the proverbial blind eye if such political aspirations were at the expense of the national movement. When the Mujama started to exert its influence over already existing institutions as a means to undermine the nationalists, the Israelis stood by.

The War of the Palestinian Red Crescent

Local health-care institutions soon became an arena of competition between the newly-registered Mujama and the national movement. One such institution was the Gaza branch of the Palestinian Red Crescent Society (PRC). The PRC was founded in 1972 as a welfare and relief organisation, funded, administered and used by Palestinians in Gaza. Its political importance lay in the fact that it was considered a national institution and therefore aligned with the PLO and its supporters. The organisation was also perceived as liberal and progressive and was popular with the local community. Its director was a local man, Dr Haider Abdel Shaffi, who was identified with the Palestinian left, a committed secularist, one of the most respected political figures in the Gaza Strip and an important advocate of Gazan national rights.

Some of the most serious internal political violence in Gaza was precipitated by the elections for the administrative committee of the PRC in December 1979. Anyone was allowed to field candidates for the twenty-one posts available. The Mujama, their Islamic supporters and rightist elements saw this as an opportunity to gain influence in a key national institution and put their own candidates up for election. When the results were called, however, the nationalists took the majority of seats while the Islamists garnered only enough votes to win three. The results infuriated the Islamists: 'They were extremely indignant and filed a complaint with the Israeli Ministry of the Interior accusing us of rigging the election to the benefit of the leftists,' said Dr Haider Abdel Shaffi.[2] The complaint was filed by a well known conservative and Islamic supporter, Assad Saftawi, who was already a committee member.[3] The Israelis investigated the matter, eventually clearing the organisation. The administration of the PRC was understandably alarmed by the fact that a committee member had brought such charges to the Israelis, and Saftawi was called upon to explain himself. He was dismissed from his post by the executive committee, although he himself alleges that he resigned after being hounded by the communists. A former supporter of the Muslim Brotherhood, Assad Saftawi was by this point linked with the Fatah movement. His Islamic credentials, however, were boosted by the activities of one of his sons who later became involved in the Islamic Jihad organisation. In the early 1980s Saftawi was in close alliance with Sheikh Mohammad Awwad, the director of the Islamic University in Gaza, and known to be sympathetic to the forces of political Islam.

The events that followed the defeat of the nascent Islamists in the PRC elections were evidence enough that Mujama strategy had many facets. Infuriated by the nationalist victory at the PRC, Mujama supporters like Sheikh Mohammad Awwad were reportedly further incensed by the rumour that the nationalists were going to establish their own university in Gaza. It was reported that by this point Sheikh Awwad and his colleagues 'felt more and more like a besieged fortress of righteousness in a sea of iniquity'.[4] Thus, on 7 January 1980, Sheikh Awwad and his Mujama supporters called a meeting at the Islamic University to discuss the nationalists' activities. The meeting was dominated by Awwad's speeches vilifying the nationalists. His fiery rhetoric was warmly received. One of those present described what happened next:

> Sheikh Awwad collected the religious people together and preached to them about the atheists who were attempting to deviate from the aims of the university. Sheikh Awwad accused Dr Haider Abdel Shaffi of being the strongest opponent. The Sheikh led the Maghreb prayer. Afterwards, they marched to the offices of the Red Crescent and set them on fire.[5]

A demonstration then started out from the grounds of the university. Most of the people involved in the march and subsequent attacks were Mujama supporters. The demonstrators, ignoring the Israeli army soldiers stationed along their way, set off in the direction of the PRC building. According to Shalom Cohen, 'Thousands of demonstrators took to the streets, shouting Allahu Akbar (God is Great), down with Communism, long live Islam.'[6]

During the demonstration the Mujama militants attacked cafes, video shops and liquor stores. When they arrived at the offices of the PRC they set the building on fire. The offices were destroyed, including approximately 80 per cent of the books in the library, one-third of which were Islamic texts. Throughout the attack the Israeli authorities failed to intervene. This was noted and viewed with a mixture of fear and outright disapproval by Gaza's secularists, as illustrated by the PRC statement following the incident:

> The tacit approval of the authorities, if not their actual connivance in what happened, is displayed by their attitude of non-interference. While usually they display great alertness in combating even peaceful demonstrations of young students within school. Here they stood indifferently watching a violent destructive demonstration marching to its objective. Their failure to track and punish the culprits is added testimony to their complicity.[7]

According to Cohen, the Israeli army did not step into break up the disturbance until the demonstrators had marched on the home of Dr Haider Abdel Shaffi when 'the soldiers and policemen fired in the air and the demonstration finally dispersed'.[8]

This telling incident presaged the future path of political Islam in Gaza. The action of the nascent Islamists, in conjunction with conservative religious elements like Sheikh Awwad and Assad Saftawi, were a clear indicator that the Mujama movement and its supporters were sufficiently well organised to orchestrate a violent attack against fellow Palestinians. The PRC incident was a warning to Gaza's secular political activists of what was to come. Two days later the offices of the secular *al-Quds* newspaper were set on fire, and a cinema, billiard hall and bar in Gaza were closed by Mujama activists, reflecting the growing tension between the PLO and Islam.

The attempt to win influence over and to control the PRC was just one element of a wider policy and was soon followed by the targeting of another institution: the Islamic University of Gaza (IUG). In the case of the university the Mujama was able to establish itself both in the administration, by adroitly manoeuvring for the removal of secular elements, and in the student body where opposition was eliminated by violence. The process began shortly after the PRC débâcle as Dr Haider Abdel Shaffi notes:

> Following the incident, they [the Mujama] started to assert their presence and power on the university grounds. It seems that the Red Crescent incident was the starting point of such a phenomenon. They became much more visible … and in fact eventually controlled the university.[9]

Liberation Through Education:
the Islamic University of Gaza

It should have come as no surprise that the Mujama coveted control of an educational institution like the university. The idea of education was at the heart of its philosophy and viewed as an essential tool through which to spread the message of Islam. If the illiterate and uneducated were taught to read the Qur'an and other religious literature then their hearts and minds would follow Islam. Whether improved education could in fact be equated with an increase in religiosity was not important; the objective of the Mujama leadership was to make its mark in Gaza. The university would provide an opportunity to carry on with the principal aim of education while at the same time make on impact on the local political scene. The Mujama's attempt to gain influence over the IUG also highlights the connivance of the Israeli authorities who were happy to see Gaza's only university as a battle-ground between Palestinian Islamists and nationalists. The Israelis preferred to have the conservative and traditionalist Mujama sympathisers, rather than Gaza's leftist or progressive forces, in key positions of power.

The idea of founding a university in Gaza had been raised from time to time by political representatives since about 1963. Earlier proposals by Gaza nationalists had always been vetoed by the Israeli authorities. Only one institution of higher learning existed in Gaza at the time, and this was the al-Azhar religious college run by Sheikh Mohammad Awwad. The college was not renowned for its academic excellence but it was a local institution enjoying a close affiliation with the newly-formed Mujama organisation.

The political events of 1978, primarily the Palestinian rejection of Sadat's peace initiative, also emphasised to political leaders the real need for an indigenous institution of higher education for the area. Previously, the majority of Gazans wanting to continue in higher education had gone to Egyptian universities. Following Palestinian protest at Sadat's peace treaty with Israel, Sadat ordered Egyptian universities to close their doors to Gazan students.

The need for a Gaza-based institution of higher education became acute. The new institution would have to accommodate the 1,000–1,500 students who had previously studied in Egypt. The outcome, which had been widely discussed in Gaza's political circles, was the transformation of the al-Azhar-affiliated religious institute into the Islamic University of Gaza. At this stage permission for the founding of the university had not been received from the Israeli authorities.

The apparent religious orientation of the institution, however, caused conflict in political circles. In an attempt to pacify the nationalist and progressive leftist elements, a consultation committee was established by Sheikh Awwad and his religious colleagues, in which the secularists would be allowed to play a part. According to a former dean of the IUG, the committee and the Board of Trustees 'gave the impression that the new university was representative of the political spectrum of Gaza. One can say that at this point in the fortunes of the university it appeared to be a secular as well as a religious institution.'[10]

Even in this early period, however, appearances were deceptive. Friction over the religious orientation of the university was persistent.

The university would also fall increasingly under the influence of leaders and activists from the Mujama. This was Gaza's only institution of higher education and the Mujama were keen to establish its hegemony over it. There were disputes over the segregation of the sexes in the university, over the basic curriculum and the pervasive influence of Mujama activists in the student body. Any expression of a secularist viewpoint or perspective was stifled and the university became more 'Islamic' than ever.

By 1981 tensions within the IUG administrative system had reached a peak. In the consulting committee, drastic action was taken over secular protests against the Islamists' monopoly over policy. The Mujama-backed leadership, confident of its position within the university, moved to eliminate the secularists. To this end a strange coalition was forged between the Mujama figures in the IUG and the Israeli authorities. Secular figures in Gaza assert that this coalition of interests soon acted to stop the nationalists. In February 1981 the Israeli authorities, at the behest of the Mujama leaders in the university, ordered the removal of seven of the thirteen members of the consulting committee. The seven were ordered to the headquarters of the civil administration in Gaza and told to resign from their posts. The collusion of the authorities in supporting this Mujama-backed move did not go unnoticed as a Palestinian press report at the time illustrates: 'One claims the removal was a coincidence of the authorities suppression of Palestinian educational opportunity and Awwad's desire to "control the university and fill the staff with Sheikhs rather than Ph.Ds".'[11]

It was no coincidence, however, that the administration of the IUG was moving inexorably forward towards the idea of a governing body consisting entirely of Mujama members and supporters. The leading lights within the university administration were already identifiable Mujama figures, like Dr Mohammad Saqr, Dr Abd al-Aziz Rantisi, and Dr Mahmoud Zahar.

Soon, the Islamic tone encouraged by the Mujama was clear, from the highest to the lowest employee in the university. Even most of the porters, doormen and gatekeepers (over fifty of them) were Mujama members or supporters. These men were paid to grow and maintain their beards in the Islamic fashion and encouraged to dress accordingly. The doormen soon developed a reputation for violence, with newspapers reporting in 1983 that they aided armed gangs who attacked striking teachers and students on the campus: 'University gatekeepers and student supporters of the Islamic bloc broke the strike line and injured fifteen striking students and teachers.'[12]

The Mujama Takes its Message to the Students

How can uncovered women and men with Beatle haircuts liberate our holy places? [Mujama slogan, 1980s]

Students attending the IUG were also at the receiving end of a decision by the Mujama and other religious conservatives to ensure that the university was a fully Islamic institution. From separate entrances for women and men to the way in which certain ideas and courses were taught, behind the walls of the institution the message of Islam was all pervasive. Organised student life was dominated by Mujama activists and their supporters. Mujama students easily identifiable by their beards and Islamic inspired forms of dress contested Palestinian nationalist activity among their fellow students wherever they found it. They quickly achieved dominant status and suppressed dissident voices within the student body. Leftists, liberals or progressives expressing a view that was in any respect contrary to that of the Mujama were dealt with severely. The story of one particular student, who was beaten, publicly ridiculed and ostracised illustrates the bitter lengths to which Mujama members were prepared to go to in order ensure a compliant student population.

When the university was established in 1978 it had only 148 students, but by the mid-1980s student numbers had reached 4,500, making it the largest campus in the occupied territories. By this stage the Mujama-inspired campaign to encourage Islamic dress among the student body was in full swing. Women were obliged to wear full Islamic dress, including the *hijab* (head-scarf covering the hair and shoulders) and *thobe* (long overdress covering the whole body). There is no doubt that a large number of women at the university welcomed the dress code, feeling that it gave them freedom to move around in public without being harassed; but others did not. Leftist or progressive women were easily identified by their refusal to wear the *hijab* and suffered at the hands of Mujama activists. For example one such woman was beaten by them and ostracised by her fellow female students. In 1983 attacks by Mujama supporters on students reached an unprecedented level when seventeen nationalists were badly beaten in clashes on the campus and ordered to halt their political activities.[13]

As with every other university in the occupied territories, the opportunity to participate in political activities was greatly cherished by students. At the IUG a student council was formed as early as 1979–80 with a nine-member executive committee. Regular elections were held and the result was always the same: the overwhelming majority of votes went to the Mujama-backed Islamic bloc. This enabled the nascent Islamists to hold all nine seats in the student council and thereby exercise a decisive influence over student issues. In the 1985 election, out of 2,283 students who voted, 570 did so for the Student Youth Movement, 150 for the Voluntary Work Committee Coalition, and 60 for the Independent Muslim Group. The remaining 1,503 votes went to candidates representing the Mujama.

The nationalists were ridiculed publicly by Mujama student activists. As early as 1981, Mujama students were singling out activist supporters of the Palestine Liberation Organisation. According to students, they called the PLO a coalition of atheists and declared that the Islamic world view was more important than Arafat. Mujama supporters in the university also used to mock the nationalists with slogans like '*sulta wataniyya, salata wataniyya*' which, roughly translated, means that the nationalist movement with its many factions is nothing more than a salad of nationalisms and ideas. Mujama slogans also mocked nationalist students for their secular forms of dress and social behaviour.

Such jests and taunts were verbally intimidating only and it could no doubt have been argued that they were no more than a indicator of a robust political atmosphere at the university. However, the creation of this atmosphere was intimidating and authoritarian; nationalists were prevented from meeting the Mujama with their own rejoinders and strenuous efforts were made to prevent them from organising their own political activities. The secular democratic forces in the university were not given the same freedom as the Mujama by either the pro-Islamic administration or the Israeli authorities. Nationalist students were often barred from the university. It is alleged by former students of the university, that the authorities stood by and allowed the Mujama student group to publish and distribute inflammatory articles and pamphlets against the nationalists and leftists. It was also common knowledge that the Mujama began to keep a cache of weapons such as axes and knives on campus to be used against secular democratic elements. Even the Israeli authorities were privy to this information but they did nothing to stop the Mujama.

Bassam the 'Bad Muslim'

One of the students the Mujama singled out for attack was a man whom I will call Bassam to protect his identity. I interviewed Bassam in the Gaza Strip in November 1989 and he told me about his background and his experience at the hands of the Mujama. In the early 1980s Bassam was a mature part-time student at the university. Bassam has a large family, works as a teacher in a United Nations and Relief Works Agency (UNRWA) school and lives in one of the largest refugee camps in the Gaza Strip. He described himself as a Palestinian nationalist supporting the views expressed by the Popular Front for the Liberation of Palestine (PFLP). Bassam was the victim of a vicious attack by Mujama activists who scarred his face with pure nitric acid.

Bassam's crime was his world-view. He questioned the role of the Mujama in the IUG and its influence on the material taught in the degree courses. 'I used to hear some of the religious lecturers deviate from accepted truths about science like Darwin's theory of evolution.[14] They would say that the Jewish community in England asked Darwin to connect Man to the Apes.' That the nascent Islamists were willing to promote radical anti-Jewish perspectives as part of a university degree course and at the same time collude with the Israeli authorities to remove the secularists seems strange. To refute the theory of evolution from a religious point of view is not out of the ordinary, but to connect the idea with conspiracy theories about the Jewish people was dangerous and irresponsible. Such expressions of hostility were not limited to the theory of evolution but extended to the history of political thought in the West and the development of ideas linked to a secular conception of the world. 'Another example I can give you is of the economics lecturer who said that proof of the laws of historical evolution and Hegelianism were complete nonsense and false,' said Bassam.

When Bassam felt compelled to dispute the opinions of a lecturer in class he was accused, both by the lecturer and fellow students, of being a 'communist and a bad Muslim'. He was also threatened. In 1981, when he attempted to run in the student council elections, the university refused to let him stand. Bassam says: 'We surmised that they were afraid we might win and therefore influence the younger members of the student body'. Although he was aware of the ideological generation gap between the mature students, who were more secular in outlook, and the younger students, who were supporters of the nascent Islamists, Bassam continued to be active politically. As the years passed he and his friends felt increasingly isolated and marginalised. By 1983 he knew he had been singled out by the Mujama:

> It reached a point where friends would stay at my house to protect me and certain members of my family would not even speak to me because they believed what the Mujama was saying about me. Nevertheless the attack came, and they threw nitric acid in my face.

Yet this was not the end of Mujama pressure on Bassam the 'bad Muslim'. Uncertain that the acid attack would ensure his compliance the organisation kept up its harassment:

> They did not leave me alone. This peace from them only came after a final act of submission on my part. Contrary to my strongest [political] principles I went to the mosque on a Friday and prayed along with the rest of the congregation. This act proved to my attackers that they had achieved their victory. I felt safe again and that my family would no longer be talking about the 'atheist'.

While Bassam's case was unusual it does give an indication of the lengths to which Mujama elements were prepared to go to in order to secure their political dominance in Gaza. The organisation secured its power on the IUG campus and continued to extended its influence in the wider community. In controlling the university, the Mujama had the potential to influence Gazan society, training its professionals and shaping the minds of its youth. The Mujama had a captive audience at the IUG, and the campus became a stronghold for the movement.

The Mujama made a variable impact in other national institutions in Gaza. It contested elections in professional organisation targeting in particular the medical and engineering associations. Despite some initial inroads, the associations proved increasingly resilient to pressure and the Mujama's position in them declined throughout the decade. In the medical association elections, for example, the following results were recorded: in 1981 and again in 1983, the Mujama won five of the eleven seats; in 1985, however, its number of seats dropped to three and by 1987 it had only one.[15] There was some support for the Mujama in staff associations established by the UNRWA programme for its school teachers and other workers, but blue-collar workers in institutions such as Gaza's Trade Union Association were not targeted by the organisation. The nascent Islamists preferred to address the rights of workers in sermons given at local mosques.

Arms and Arrests

The Mujama suffered a temporary setback in 1984 following the arrest and trial of Sheikh Yassin and five of his supporters. Yassin was accused of: membership of a Muslim fundamentalist organisation; promulgating jihad to destroy Israel; receiving funds from Jordanian sources; and possession of sixty rifles. Sheikh Yassin, Abdel Rahman Timraz, Mohammad Shihab, Mohammad Mohrah and Ahmad Samarah were all found guilty by the judge of the military court in Gaza. Their prison sentences ranged from nine to thirteen years. Sheikh Yassin, however, served no more than a year in jail. He was released in 1985 as part of the Popular Front for the Liberation of Palestine–General Command (PFLP–GC) prisoner exchange with Israel. Although forbidden officially to remain at the head of the Mujama organisation once released, he appointed his close associates, Dr Abd al-Aziz Rantisi and Dr Ibrahim Yazouri, to take his place, in this way remaining the movement's guiding force and spiritual mentor.

The discovery of the arms cache and the Jordanian funding, should not, however, have surprised the Israeli authorities. The arms, if they had been used, were in all likelihood intended for Palestinian rather than Israeli targets. There was no evidence to suggest that the Mujama were preparing to wage a war against Israel. So far as funding was concerned, the Israeli authorities, by permitting the registration of Mujama as a charity, were tacitly approving the transfer of funds to the organisation. The Muslim Brotherhood in Jordan acted as conduit for moneys secured in Jordan and the Gulf states. It was hardly surprising, therefore, that the group was in possession of 12,000 Jordanian dinars from Dr Yousef al-Athm in Jordan.[16]

The Mujama quickly recovered from this set back and with the release of Sheikh Yassin in 1985 continued its activities in the Gaza Strip. The effects of its Islamisation programme were increasingly evident. Cinemas, liquor stores, restaurants selling alcohol, and casinos were closed in the face of mounting Islamic pressure on their owners and managers. Those who resisted had their premises vandalised or destroyed by Mujama cadres. In 1986 attacks on nationalists, particularly leftists, increased. Acid attacks, stabbings and beatings were perpetrated against an increasing number. One such individual was Dr Rabbah Muhanna, who was severely beaten and subsequently hospitalised. Commenting on the attacks, Dr Muhanna stated: 'I criticised their tactics at meetings which we held, I argued that they were collaborators and a danger to us all. At one of these meetings they attacked and beat me.'[17]

Other aspects of Gazan life were also disrupted by the Mujama activists. Weddings which they deemed inconsistent with Islamic tradition were attacked and some forcibly disrupted. The playing of music was declared forbidden, as were other Western-inspired traditions such as the dresses that brides wore and the mixing of the sexes at celebration parties. Islamic dress was increasing throughout the Gaza Strip and the Mujama encouraged more and more Palestinians to abandon Western fashions in favour of more modest and conservative clothes. By 1987 the influence of Islam was palpable also in terms of politics, with increasing evidence of the return of Gaza to the 'straight path of Islam'. As the former mayor of Gaza, Rashad Shawwa remarked at the time, 'If you have to be religious in order to liberate Palestine then I'm prepared to be religious too'.[18]

Islamic Jihad:
Putting Palestine First

The notion of an Islamic movement committed to the act of jihad (holy war) against the Israelis altered the nature of the Palestinian conflict with Israel in the occupied territories. The rise of the Palestinian Islamic Jihad (consisting of a number of organisations) politicised the conflict in a way not seen since the days of Sheikh Izz ad-Din al-Qassam. This independent, Islamist movement views itself as a vanguard for Islam in a battle to wrest control of Islamic land back from the Jewish people. Islamic Jihad is an activist movement and committed to a revolutionary political programme. The movement represents a number of groupings embracing the same broad ideological stance. The label of Islamic Jihad is both generic and specific, referring to a movement as well as number of groups active in the Palestinian arena. The four groups which emerged under this name during the 1980s are: Islamic Jihad (Shqaqi–Auda faction), Islamic Jihad Jerusalem Brigade, Islamic Jihad Battalions and Islamic Jihad Palestine (Amar faction).

Islamic Jihad (Shqaqi–Auda faction) was the first group to emerge in the early 1980s led by two Palestinians from the Gaza Strip called Fathi Shqaqi and Sheikh Abd al-Aziz Auda. The faction is the largest of the Islamic Jihad groups and is based in the Gaza Strip. The military actions of this faction are commonly cited as the catalyst for the Palestinian uprising in December 1987. Islamic Jihad

Jerusalem Brigade is led by Sheikh As'ad Bayyud Tammimi, originally from Hebron in the West Bank and deported to Jordan in 1970 by the Israeli authorities. From his base in Amman, and assisted by his two sons, he ordered a series of attacks in the name of his organisation in the late 1980s. Sheikh Tammimi is a veteran of Palestine's Islamic movement, having enjoyed links with both the Muslim Brotherhood and the Liberation Party in the 1950s and 1960s. The Islamic Jihad Battalion was established in 1985 by Bassam Sultan. The organisation has a small membership and enjoys close links with Fatah. It is widely believed that the establishment of the organisation was encouraged by Fatah leaders Abu Jihad and Munir Shafiq as a nationalist foil to growing support for the Shqaqi–Auda faction. Islamic Jihad Palestine (Amar faction) is led by Jamal Amar, a former member of Fatah. Amar established the cell during a lengthy prison sentence and is currently based in Sudan.

Islamic Jihad put Palestine first in the debate about political Islam in the occupied territories. In many respects this new movement was the antithesis of everything that characterised the Mujama: (i) it was revolutionary and its number one priority was to end Israeli rule; (ii) it was small, and its leaders filled an intellectual gap that had arisen in Islamic circles, and (iii) it was anti-establishment at a time when the mainstream Mujama movement was seeking to epitomise itself as the sole political, religious, and social establishment in the Gaza Strip.

Islamic Jihad challenged nationalist sentiments about Palestine, appropriated them and used them to support its call for liberation. Palestine, was a priority, its liberation from Israeli occupation a prerequisite for the transformation of society and Islamic ascendancy.

The Islamic Jihad faction, founded by Shqaqi and Auda, was formed in the Gaza Strip in the early 1980s. It is the largest faction of the movement. These two young radicals had been involved previously in the mainstream Mujama movement. The new group arose during a period of dispute within the nascent Islamist movement at the IUG. At the centre of the dispute were two issues. The first and most important revolved around the attitude of the Mujama towards the Israeli occupation of Palestinian/Islamic land and the call for jihad against Israel, the second focused on the stance of the movement towards the Iranian revolution and its relations with external actors.

Described by the Israelis as 'ideological formulators and spiritual leaders',[19] Sheikh Auda, in his thirties and from a refugee family, lectured at the Islamic University. He was also the imam at a mosque in Beit Lahiya near the Jabaliyya refugee camp. Auda and Shqaqi had become friends during their years as students at Zagaziq University in Egypt. Both men had a strong political commitment to Palestine and sought to articulate this through their religious beliefs. During their time as students they were attracted to the ideas expressed by Egyptian radical Islamic groups such as al-Gama Islamiyya and Islamic Jihad which had split from the mainstream Muslim Brotherhood movement. These groups took a radical activist approach to the realisation of their goal. Both Auda and Shqaqi were attracted to this idea; they believed that while preaching had a role, their main objective should be liberation of Palestine through Islamic revolution and military struggle. Their activist stance is encapsulated in the following quotation:

> It is futile for the Islamists to dream of complete independence or a comprehensive civilisational revival, while the centre of colonial operations remains fully entrenched, fully fortified and fully equipped in Palestine to do what it pleases in our land, and hell-bent on imposing 'the Israel era' in our region.[20]

When they returned to their homes in the Gaza Strip and involved themselves in the local Islamic movement, Auda and Shqaqi questioned aspects of Mujama's policy. Given the authoritarian nature of decision-making and policy formulation in the Mujama, voices of dissent were not welcomed. Nevertheless, the two stood up and made their criticisms. As a university colleague of Auda's noted, the Sheikh felt compelled to speak out, 'because of the [Mujama] policy of distraction from the occupation. These disaffected members felt that Mujama was not answering the most important question, what to do about the occupation?'[21]

Sheikh Auda and his supporters believed that Palestine as an Islamic land seized by infidel rulers was the central issue for local Muslim organisations. To ignore Palestine was to ignore the call to jihad as a religious obligation. In an Islamic Jihad pamphlet, Auda wrote:

> What is now taking place in the Holy Land is not just a battle for the Palestinian people alone. It is the battle for Islam, a battle for the future of the entire *umma*. It is a battle against the forces of arrogance – against the colonial hegemony over our world.[22]

Auda emphasises the pivotal place of Palestine in the wider Islamic struggle for liberation in the twentieth century: 'We consider the central cause of the Islamic movement to be the Palestinian cause. There is an inseparable connection between serving Islam and serving Palestine.'[23]

The debate over the issue of Palestine and the Islamic movement ran in parallel with the internal conflict between the movement's leadership and young radical membership over their stance on support for the Iranian revolution. Initially, in the post-1979 euphoria that swept the Muslim world, the Mujama had declared its support for the revolutionary ideals of Khomeini. Furthermore, in the wake of Iranian attacks on the regimes in Saudi Arabia and other Gulf states that enthusiasm waned. Iran's attempt to appoint itself as the vanguard and custodian of Islam placed the leadership of the Mujama in an ideological and practical dilemma: if the Mujama in Gaza pledged its ideological support to Iran it would alienate its Gulf sources of funding; if, on the other hand, it criticised the Iranian revolution, it was denying the important political and religious effects of the event on the entire Muslim world. A student at the IUG described the dilemma in more prosaic terms: 'The Mujama, probably at the behest of their Saudi paymasters, denounced the revolution in Iran. We understood why, because Iran threatened Saudi Arabia and the Ikhwan abroad. So the Mujama were ordered to stop supporting Khomeini.'[24]

Sheikh Auda and his colleagues, however, saw no contradiction. Auda argued for a revolutionary Islamic model, which included obligation to jihad against the Israeli occupation. Sheikh Auda, Shqaqi and their associates[25] embraced the example of the Iranian revolution as a positive role model for Palestine. For them the revolution itself, rather than the Shi'a character of Islamic politics in Iran, provided the significant example. A commitment by the Iranian republic to support the call for jihad in Palestine was also important at this juncture. Islamic Jihad was not advocating a Shi'a revolution, nor, indeed, can the Iranian revolution itself truly be described as such. The revolution in Iran was a symbol which proved that mighty regimes ruling over a subjugated Muslim people could be toppled. Iran, like Israel, had been the recipient of some of the largest American aid in the region and was closely aligned to the United States of America. If the shah could be toppled, Israel could follow.

Throughout the early 1980s the debate within the Islamic movement in Gaza raged between those who supported and drew value from the Iranian model and those who did not. As a result of this and other conflicts Auda, Shqaqi and their associates broke away from the mainstream movement and founded the first Islamic Jihad organisation in the occupied territories. By 1983 the conflict with the Mujama over Iran had worsened. As one observer noted:

> The Mujama dismissed Auda but he did not shut his mouth. He started to preach in the mosque in Beit Lahiya in support of revolutionary Islam and Iran, and also to reveal the wicked practices of the Mujama. So the Mujama attacked him with clubs. He was hospitalised.[26]

Following the incident a colleague at the IUG claimed that Auda was accused of making trouble: 'At the behest of the university the Israeli authorities banned him for a year from the university campus.'[27] Islamic Jihad supporters at the university were marginalised by Mujama activists and referred to as 'the weakest of the earth' (*al-mustabafin fi 'ard*).

Tension between the new Islamic Jihad organisation and the Mujama remained high throughout the 1980s. Islamic Jihad established a small, cohesive military and political organisation, dominated by a cell network, and built up a core of no more than a hundred committed activists.[28] While some members were drawn from the university campus, others were recruited in the Beit Lahiya mosque and the al-Salam mosque in Rafah where Auda and Shqaqi preached regularly. New recruits were invited to home gatherings where they would be more thoroughly introduced to the ideas and practice of Islamic Jihad.

A number of important members were recruited while serving prison terms for nationalist activity in Israeli jails. Abu Amr cites the example of Jamal Amar, an ex-PLA and Fatah member, as 'one of the founders of the Islamic Jihad inside Israeli jails'.[29] Jamal Amar went on in fact to found his own faction. Ahmad Muhanna, Mohammad Jamal and Misbah al-Suri are also cited as joining the ranks of the Jihad in jail after being formerly active in the PFLP.[30] According to a former prisoner who knew Amar, the latter became active while in serving in Ashkelon jail. He started to pray, and practise the religion and to criticise nationalist prisoners for their un-Islamic attitudes. He soon built up a core of support: 'His followers numbered between twenty and forty over the years. Some of them were very Islamic in their beliefs and believed in him as a religious leader of his group.'[31] Many of Amar's recruits were drawn from the ranks of other organisations in the prisons. When he was moved to Beersheba and Gaza prisons he built up a core of support in each. He was released from prison in 1983 and subsequently promoted and supported Islamic Jihad while in exile in Cairo. From Cairo, Amar went to Tunis settling eventually in Sudan where he enjoys the support of the Islamic regime in Khartoum.

Although the ideals and objectives of the Islamic Jihad were never widely embraced, the organisation did find support in the local community and was respected by the various factions of the national movement. Indeed many of its members and sympathisers, including Ahmad Muhanna, Jamal Amar and Ramadan Shallah, had themselves been previously involved with secular-nationalist organisations. Evading Israeli capture, Shallah fled Gaza in the mid-1980s, studying in Britain and disseminating the call of Islamic Jihad in Europe. He left Britain in the early 1990s and settled in America along with other exiled supporters of the movement.[32]

The Jihad in Action:
Ways to End an Occupation

In the eighteen months preceding the Palestinian uprising, Islamic Jihad conducted a military campaign in the Gaza Strip. This wave of attacks alarmed the Israeli army but popular support for the organisation was so high that Islamic Jihad claimed later that it was its activities in October 1987 that provided the spark for the Intifada which galvanised the Palestinian population. This claim was strengthened by the vanguard role played by Islamic Jihad in the early weeks of the uprising.

The first attacks attributed to and claimed by Islamic Jihad in Gaza took place in September and October 1986. The victims in each case were Israeli taxi drivers working in the Gaza Strip: Haim Azran and Yisrael Kitaro, both from Ashkelon, were stabbed to death.[33] The attack was meant as a warning to Israelis to stay away from Gaza, formerly popular for its markets and cheap labour. The murders alerted the IDF to a new and dangerous force. In December 1986 the Israeli army swooped on the Gaza Strip and arrested more than fifty alleged members of Islamic Jihad, among them Khaled Jayidi, Abdel Rahman al-Qiq and Imad Saftawi, the son of Assad Saftawi. All three were charged with the murders of Azran and Kitaro, as well as further murder attempts and grenade attacks on the IDF.

The trial of the three opened on 12 May 1987. The accused admitted membership of Islamic Jihad but denied the other charges. The court proceedings, however, were soon overshadowed by a spectacular escape mounted by six Islamic Jihad detainees (including Imad Saftawi) from Gaza central prison on 18 May. The jail-break was the first of its kind, astounding the Israeli authorities and highlighting the level of Islamic Jihad's organisation. The inability of the Israeli authorities to recapture the escapees pointed to the local support that the organisation enjoyed in the Gaza Strip. It was popularly assumed at the time that the six escapees had made their way to Egypt. While this was true of three of them, the others remained in Gaza carrying out more attacks against the Israelis throughout the summer and early autumn of 1987. In July the three accused of the Azran and Kitaro murders were found guilty by the Israeli military court. After the verdicts Jayidi stood in court and declared, 'We, the members of Islamic Jihad, attach greater importance to death than life. Either we liberate our country, or we die in the attempt.'[34] Saftawi, who by this time was in Tunis, was sentenced *in absentia*.

By the summer Islamic Jihad was engaged on another campaign of attacks on Israeli targets. In early August a police officer, Captain Ron Tal, was killed by Islamic Jihad mujahidin as he walked in Gaza city. Throughout August and September grenade attacks on Israeli army patrols and Shin Bet vehicles were reported. Islamic Jihad were the prime suspects. Shin Bet moved against the organisation on 1 and 6 October 1987 in the Shujai'a neighbourhood of Gaza city. In the first incident three Palestinians were killed, two local merchants and Misbah Hassan al-Suri, one of the May escapees widely believed to be in Egypt. Al-Suri's death was not announced by the Israeli authorities until twelve days after the incident. A rumour circulating at the time, which was not officially suppressed, was that al-Suri had been taken alive and had died in detention after he had revealed the names and whereabouts of other Jihad activists. Since the Israeli authorities did not explain their delay in announcing al-Suri's death the rumour was given credibility following events in Gaza city on 6 October.

Shujai'a was again the location of a Shin Bet clash with Islamic Jihad. This time a fierce gun-battle raged for several hours. One Shin Bet officer, Victor Arjwan, and four members of Islamic Jihad, Fayez Hammad Gharabli, Mohammad Said al-Jamal, Sami Mohammad ash-Sheikh Khalil and Ahmad Omar Ahmad Hilles, were killed. The four Islamic Jihad activists were immediately declared martyrs in the wave of popular support after the event. Islamic Jihad called its first general strike in Gaza to commemorate the deaths and large numbers of demonstrations and sermons were held at which eulogies were delivered for the martyrs. As Schiff and Ya'ari note, the deaths of the four Islamic Jihad fighters were a potent symbol for many Palestinians in Gaza, transforming the clash with the Shin Bet into a 'legend of valour, replete with the motifs that speak to the hearts of young men: pride and courage, the spirit of self-sacrifice, and a martyr's death on the altar of the nation's freedom'.[35]

All through the rest of October and November the Israeli authorities tried to close the net on Islamic Jihad, but the organisation was an elusive quarry. The authorities imposed curfews, demolished the homes of the October martyrs, conducted house-to-house searches and even announced the arrest of Sheikh Abd al-Aziz Auda. Islamic Jihad responded by organising more general strikes, printing communiqués condemning the Israeli authorities and holding large demonstrations to protest the deportation order against Sheikh Auda. Islamic Jihad were setting an example for the Palestinians of Gaza. Against the highest odds they were beating the Israeli occupation at its own game. The Israeli authorities appeared powerless to stop the wave of mass sentiment that gripped the Gaza Strip in November 1987, a sentiment that was empowered by political Islam.

Foundation Stones for Political Islam

The following section will deal with the structures of the Mujama and Islamic Jihad. There is considerable dispute among scholars as to whether the Mujama and Muslim Brotherhood are one and the same thing. On a general level there is evidence to suggest that the Mujama organisation both embraced and practised the philosophy of the Muslim Brotherhood as outlined by Hassan al-Banna. Sheikh Yassin, the leader of Mujama and of the reformist socio-educational Islamic revival in Gaza, is known generally to embrace the philosophy of Hassan al-Banna, in particular al-Banna's belief that the revival of Islam should be dependent on preaching and education and the Islamisation of society. Sheikh Yassin and his colleagues had enjoyed a close association with the Muslim Brotherhood and regarded their activities as an extension of this work. The Mujama facade was constructed primarily to win permission from the Israeli authorities for the group's activities. While the Israelis were happy to extend a licence to an organisation with charitable status and to all intents and purposes dedicated to welfare and education work, they might have rejected an application from the Muslim Brotherhood.

Charity Begins at Home

The official registration with the Israeli authorities of the Mujama as a charitable society was an act of great significance. It left it free to establish a formidable organisational base for the nascent Islamist movement in Gaza. By legalising and bestowing official legitimacy on the organisation the Israeli authorities were also knowingly allowing the Mujama to proceed with its political as well as charitable plans. Unlike other Palestinian political factions, the Mujama was not proscribed and so was free to organise, recruit and receive funds. Israeli policy in this respect echoes that adopted by King Hussein in 1957 when, following an attempted coup, the king proscribed all political parties, except the Muslim Brotherhood which continued its activities under Jordanian charity laws. Both King Hussein and the Israelis were to regret this policy of encouraging Islam at the expense of political pluralism.

Its charitable status meant that the Mujama was able to establish rapidly and openly an organisational network rivalling that of the other political groups in the local arena. While it took the PFLP, the communists or Fatah decades to establish clandestine local institutions for health, welfare and education against the wishes of the Israelis, it took the Mujama no more than a few years to cover the same ground. As Schiff and Ya'ari note, 'In the space of a decade, Yassin built the Islamic Congress (Mujama) from a fledgling charitable association into an empire that ruled most of the religious life in the Gaza Strip.'[36] The Mujama was successful in its attempts to promote Islam in the lives of many Gazans. By targeting the young the organisation made inroads into the most significant strata of society.

The type of activities undertaken by Mujama cadres were restricted by its rigid organisational base. Following traditional lines of organisation, the structure of the movement was authoritarian and pyramidal. It was headed by a president, general secretary, treasurer and other administrative officials in a way that any other organisation might be staffed. The leader, however, surrounded by his close aides and advisers, commanded complete authority. The administrative officers simply ensured the distribution of funds to all Mujama-run or sponsored projects in the Gaza Strip. There was no obvious internal democracy in the Western sense of the word. The leadership was self selecting, not elected. Those who acted as second-in-command were appointed by Sheikh Yassin, and there is no evidence to suggest that the membership was consulted on major issues of policy or strategy.

The Mujama leadership ran two parallel organisations under the same name. On the one hand there was the public face of the Mujama, with its own offices located in Gaza city the front for the charitable organisation and welfare activities. On the other hand, the political activities of the movement were directed from the home of Sheikh Yassin and the Jawrat al-Shams mosque. Sheikh Yassin appears personally to have been in control of political matters, not just to have fulfilled the function of symbolic figurehead or spiritual guide. Nevertheless Yassin did delegate some authority to a few chosen lieutenants. These men set the internal agenda for both sides of the organisation.

From 1977–87 the growth of the parallel charitable and political organisations continued apace and made a considerable impact in the Gaza Strip. The charitable wing established a commendable welfare structure: crèches, kindergartens, clinics, drug rehabilitation programmes and youth clubs. During religious festivals sweets and toys were distributed to children and play parks were organised. In Khan Yunis, for example, the Mujama set up a clinic staffed by its own doctors, a dental service for the refugee camp, and ran a kindergarten. The Khan Yunis branch of the organisation was large and through its work in the community made inroads into the political support of the nationalists. The Khan Yunis activities were directed by Dr Abd al-Aziz Rantisi and later by Ahmad Nimr. Again, in a facility just north of Shatti camp in Gaza city, the Mujama rented a building with three rooms and an external floodlit pitch. The organisation was legally independent and was called 'The Islamic Society', although the local population viewed it as part of the Mujama. It was headed by Khalil Koka. On its premises a play group was organised, classes in Qur'anic studies were held regularly for young men, and sporting activities, especially football, were a regular fixture, always drawing a crowd of eager young players.

The Mujama set up a formidable welfare, education and sporting network in the Gaza Strip. There was no need to rent huge numbers of buildings, because the mosques, including many new ones built or converted by Mujama supporters, offered a foothold in every neighbourhood, village and camp. The mosque was used not only for worship and Qur'anic classes, but also to house libraries and sporting equipment. The rate of mosque building throughout this period increased rapidly. The Mujama's support of non-Waqf mosque building was funded in part by the Israeli authorities and in part by Saudi and Kuwaiti donors and staffed by imams loyal to Mujama leader Sheikh Yassin. A conservative estimate would be that around fifty mosques were built during this period. The construction of a new mosque normally entailed little more than the conversion of an existing building or the erection of a small concrete structure although there were larger projects, namely the mosques in Nussierat and Shatti camps, and one near Mahmoud Zahar's home in Gaza city.

Membership and Recruitment

In 1985 it was estimated that the membership of the Mujama in the Gaza Strip was two thousand. Out of a total population of 600,000 this looks insignificant although, since female membership was not encouraged and more than half of the Gazan population was then under fourteen, the population of potential members was in fact no more than 150,000. Even so these figures give no pointer to the mass-based popular movement into which the Mujama was to develop after the outbreak of the Palestinian uprising two years later. Until that point in fact, the movement's membership remained relatively small in comparison to that of rival political movements, such as Fatah or the PFLP, although it had already established a framework that would allow it to recruit with ease.

It is of some interest to note the background of the 2,000 members and the particular socio-economic characteristic(s) they share. Broadly speaking many of the 2,000 were employed in the very occupations that epitomised the priorities of the movement: religion, service to the community and honest trade. They were involved in religious affairs, as imams or other employees of the Waqf, giving them, in turn, control over 'an extensive network of property that Mujama then leases to local inhabitants'.[37] Other members were physicians, educators, merchants or pharmacists.

A profile of the leadership of Mujama reveals some interesting facts. Apart from the men previously discussed, including Sheikh Ahmad Yassin, Dr Ibrahim Yazouri, Dr Mahmoud Zahar, Khalil Koka and Dr Abd al-Aziz Rantisi, the Mujama leadership included amongst its members Sheikh Salah Shihadeh, Dr Mohammad Siam, Fadel Khaled Zabout, Ibrahim Abu Salem and Ahmad al-Alami. All these men shared a similar life-history: all were born in the period directly before or after the 1948 war; all were the children of families that fled their homes and settled in refugee camps in the Gaza Strip; each had an impoverished childhood; all would have been barred from any role within Gaza's existing political structures because of their status as refugees; finally, all were educated in Egypt and returned to the Gaza Strip with the kind of professional skills that enabled them to help the community, predominately in medicine, education and science. For example, Mahmoud Zahar studied medicine in Cairo, Ahmad al-Alami took an engineering degree in Cairo, Zabout studied at al-Azhar in Cairo and then taught at the Islamic University in Gaza, while Yazouri studied pharmacy and Rantisi medicine. All of these men studied during the latter half of the 1960s to the first half of the 1970s. Generationally speaking only their leader, Sheikh Yassin represented the old Muslim Brotherhood.

Another distinguishing feature of these men is their lack of formal religious training. Like Sheikh Yassin himself, they are all secularist by education and have, for the most part, turned to Islam as a political force later in life. Their religiosity and spirituality is realised through a path that is political rather than metaphysical. The leadership is also an all-male preserve; there are no parallel positions of power for women attracted to the call of the movement.

Finances

Fund-raising was obviously a very important aspect of the Mujama's work. Each project, whether it was a kindergarten, library, mosque or clinic needed funds. The residents of Gaza were encouraged to contribute through the system of *zakat* (a voluntary 7 per cent tax on income). Through the *zakat* committees in the Gaza Strip the Mujama was able to control the funding of projects for the poor. Locally-raised money could not, however, meet all the expenses incurred by the organisation's expanding welfare and charity structure. Other sources of funding were the Gulf states (particularly Saudi Arabia and Kuwait), Jordan (often acting as a conduit for Mujama funds from the Gulf), the Palestinian Muslim communities of the United States of America and, indirectly, Israel.

The issue of funding came to the fore during the 1984 trial of Sheikh Yassin. The Israeli authorities alleged that 'the accused received 12,000 [Jordanian] dinars (about US$30,000) from Jordanian-parliament member Dr Yousef al-Athm to buy weapons in Israel, while visiting in Amman.'[38] The allegations, assuming they were valid, give some idea of the size of funds that were being channelled through from Jordan to the Gaza Strip. Dr Yousef al-Athm admits that he helped with funding, although not necessarily for the purchase of arms: 'According to the circumstances we would try and send money; we got funds from everywhere we could, but mostly from the Arabs and Muslims'.[39] Al-Athm saw funding to the Islamic movement in Gaza as part of the general strategy and framework of support between the Muslim Brotherhood in Jordan, the West Bank and Mujama in the Gaza Strip. The funding from Jordan was one way of restructuring the organisational links that had been broken in 1967.

The Mujama's sources of funding from the Gulf are less clear. Nonetheless, there is evidence that the organisation was funded by individuals or Islamic organisations in Saudi Arabia. Saudi funds found their way to the Gaza Strip through such institutions as the IUG. A lecturer at the university states that Mujama figures went on regular tours of the Gulf states in an effort to raise funds for the university as well as other projects. According to this lecturer, 'Mujama received funds from the Rabitat al-Alam al-Islami',[40] a charity based in Saudi Arabia and funding Islamic organisations throughout the world. The lecturer also mentions the Jami'a al-Amr bi'l Marouf wa Nahi an al-Munker (Society for Orderly Virtue and Avoidance of Sin), part of the religious police in Saudi Arabia, whose members raised money for Mujama projects. Dr Mohammed Saqr, a former president of the IUG, admitted to additional funding from Gulf sources: 'We got donations from Saudi Arabia, Qatar and Kuwait.'[41] The organisation also benefited from the generosity of former brothers from Gaza who had fled during Nasser's crackdown the 1960s.

While Israel could not be seen to be funding the Mujama directly it is clear that money from the Israeli authorities was intended to bolster the Mujama in its anti-nationalist campaign. The funding came through the mosque-building programme and other activities which were under Mujama control. As an Israeli military governor for the Gaza district, Brigadier-General Yitzhak Sager, stated, 'The Israeli government gave me a budget and the military government gives it to the mosques ... The funds are used for both mosques and religious schools, with the purpose of strengthening a force that runs counter to the pro-PLO leftists.'[42] As long as the Mujama directed its attacks on the local Palestinian population the Israeli authorities were unconcerned. Speaking in 1986 a senior Israeli military figure said of the rise in local tensions between the Mujama and nationalists: 'Fundamentalism exists, but we're not concerned … [There] is no reason to talk about a growing wave of religious fanaticism.'[43] Indeed it is widely alleged that the Israeli authorities considered themselves to enjoy good relations with the Mujama during this period.

There is no question as to the existence of Israeli–Mujama collusion. From the late 1970s onwards the real issue was its extent. It is alleged that:

> The [Israeli] military government accepted them [the Mujama], knowing that they were being used *inter alia*, for political activity and bringing money from abroad for their activities. The military government believed that their activity would undermine the power of the PLO and the leftist organisations in Gaza. They even supplied some of their activists with weapons.[44]

The funding link between Israel and the Mujama was common knowledge in Palestinian political circles and tainted the Mujama in the eyes of the rest of the Palestinian population. Nevertheless, so long as Mujama's anti-nationalist anti-leftist campaign continued, the Israeli authorities turned a blind eye or offered financial support. The link between Mujama and the Israelis did, however, affect the organisation's ability to win popular support for its cause in the Gaza Strip. These collaborationist tendencies were not ignored by Gazans and would haunt the leadership of this nascent Islamist trend in later years.

Ideology

Any examination of the Mujama's ideological outlook must begin by acknowledging that the Palestine issue, particularly in the context of a movement for national liberation, did not appear on the ideological agenda of the movement. This ideological agenda was not indigenous in nature, its inspiration being the philosophy or ideology of figures or movements from outside Palestine. In this context the Mujama could more properly be described as a Muslim rather than a Palestinian–Muslim movement.

The tenets embraced by the Mujama reinforced the ideological link to the Muslim Brotherhood in Egypt. The conservative–reformist approach it espoused was in ideological opposition to the radical–revolutionary rhetoric of many in the Palestinian national movement. Mujama ideology was not fundamentalist but instead advocated a gradual change based on principles of re-Islamisation, that would eventually reform and change the political system. The movement did not print its own books or tracts; the material it circulated was Egyptian in origin, primarily the works of Hassan al-Banna and Sayyid Qutb. Other religious literature, the Qur'an and stories of the *hadith*, were read regularly but there is no evidence to suggest any substantive contribution to literature from the leadership of Mujama itself. The publication of books, newspapers or leaflets would have been extremely difficult given the military occupation. Printing presses and publications had to be licensed by the Israeli authorities and subject to Israeli military censorship.

The Mujama relied instead on the sermon in the mosque and on word-of-mouth. It could be said that it represented a trend advocating ideological oration. The Friday Sermon became an occasion for the leadership to transmit its position on a variety of issues. Each sermon would address a particular theme, relating it specifically to an Islamic message. The preachers would also use the occasion to disseminate the ideological position of the Mujama. Some preachers and sermons were so popular that recordings were made and later sold on cassette. These sermons, however, have always provided a simplistic rendition of Mujama rhetoric based on mass appeal.

Ideology was related to particular themes: family, religious practice, education and welfare. Members were encouraged to embrace a life of Muslim piety. Such piety, Mujama argued, would set an example for others in society, promote the rightful place of Islam and eventually gain momentum resulting in the establishment of an Islamic state and resurrected Caliphate. This simple Islamic message of religion through reform argued that a belief in the role of Islam in every sphere of life must be acknowledged. Mujama therefore rejected secularist notions of separation between religion and politics.

Islamic Revival in the West Bank

Following considerable decline in the activities of both the Muslim Brotherhood and the Islamic Liberation Party, political Islam revived in the West Bank in the second decade of the occupation. Developing through its own momentum rather than in concert with the movement in Gaza, the Muslim Brotherhood attracted a new generation of supporters. These younger supporters, many of whom had grown up under Israeli occupation, used the message of the brotherhood to challenge the hegemony of the Palestine Liberation Organisation. While they were unable to force the national movement into retreat they did communicate to many West Bankers that there was a political alternative to the nationalist secular ideal. Like their counterparts in the Gaza Strip the Muslim Brotherhood in the West Bank challenged the national movement in their own institutions, in particular in the universities.

The key political player in the period from 1977–87 was the Muslim Brotherhood. The Liberation Party continued with its vow to abstain from the politics of the Palestinian issue. This did not mean that the LP was no longer active, rather that it was no longer willing to immerse itself politically in the struggle with the Israeli authorities and other Palestinian political movements, and so the Muslim Brotherhood, revitalised by younger and more broadly-based cadres, expanded its activities most discernibly in Nablus, Ramallah, Hebron and even Jerusalem.

The brotherhood faced a formidable obstacle, however, in the popular Palestinian nationalist and leftist support in the West Bank. Here the process of the secularisation of Palestinian society was apparent at every level, from patterns of consumption to leisure activities. The relationship with the occupier through the demand for Palestinian wage-labour in Israel also 'transformed the whole relationship between family expectations, children's education and the demands of the labour market'.[45] The increasingly secular nature of society extended to the establishment of a mass-based national movement in the West Bank and the founding of a large number of 'national institutions'[46] throughout the 1970s and 1980s including universities, hospitals, research centres, newspapers and magazines. West Bank intellectual trends supported further secularisation and looked upon the brotherhood with their attendant prescriptions for societal and political reforms as reactionary. While some parts of the West Bank, particularly the rural areas and towns like Hebron, remained traditionally conservative, urbanisation and the impact of urban growth on proximate rural areas meant that politically and socially the impact of a more secular society was felt by everyone. However, the heightened atmosphere of political competition over national institutions between groups such as Fatah, the PFLP, DFLP and communists, particularly in the wake of the Israeli invasion of Lebanon and the subsequent ousting of the PLO in 1982, exposed a weakness in the nationalists' organisation.

Lebanon and the Weakened Links of Nationalism

The Israeli invasion of Lebanon in June 1982, the forced exile of the PLO and PLA and the subsequent massacres at Sabra and Shatilla led to a breakdown in the Palestinian national movement. The trauma of Lebanon could be seen throughout the PLO and nationalist organisations from 1983–87. The dislocation of the PLO, the leadership and headquarters were now situated in Tunis, the continued involvement of the Palestinians in the Lebanese civil war and the defeat suffered at the hands of the Israelis and their Lebanese allies were all immense. Internal factional disputes gripped the movement, in particular Fatah, undermining its authority and legitimacy. This period of bitter internal political feuding harmed the national movement leaving it vulnerable to political challenge. The Muslim Brotherhood was only too willing to take advantage of these divisions to gain a foothold in the political arena and, exploiting the protracted conflict between Fatah and the PFLP that lasted throughout the mid-1980s, forged an alliance with Fatah against the PFLP. While the alliance was never permanent and was normally constructed within the realms of elections or other forms of power struggle, it was important in helping promote the message of the Islamists. It was in the universities that displays of power-brokerage as part of complex political relationships were most evident.

Campus Clashes and the Muslim Brotherhood

On the university campuses of the West Bank the forces of political Islam, particularly the student-affiliated bodies of the Muslim Brotherhood, were able to make a political impact both in terms of raising the profile of the movement in relation to other political factions and in successfully contending student elections. The growth of an Islamic base among the student population of the West Bank was a reflection of what the brotherhood believed to be the radicalisation of youth which culminated in a critique of the old nationalist slogans and an embrace of Islam as a political solution. As one leader of the Islamic bloc at Birzeit University (a coalition dominated by the Muslim Brotherhood, also including Islamic Jihad and Liberation Party students) was quoted as saying:

> We tried the fiasco of liberalism in 1948 and we lost half of Palestine. We tried socialist constitutionalism in 1967, and we lost the rest of Palestine.

We need to be more doctrinaire if Israel is to be overthrown. We need an Islamic state founded on the principles of the Qur'an.[47]

The brotherhood's attempts to penetrate positions of power within the university system as a whole met, however, with only mixed success. The corridors of power in Birzeit and Bethlehem universities were not as welcoming to the kind of militant Islamic elements that had managed to dominate the IUG. The examples which follow of Najah and Birzeit universities illustrate, however, the length to which the brotherhood was prepared to go in order to establish a foothold amongst Palestinian youth, the vanguard of the future.

Najah University and a Battle of Wills
Throughout the 1980s the Muslim Brotherhood found fresh support among the student population of the West Bank. Nowhere was this more apparent than at Najah University in Nablus. Nablus has always been popularly considered as the centre for the national movement but the Muslim Brotherhood also has had a long history of activity in the city.

Najah College was established in 1977 but an educational facility of this type had existed in the city since 1918. The idea of the university, according to one administrative official, was based on a desire by the notable families of Nablus 'to improve the educational lot of the people'.[48] The notable families, in particular the Masris, later came to dominate the university and shape its policy as an educational institution. By 1986 some 4,000 students were registered and the institution was popularly known as the Najah National University. The student body (55 per cent male and 45 per cent female) came, for the most part, from the town and from the surrounding region indicating a large number of students from a rural background. Religion has often dominated politics within the university and remains a potent symbol and rallying-point for many of the students. Religiosity and its relationship with politics has been complex. As the Palestinian sociologist Iyyad Barghouti high-lighted in his study of Najah students, 'Religious observance is still negatively related to political activism'.[49] Nevertheless, the expression of differing political perspectives is seen as a natural right by most students and politics have given the university a stormy history.

According to students and lecturers interviewed at Najah, the rise of the Islamic bloc was apparent by 1981, and the period that followed was characterised by a series of clashes between this bloc and nationalist students on the campus. By January 1982 the Islamists had organised themselves into a formidable political grouping ready to challenge the hitherto undisputed authority of the nationalist students and to enter into conflict. On 9 January 1982 the Islamic bloc physically attacked a nationalist lecturer, Mohammad Suwalha. Suwalha was branded an enemy of Allah because of his leftist views. He was either pushed or forced to jump out of a third floor window of a university building. Another lecturer who witnessed the incident declared:

> Some of the Islamic bloc gathered on the campus. I went and asked them what they were doing. They said they wanted Mohammad Suwalha. They said they wanted the university to dismiss him. They said he was a communist and an immoral person ... We tried to resolve the issue but the students would not listen and they went to attack Suwalha.[50]

Following the incident clashes erupted between the Islamic bloc and the nationalist students. The university administration, unable to contain the violence, announced the voluntary closure of the campus for two weeks. The conflict was eventually resolved only through the involvement of the notable families, who dictated a settlement.

The Islamic bloc created considerable tension in the university. Its grievances stemmed from claims that the university authorities were supporting the rights of lecturers to express leftist political views. In the previous year the university administration had reinstated four lecturers dismissed on account of holding such views. The reinstatement appeared to be the result of pressure applied by Nablus mayor, Bassam Shaka, on the university president, Hikmat al-Masri. According to one newspaper report at the time:

> It was Shaka who lobbied on their [the sacked lecturers] behalf, using the vociferous support of the left-wing students and the pressure of other left-wing groups in the town. The reinstatement of the four lecturers ordered by Hikmat al-Masri after the Shaka lobby efforts incurred the wrath of the Muslim Brothers who had previously supported him.[51]

The controversy over the Suwalha incident illustrates the determination of the Islamic bloc both to frustrate any attempt to marginalise their influence and their strong desire to ensure the elimination of leftist influence. The members and supporters of the Islamic bloc openly challenged arguments in favour of the right to political expression, by either lecturers or students. Political pluralism was a luxury they could not afford in their fight to strengthen their position after the years of political dormancy. And, like their counterparts in the Gaza Strip, the new Muslim Brotherhood activists in the West Bank were prepared to resort to violence in the name of politics. Once again, the Palestinian left was identified as the main target; its elimination was crucial in the endeavour to re-Islamicise Palestinian society.

The Suwalha incident was eventually put aside and for the rest of the decade political competition among the students was confined to the ballot box – in the annual elections for the eleven posts on the student council.[52] In the five years before the closure of the university in 1987, the Islamic bloc (consisting of the Muslim Brotherhood and Islamic Jihad) commanded a majority on the council only once as a result of the 1982 election following the Suwalha incident. According to nationalist students, an electoral alliance with Fatah and the subsequent split in the national ranks was what enabled the Islamic bloc to defeat the leftist-based coalition at this point. One lecturer noted the temporary nature of this electoral alliance: 'There is a lot of common ground between Fatah and the Islamic bloc but there has never been any formal coalition between them.'[53] This alliance highlights a truth which continues to permeate localised politics: at the level of the day-to-day contest between factions a series of unlikely political relationships emerges on a temporary basis in which the usual ideological objections are suspended in the battle to eliminate a common opponent. This relationship is epitomised by the Arabic saying, 'My enemy's enemy is my friend'. Subsequent student council elections at Najah saw control of the student council revert to the nationalist and more specifically the Shabiba (Fatah youth) faction. in the 1986 and 1987 elections at Najah the following votes were cast: in 1986 the nationalists (including Fatah and the PFLP and DFLP) gained 62.6 per cent of the vote, the Islamic bloc 37.4 per cent; in 1987 the nationalists and Islamic bloc won 58 and 42 per cent respectively.[54]

Between the 1986 and 1987 elections, then, there was a 5 per cent increase in the Islamic-bloc vote which, according to one student council member, can be attributed to Israeli interference in the elections rather than to an increase in support for the Islamists: 'Before the election day the Israeli authorities arrested the Shabiba leadership (about 100 students in total), there were no arrests among the Islamic leadership and their leadership on the university campus'.[55] In a policy similar to that operated in the Gaza Strip where the Israelis turned a blind eye to the activities of the Islamic movement, the Islamists at Najah were less likely to be arrested than the nationalist or leftist activists. Lecturers at the university stated that the army never interfered when activists from the Islamic bloc were agitating on campus:

> There was no interference whatsoever by the Israeli army, they have never stopped the Islamic bloc from trouble-making ... The Israeli authorities promoted and encouraged divisions to indirectly strengthen one current over another. They were trying to maintain a balance of power and prevent the nationalist movement from becoming too powerful.[56]

The accommodation of Islamist and nationalist opinion, exacerbated by the Israeli policy of divide and rule practised during this period, was not just a problem for the student body at Najah. Even the so-called bastion of nationalism and liberalism in the West Bank, Birzeit University, was not exempt from the Islamic-nationalist power struggle. As at other university campuses in the West Bank the tensions between the Islamic and nationalist groups evolved into conflict rather than political accommodation.

The Emirs of Birzeit

Founded in 1922 and with a student population of around 4,000 by 1975, Birzeit University is regarded as a bedrock of academic and student liberalism. Liberalism, however, did not characterise the challenge that was mounted by the Islamic bloc at the university throughout the 1980s. As the former president of the student council and deportee Marwan Barghouti noted, 'The Muslim Brotherhood leadership set out actively to conquer the nationalist students of the university campus by encouraging the growth of the Islamic student bloc.'[57] The emergence of an Islamic bloc, mainly fronted by young supporters of the Muslim Brotherhood, was first noted in the late 1970s. According to lecturer Munir Fasheh:

> Until 1977 or 1978 most of the people at the university had not heard of any separate or distinct religious group ... The first sign ... was the student election of November 1979. There were two slates, one nationalist and the other religious. About 90 per cent of the students voted and the religious slate got 43 per cent of the vote. That was the first measure of where things stood.[58]

In June 1983 the presence of the Islamic bloc on the campus led to fierce clashes and violence. Conflict erupted after Islamic-bloc activists and their supporters stormed the campus, damaged property and attacked fellow students. The Birzeit trouble was linked to a pattern of problems and difficulties between the Islamic bloc and nationalists at the IUG. A local newspaper reported, 'The pitched battles on Saturday 5 June, ended after Islamic students, many from the Gaza Strip, had wrecked part of the campus during a march, injured dozens of students and threatened university officials. They were driven off by national students.'[59]

Following the incident the university authorities, like their counterparts in Najah, announced the voluntary closure of the campus, a significant indicator of the seriousness with which these Islamic bloc–nationalist clashes were viewed at institutions of higher education in the West Bank. Nevertheless, when Birzeit University reopened, the Islamic bloc continued its activities on campus and stood in opposition to Birzeit's nationalist tendency in student elections.

The Islamic bloc won, on average, a third of student support. Its ability to win hearts and influence grew with the high level of commitment among its members and its rigorous application of beliefs. Within the university a pattern of support for one political group over another emerged on a faculty-wide basis. The faculties of Engineering and Science became known as Islamic bloc strongholds while Arts and Humanities students were generally associated with the nationalist/leftist tendency. Throughout this period, Islamic cohesiveness allowed Islamic bloc students at Birzeit to carve a place for themselves in a localised political arena and the university became an important political training ground for the movement. Indeed, by the end of the decade Islamic student leaders of Birzeit active in the early 1980s had become leading figures in the nation-wide movement. Leftist student leaders at the university were impressed by the abilities of their opponents, as Bashir Barghouti, a student leader known to support the Communist Party noted:

> The Islamists were very good at organising. This we could see during the election campaigns, when they would hold large marches which were organised and directed by Islamic supporters outside the campus. Also, the Islamic bloc used the mosque in Birzeit village as its headquarters and people from all over the region would meet up there. The leaders on the campus were called 'emirs' and in each faculty there was an emir from the Islamic bloc who led the students. This meant that power was very centralised and the emir must be obeyed unquestioningly.[60]

The Islamic bloc at Birzeit was led by Mustafa Lidawi, from Jabaliyya camp in the Gaza Strip. Lidawi enrolled for courses in 1984 and by 1986 was the most significant figure in the Islamic bloc.

He quickly gained a reputation for his sermons in which he called on fellow Muslims to support the Islamic movement. Activities centred around the organisation of meetings and prayers. Religious activists would encourage students to participate in the Friday prayer held in the campus grounds. Book-fairs were held where Islamic texts were sold and lectures given by supporters. The Islamists even had their own band, consisting of drummers who would lead marches of the brotherhood at various rallies, events and demonstrations. Activities concentrated on winning the hearts and minds of students while the nationalist students continued to focus on opposing the occupation authorities. The Islamists did not organise or attend marches or demonstrations against the Israeli authorities. Rather their presence was felt in the lecture halls and in the high profile of supporters calling for regular prayers and the observance of other religious injunctions.

Students and the Politics of Islam

The Islamic movement had varying success at other West Bank universities. At Bethlehem University, a Christian institution with a Muslim student majority, sectarian politics was never a real issue during this period. The national movement was strongly represented on campus and the student council was dominated by the PLO factions. The Islamic movement did not make a significant impact. At Hebron University the opposite was true. The traditional and conservative nature of the city was reflected in the student body. The Islamists dominated student politics and local heroes such as Dr Abdullah Azzam, who was killed during the war in Afghanistan, were lauded. The students erected a shrine to Azzam's memory and he was often cited as a true example of mujahidin spirit. The teaching staff also tended to favour the Islamic movement; many devoted student followers preached in local mosques, particularly in the Ibrahimi mosque also used by Hebron's Jewish settler population. The student council elections at Hebron always brought victory for the Islamic bloc. There was, however, no discernible tension or conflict between the Islamic bloc and the nationalists. Many Islamic activists shared close links and alliances with religiously-minded leaders and activists from Fatah while the absence of any leftist forces in Hebron deterred serious disruptions or clashes at a local level. Support for the Islamic movement at the university was neither dented nor bolstered by the tide of political events in the area and remained fairly constant throughout the 1980s.

The Palestinian universities of the West Bank became useful bases for the revival of political Islam, and in particular the Muslim Brotherhood, during this decade. In other areas of activity the brotherhood was less successful. It was not able to rival the welfare, or education structure established by the national movement during this time nor did it seek to gain influence in any of the professional associations, trade union groups, women's co-operative project or non-governmental institutions. The universities represented not only the most visible success of the brotherhood in its revivalist tendencies but its only political achievement. The nationalist community of the West Bank was resilient to the incipient challenge of political Islam, while the ascendancy of the West Bank intelligentsia inhibited any significant swing of popular support away from the PLO at this period.

The Journey into the Lion's Den: Islamic Jihad in the West Bank

The formation of Islamic Jihad cells and activity throughout the period leading to the outbreak of the Intifada in 1987 was limited but spectacular. Indications that Islamic Jihad was operative in the West Bank appeared in 1983 and continued sporadically over the next few years. While influenced by the Shqaqi–Auda faction in the Gaza Strip, the activities of the Islamic Jihad Jerusalem Brigade in the West Bank were directed, in the main, from Amman and commanded by Sheikh As'ad Bayyud al-Tammimi. Nevertheless, compared to Gaza, the heartland of the organisation, only a few cells were established. Unsurprisingly, Islamic Jihad made no significant inroads politically into the power structures of any local institutions. Unlike the Muslim Brotherhood, which spent the 1977–87 period in a battle of wills with the national movement and virtually ignored the policies of the occupation authorities, the main target of Islamic Jihad was Israel. The application of jihad, liberation through struggle against the usurpers of Islam, was a philosophy widely and reverently embraced by its activists.

The first Islamic Jihad attack in the West Bank was significant in that it was against an Israeli civilian, rather than a military target. A Yeshiva student, Aharon Gross, was stabbed to death in the centre of Hebron in July 1983. That the attack was in Hebron, the centre of Israeli settler activity and focus of continued religious tension over Jewish and Islamic claims over the Ibrahimi mosque was probably no coincidence. Following the attack Islamic Jihad issued a communiqué claiming responsibility. Despite an immediate search and murder enquiry the assailants were never apprehended. The action was applauded by sections of the Palestinian community, and on the Friday following the murder of Gross hundreds of worshippers at Jerusalem's al-Aqsa mosque demonstrated their support for Islamic Jihad. The demonstrators shouted 'Allahu Akbar', and as a newspaper report noted: 'Despite a few pro-Arafat slogans, police sources noted on Friday that the tone of the demonstrators was more religious than political.'[61]

The specific dynamic of religious dispute between Muslim and Jew was evident in Islamic Jihad attacks in the West Bank. The nature of the religious conflict, the belief in jihad and the history of hostility dominated the planning of these incidents. The sacrifice of life in the name of jihad encouraged within the cell system of the organisation meant that activists were willing to take significant risks and were even prepared to walk into the lion's den.

This lack of fear in the face of Israeli military might was clearly illustrated in October 1986. During a military passing-out ceremony for Israeli soldiers at Jerusalem's Western Wall (the site most holy to Judaism), Islamic Jihad struck. Islamic Jihad mujahidin took their positions amongst the milling crowds that filled the plaza directly in front of the wall. As soon as the military ceremonies were under way the Jihad attackers threw a number of hand grenades into the crowd of soldiers and civilians. The soldiers escaped but the father of one recruit was killed and others were injured as the grenades exploded.[62] From its base in Jordan the Islamic Jihad Jerusalem Brigade issued a communiqué claiming responsibility for the attack. The Israeli authorities responded swiftly by arresting and interrogating hundreds of Palestinians, particularly from the Old City of Jerusalem. Among them were a few young men who were the alleged perpetrators of the attack. According to a press report, the three 'were held incommunicado for forty-five days. After savage torture, one of them is reported to have confessed that they had instructions from their leadership based in Jordan.'[63]

The three prisoners allegedly confessed to a link between the PLO and Islamic Jihad Jerusalem Brigade. An Israeli newspaper reported that 'the suspects had been recruited in Jordan by the Fatah organisation in December 1985. They had then been trained in Jordan before King Hussein closed Fatah's operational office in Amman.'[64] The suspects were not denying that they belonged to Islamic Jihad

Jerusalem Brigade, just that they had been recruited originally by Fatah and trained in Jordan under al-Tammimi's guidance at Fatah facilities. The claim added to the suspicion that elements in the Fatah hierarchy, including Abu Jihad and Munir Shafiq, were keen to support the Islamic Jihad tendency to counteract the flow of Fatah supporters reportedly leaving the movement to join the Muslim Brotherhood. The leader of Islamic Jihad (Shqaqi–Auda faction), Sheikh Abd al-Aziz Auda, asserted, however, that while his movement was not part of the PLO it did maintain 'good relations with all the PLO factions' and that the relationship was based on a common goal: 'The Islamic Jihad co-operates at all levels, and battlegrounds in the confrontation with the Jews. However, we differ with these others over the settlement, recognition of Israel, and any dialogue with the Zionists and Jews.'[65]

There was evidence that as far back as 1982 Fatah had already acknowledged the growth of the Muslim Brotherhood as a threat. One reason for the much-lauded reconciliation between the PLO and King Hussein was that 'the Jordanian government and the guerrilla movement ... are becoming desperate as the loyalties of West Bank Palestinians slowly slip from their control.'[66] Hanna Nasser, a member of the PLO Executive Committee was quoted as admitting that 'fundamentalism had cut into PLO support' and acknowledged that the trend towards Islam had been growing in the occupied territories 'among young people who feel that no answer to the occupation has been found by traditional nationalist groups'.[67] While the evidence of three suspects does not necessarily imply that an organisational link exists, and indeed figures within Islamic Jihad deny any relationship at this level, there is some evidence to suggest that Fatah training facilities in Jordan were made available to certain wings of the Islamic Jihad movement. Fatah had also trained Liberation Party members who were arrested by the Israeli authorities in 1981 on murder charges.[68]

Islamic Jihad was involved in sporadic activity in the West Bank throughout 1986 and 1987. In August 1987 an Islamic Jihad cell based in Bethlehem was uncovered by the Israeli authorities before attempting to car bomb the Israeli Ministry of Justice. A young woman, Atif Aliyan, had been recruited to drive the car in a suicide mission to Jerusalem. The Shin Bet discovery alerted the authorities to the very real threat that Islamic Jihad posed to the internal security of Israel. If Islamic Jihad were able to recruit activists willing to sacrifice their own lives for the struggle then Israel's security could be weakened severely. This message was not lost on the Israelis as they sought to contain the threat of Islamic Jihad in the months preceding the outbreak of the Intifada. By this time, however, the message of sacrifice championed by Islamic Jihad had already inspired many thousands of young Palestinians who would also turn on the occupation, creating a popular myth of invincibility in the face of Israeli military might.

Conclusion

The decade before the outbreak of the Palestinian uprising in 1987 had created opportunities for the Islamic movement to establish itself organisationally in the Palestinian arena. By the end of the decade the phenomenon of political Islam had emerged as a dynamic force which would alter the configuration of power and its structures in the occupied territories and compel both the Palestinian national movement and the Israeli occupation authorities to reassess the conflict between them.

The Mujama, led by Sheikh Yassin, would become a formidable political force in the Gaza Strip, rivalling that of the national movement. Political Islam was fast becoming a challenge to the national movement, which by 1982 was severely weakened and factionalised following defeat in Lebanon at the hands of the Israelis. The challenge was conservative in nature and ambitious in political activity. The Mujama would provide a meaningful alternative to the PLO in Gaza. It quickly gained a popular local reputation for its honest leadership, untainted by allegations of corruption. It also made an impact on the heart of the Gaza community, in the refugee camps and among the poorest groups, who it provided with welfare assistance and religious support. Through the re-Islamisation of Gazan society, the Mujama would make its eventual political gains. Through encouraging the secularised youth of Gaza to return to the mosque, to make the mosque part of their daily life, the Mujama would eventually win the loyal support of thousands of young men.

Islamic Jihad, developed after splitting from the Muslim Brotherhood, established itself as a meaningful political actor. Its message and vision of political Islam did inspire Palestinians to take some sort of control over their destiny and in turn they were encouraged to find ways of resisting the occupation. The ethos of political violence embraced by Islamic Jihad contrasted with Mujama's facade of gradual reformism. The presence of Islamic Jihad and its vision of unity of struggle and philosophy of avoiding internal dispute with other political factions also reflected negatively on the Mujama as the latter's campaign of attacks and violence against secularists, nationalists, leftists and ordinary Gaza residents, grew as the decade progressed. This reality jarred with the facade of quietist reform, preaching and education which the movement professed. Popular support would not be won through the forced assimilation of Gazans into an Islamic vision of society preached by the Mujama. Towards the end of the decade there was movement within the organisation to recognise this fact and the Palestinian uprising or Intifada, as it became known provided a unique opportunity to transform the message of political Islam and harness it to a deep-seated desire among the Palestinian communities of the Gaza Strip and West Bank to end Israeli occupation irrespective of the political outcome.

The Intifada and the Peace Process:
Islamic Challenge or Nationalist Victory?

The outbreak of the Palestinian uprising in December 1987 took everyone by surprise. After the event conventional wisdom on the subject admitted that the explosion of anger and frustration was inevitable after the Palestinians had lived under Israeli rule for so long. Yet, in addition to reflecting a basic and instinctive rejection of Israeli military rule, the uprising (Intifada) reflected a complex rubric of changing attitudes towards the prevailing political order outside as well as within the Israeli occupied territories.

The Intifada, then, was more than the 'shaking off' (of Israeli occupation) that its Arabic name implies. It marked changes also in political relations within Palestinian society. In terms of nationalist and Islamist relations within the West Bank and Gaza Strip it signalled an important watershed reflecting power struggles, internal democratisation, an increase in the acknowledgement of populist sentiment and a corresponding decline in the vanguard and often elitist approach to politics. The Intifada both forced responses from political actors and created opportunities for them to capitalise on the unprecedented internal political changes.

The Islamic movement was, as we have seen, already playing an increasing role in Palestinian affairs. Islamic Jihad in particular played a significant role in the first months of the uprising with the Shqaqi–Auda faction co-operating with nationalist groups to mobilise people and direct their protest towards more concrete actions such as forming committees. The Israeli authorities responded to the threat by deporting a number of Islamic Jihad leaders, including Fathi Shqaqi and Sheikh Abd al-Aziz Auda, in January 1988 and, over the next two months, imprisoning members and supporters. By the late spring the various factions of Islamic Jihad were in a weakened state and it would take several years for the organisation to recover fully from this early setback.

It was, then, the emergence of the Islamic Resistance Movement (Harakat al-Muqawama al-Islamiyya), better known by its Arabic acronym Hamas, that posed the greatest challenge, not only to the Israeli occupation, but also the hegemony of the secular-nationalist movement. Hamas, seeking to step into the political shoes of Islamic Jihad in harnessing popular support, would come to represent the potent force of political Islam in the West Bank and Gaza Strip.

Message from the Mosque:
the Hamas Phenomenon

The spontaneous outburst of protest and demonstration which became known as the Intifada reflected the increasingly desperate situation Palestinians faced after twenty years of Israeli occupation. The uprising, in a sense, was an event waiting to happen and the death of Gazan day-labourers in a traffic accident with an Israeli vehicle but the catalyst that set it off. In Gaza hundreds and then thousands of Palestinians took to the streets. Within days, protest had swept through the West Bank and the uprising had begun in earnest. They wanted just one thing: an end to Israeli occupation.

Out of this confusion journalists, policymakers, noting the role of the mosques were now playing in political mobilisation, at first jumped to the conclusion that the Intifada was an Islamic revolution. The loudspeakers fixed to the minarets, normally used to call the faithful to prayer, transmitted orders to the population, announced strikes and warned of approaching Israeli forces. The military authorities were quick to respond by cutting wires or confiscating the speakers themselves and local preachers were arrested for allowing their mosques to be used in this way.[1] Reports of other cases of disregard for traditional Islamic practice were widespread.[2]

These potent Islamic emblems of the first weeks of the Intifada did not, however, signify any unified Islamic political structure. Protest was general and undirected. The national movement took time to catch its breath but was soon organised under the auspices of the PLO-backed United National Leadership of the Uprising (UNLU). The UNLU included Fatah, PFLP, DFLP and the communists and was organised to realise nationalist objectives. It took much longer for a coherent Islamic response to emerge. The leaders of Mujama were unable initially to harness their organisational structures to the new political situation, and were for a long time trying to gauge whether or not the political protest would continue. Thus Islam did not form part of a grand political strategy to end the Israeli occupation and establish an Islamic state in the whole of Palestine.

It was perhaps inevitable that a link should be made between Islam and the Intifada: religion was a cultural part of the Palestinian process of demonstration as the protest at one funeral or death led inevitably to another in the cycle of conflict in the occupied territories. To the casual observer it must indeed have seemed as if the Intifada were an Islamic uprising; but this view was mistaken and based on an alarmist vision of the changes then taking place. Islamic influence in the first events of the Intifada was rather unclear, representing a cultural rather than political or ideological response to events.

The emergence of a new Islamic force in the context of the Intifada took some months and was the result of a number of factors as well as pressures on the leadership of the Mujama movement, including the respected Sheikh Ahmad Yassin. Mujama had already mounted a challenge to the political monopoly of the PLO; the new organisation, Hamas, would openly compete with it. The emergent Hamas was run by the same personalities previously prominent in Mujama. Mujama had been caught out by the strength of feeling and determination expressed by all Palestinians in the first weeks of the Intifada. The nationalist movement and the already active Islamic Jihad group had, from the very first days of the demonstrations, quickly harnessed popular support through the formation of small local committees and through leaflets.[3] The leadership of Mujama, however, was slower to respond. It deliberated over the significance of the events and their implications for the future of the organisation, counselling caution as it grappled with the change in political forces. Mujama's record on the question of anti-occupation activity was bound to mean that figures like Sheikh Yassin would take time to determine the appropriate reaction.[4] It was therefore some months before a co-ordinated reaction to the uprising was forthcoming. Following negotiations with Mujama's Muslim Brotherhood counterparts in the West Bank, Hamas, or the Islamic Resistance Movement, was established in late February 1988.

Hamas and the Intifada

The emergence of Hamas added a new dimension to Palestinian politics. The new organisation was not willing to subsume itself within the framework of the PLO and threw down the gauntlet in the struggle for political power. Here was an activist Islamic organisation operating publicly and openly challenging the authority of the national movement in a competition to win popular support. Hamas is an indigenous group, yet tied to the wider trend of political Islam in the region. In its covenant, published in August 1988, Hamas describes itself as 'a wing of the Muslim Brotherhood in Palestine'.[5] It was clear from the outset that Hamas would find it hard to ignore its legacy and links with Mujama, and some nationalists have argued that the new organisation was in fact just the old group in a different guise.[6]

Hamas quickly attracted a large following. Young men joined up in droves, many of them already Islamic activists, others disaffected supporters of PLO factions. The organisation generated a special appeal among the Palestinian population. Of the young men who flocked to its ranks, many had refugee backgrounds and saw an opportunity for self-identity and esteem *vis-à-vis* the rest of society through their association with this religious organisation which put a mark of holiness on them. Of note, however, is the fact that Hamas was able to draw considerable support also from the Palestinian middle classes, white-collar workers and professionals.

Its growing membership saw Hamas through many vicissitudes as the Intifada took root in the West Bank and Gaza Strip and became a way of life. The establishment of a new political reality throughout the area resulted in a number of recognisable phases in the development of Hamas from the late 1980s onwards: (i) Hamas' reaction to the Intifada and the nationalist initiative; (ii) the links with Israel; (iii) the Sasportas–Sa'don killings and the Israeli crackdown; (iv) challenge and confrontation with Israel and the nationalists; (v) the Gulf Crisis, and (vi) the effects of the peace process.

Hamas' Reaction to the Intifada

The first period of Hamas activity in the Intifada was characterised by reaction to the immediate situation rather than the initiation of anti-occupation policies and an attempt at a national leadership role. Hamas had to catch up with the nationalists and Islamic Jihad. The

United National Leadership of the Uprising (UNLU), a coalition including all the nationalist factions of the PLO, had marshalled popular support, directing it to specific actions and goals through its regular leaflets. Hamas set about covering similar political ground and its first significant public activity was to issue leaflets in its own name. In its fourth leaflet, for example, it called all the Palestinian people to rally together under the banner of Islam to end the occupation:

> At this time the Islamic uprising has been intensified in the occupied territories. In all the villages, all the refugee camps, our martyrs have fallen ... But they have died in the name of God and their cries are those of victory ... In the name of God, God is Great, The Hour of Khaybar has arrived, Death to the occupation.[7]

Hamas was able to establish a strong organisational framework relatively quickly. In the first months following its establishment it was relatively free to do as it pleased, without Israeli interference. Members and supporters were not subject to prohibition, deportation, mass arrests or the administrative detention of their leaders. Hamas was, in short, only subject to the same general punishments meted out to the population as a whole through curfews, relaxation of open-fire orders and other measures.

Without the charismatic presence and the experience of Sheikh Ahmad Yassin it is hard to imagine that Hamas could have made such an impact on political life in the Gaza Strip. Although Yassin acted primarily as spiritual leader of the new organisation, he appointed those closest to him to take charge of the new organisation's more temporal and day-to-day affairs. For administrative purposes Hamas was initially divided into three chapters: (i) the political wing; (ii) the intelligence gathering sector, and (iii) a military wing named after the 1930s radical leader Sheikh Izz ad-Din al-Qassam, the military and intelligence wings later being combined. The distribution of power within this organisational triangle was never fixed and since the group's inception has passed from one point of the triangle to another, meeting situations as needed.

The political wing of Hamas was staffed by some of Sheikh Yassin's closest Mujama associates including Ismail Abu Shanab, Ibrahim Yazouri, Dr Abd al-Aziz Rantisi and Dr Mahmoud Zahar. It concentrated on activities such as the writing, publication and dissemination of leaflets, fund-raising both at home and abroad, and recruitment. In addition it set about asserting Hamas authority over the mosques, which at this point were not dominated by any particular Islamic political faction[8] and eliminating nationalist political influence over them. In certain areas of the Gaza Strip this policy was very successful, and in the mosques it dominated, Hamas organised activities such as Qur'an classes and political meetings to work out strategies and tactics. Funds from abroad were vital to the organisation. Hamas figures in Jordan, such as Dr Mohammad Saqr and Ibrahim Ghosheh, undertook tours of the Gulf states throughout 1988 and 1989 raising millions of dollars. Supporters in Europe and America also arranged fund-raising drives and disseminated the political message of Hamas.[9]

The intelligence apparatus, known as *al-Majd* (Glory), was initially assigned a policing role in the Gaza Strip. With the breakdown and erosion of Israeli rule in the area, the first leaders of this branch, Yihyeh Sanwar and Ruhi Mushtaha, perceived the need, and the opportunity, for an internal policing function. The intelligence apparatus was later subsumed in the organisation's military wing, the Sheikh Izz ad-Din al-Qassam Brigade. The wing is responsible for executing Palestinians identified as collaborators and for attacks on Israeli targets.

When it was initially established, the Izz ad-Din al-Qassam Brigade,[10] was the smallest of the three wings of the organisation. Over the years, however, its prominence has varied with the policies of its leadership. The military wing's leadership is a closely guarded secret and it operates a cell system with a fairly fluid chain of command, so that it is rather more autonomous than other arms of the movement. According to Israeli charge-sheets the founder was Sheikh Salah Shihadeh from Gaza. He appointed a leader of operations, purported to be Nizar Abdullah, who it was claimed 'established four military squads which engaged in planting and throwing explosive charges'.[11] Other infamous figures include Yahya Ayyash, known as the 'Engineer'. The Israeli security apparatus has had difficulty in exposing and capturing either the leadership of the military wing or its members who have been active in both the Gaza Strip and the West Bank, camping out in orange groves and hillsides to escape arrest.[12]

By the sixth month of the Intifada, Hamas was still shadowing the initiatives of UNLU, making similar appeals, calls and demands through its communiqués. However, the language in which Hamas cloaked such calls was purely Islamic and designed to strengthen the myth of the Islamic nature of the Intifada:

We are with every person who truly works for the liberation of Palestine, the whole of Palestine. We will continue to have faith in Allah and His power. Every Muslim around the globe is our asset, this is our strength, this is our base, and these are our beliefs, and victory is ours with Allah's will.[13]

From its very first days the Palestinian general strike was a key element in the uprising. The withdrawal of labour from Israel, the closing of Palestinian shops, schools and offices were acts of mass defiance in which everyone could play a part. The strikes went on for several months and a retaliatory policy of forcing shops open was executed by Israeli troops. Strikes were held either as an act of protest against specific Israeli actions or as a symbolic action to show solidarity in the community. The leaders of the Intifada, the UNLU, gave strike organisation careful thought and consideration.

The leadership of Hamas immediately recognised the political significance of directing the strike and with its first leaflets started arranging localised Hamas actions, mainly in the Gaza Strip. By the late summer of 1988 the organisation was ready to call for its own territories-wide strikes independent of UNLU arrangements. The first such strike resulted in clashes between Hamas and the nationalists. Hamas supporters in the West Bank enforced the strike call violently, attacking shops which stayed open, throwing molotov cocktails at and beating up car drivers.[14] The UNLU opposed the violent imposition of any orders and in its communiqué which followed the Hamas action condemned Islamists.

If the Hamas leadership had hoped to elicit a full-scale confrontation with the nationalists over the strike issue they were disappointed. It was apparent however, that Hamas was ready to enter a new stage, one in which it would increasingly take the initiative and threaten support for the UNLU and by association the Palestine Liberation Organisation. Nationalists had hitherto sought to contain rather than confront opposition within the community. Indeed the strength of the Intifada had been its ability to unite all Palestinians around one specific issue: actively bringing an end to Israeli occupation. When Hamas publicly attacked the PLO's Declaration of Palestinian Independence in November 1988 and its acceptance of UN resolutions 181, 242 and 338 the nationalist response was once again to warn Hamas to keep its own counsel. Another UNLU leaflet urged 'certain fundamentalist quarters to place national interest above their factional concerns and interests and to correct negative attitudes which, whether intended or not, serve only the interests of the enemy'.[15]

Hamas strategy, however, was still to undermine the PLO's credibility and its claim to be the sole legitimate representative of the Palestinian people. It was facilitated by continuing close relations between the Israeli authorities and major Islamic figures, formerly with the Mujama and now heading Hamas.

Links with Israel

By the end of the first year of the uprising popular support for Hamas had increased dramatically and provided a strong base for the organisation in both the Gaza Strip and in the West Bank.[16] Hamas was now prepared to seek further control over the political arena and consolidate its position. It could do this only once the contradictory nature of its relationship with Israel was resolved. By the second year of the uprising the Israeli link was proving a hindrance to Hamas' ambitions.

The relationship between Hamas and the Israeli authorities was, however, at its strongest during the second year of the Intifada. The Israelis had been quick to extend legitimacy and status to Hamas in an attempt to marginalise the PLO. Leaders of Hamas were regularly filmed at meetings with top-level Israeli officials and the message the Israelis were sending out was that they regarded Hamas as the type of people with whom they could work. This ill-conceived policy cost Israel dearly and sent out all the wrong messages to the Hamas movement. Nevertheless, as long as Israel accorded Hamas the status of 'partner-for-discussion' nobody was likely to be prosecuted for setting up joint meetings.[17] Within a year of Hamas' establishment its spokesman, Dr Mahmoud Zahar, was attending meetings with Israeli Defence Minister Yitzhak Rabin. The spiritual leader Sheikh Yassin and others also met with Israeli government officials as well as with representatives of the civil administration in the Gaza Strip to discuss the uprising and its implications. Israeli policy makers remained intent on viewing Hamas as a moderate Islamic movement for social reform rather than an Islamist organisation with the stated goal of jihad to end the Israeli occupation of all Palestine.[18] In addition the Israelis continued turning a blind eye to the large amounts of money coming into the country destined for Hamas coffers, while at the same time actively stopping the flow of PLO funds in support of the Intifada.

Hamas claimed it had nothing but contempt for the state of Israel, but at a more a prosaic level the relationship with Israel was dominated by a shared antipathy towards the PLO and the secular national movement. The favours shown to Hamas by the Israeli authorities did not go unnoticed by the rest of the Palestinian population and were felt especially keenly by the thousands of nationalist Palestinian prisoners rounded up by the Israeli authorities while Hamas supporters were left free: 'There were no Hamas prisoners with us', noted one imprisoned communist activist from Ramallah.[19]

The Sasportas and Sa'don Killings

The tenor of the Hamas–Israeli relationship changed dramatically in mid-1989. The attitude of the Israeli authorities altered following the involvement of Hamas activists and leaders in the kidnapping and murder of two Israeli soldiers, Avi Sasportas and Ilan Sa'don signifying, according to the Israeli press, Hamas' adoption of techniques 'normally favoured by the Islamic Jihad'.[20]

The Sasportas–Sa'don killings were a significant turning point for Hamas for a number of reasons: the incident was the first in which Hamas was directly identified in an attack on Israeli military targets and indeed the first armed assault of which the organisation was accused; Hamas chose to kill Israeli soldiers at a time in the Intifada when the UNLU was pursuing a policy against assaults of this sort; the incident was a calculated and dramatic bid for popular Palestinian opinion at a time when support for the uprising appeared to be flagging. It is not clear whether the organisation's leadership had weighed up the likely response of the Israeli authorities to such an attack. Following the experience of Islamic Jihad, Sheikh Yassin would know that the reaction of the Israeli authorities would be harsh but it is probable that he weighed this against the relations Hamas had built up with the Israelis in opposition to the Palestinian national movement.

Within a month of the soldiers' deaths in April 1989 Israeli wrath reverberated throughout the whole of the Hamas movement. Three hundred Hamas activists were arrested in Gaza and the West Bank, among them Sheikh Yassin, Dr Mahmoud Zahar and other key leaders. Those arrested were charged with the kidnapping and killing of the Israeli soldiers as well as with 'assassinating collaborators and brutally imposing the laws of the uprising on the population'.[21] The move against the organisation was the first serious attempt at eliminating Hamas from the Palestinian scene. The detention of the leadership was obviously designed to demoralise supporters and weaken the chain of command in the Gaza Strip. The setbacks of April and May were further compounded by a series of moves against the organisation in the latter half of 1989. At the end of the summer of 1989 Israel announced that the civil administration would be halting all further meetings and suspending contacts with Hamas. By December the organisation was prohibited and membership in it declared a punishable offence.

Challenge and Confrontation

While Sheikh Yassin remained in prison awaiting trial, other Hamas leaders, amongst them Dr Zahar and Dr Abd al-Aziz Rantisi, were released and able to maintain a chain of command with the imprisoned spiritual leader as well as directing the organisation. Hamas took a more public position on certain issues, including projected peace initiatives between the Israelis and Palestinians with the proposal to hold elections in the occupied territories. Hamas wanted to heighten its international profile and achieve equal status with the PLO.

Throughout 1990 Hamas occupied the political scene as a major independent political force. Despite the organisational setbacks of 1989 the group was able to attract more supporters and extend its scope of activities. Soon it was strong enough to hold its own in the Palestinian political arena without Israeli help.

By this point the Intifada had become a way of life for Palestinians. The commercial strike was a daily occurrence and general strikes were called approximately twice a week. Universities and other institutions remained closed, demonstrations were a regular event and the number of casualties rose steadily. The structure of the Intifada had endured despite attempts by the Israelis to quash it. With Hamas and UNLU an established part of the local political scene, competition for popular support and power preoccupied both.

Despite attempts at localised alliances and the publication of memoranda of co-operation there was an increasing tendency throughout 1990 and 1991 towards conflict between Hamas and the PLO-supported UNLU. In an attempt to undermine nationalist unity Hamas intensified its campaign against Fatah predominance in the PLO and sought to build alliances with its old enemies in the Palestinian left – the Popular Front for the Liberation of Palestine (PFLP).

The first indication that Hamas had adopted this policy came in

April 1990 when together with the PFLP it declared a 'consolidation of the internal front and appreciation of the perceptive position of the Popular Front.'[22] This first alliance was short-lived and ended when a Fatah communiqué announced that differences between itself and the PFLP had been overcome and that the two organisations would now co-operate with each other. However, the PFLP and Hamas were later to become allies once more in a shared critique of Fatah policies.

The Gulf Crisis Rocks Hamas
and Islamic Jihad

The outbreak of the Gulf crisis in August 1990 served to polarise Hamas–UNLU positions further and set the trend for political positions maintained after the war.[23] Shortly after Iraq's invasion of Kuwait and the announcement that Western troops were being sent to Saudi Arabia, Hamas issued its first communiqué on the crisis. The leaflet of 12 August 1990 condemned the presence of American and allied forces. Yet leaflet 64, published a few weeks later, called on Saddam Hussein to withdraw his troops from Kuwait. Because Hamas had to maintain support for its Gulf funders and at the same time respond to the Palestinian sentiment expressed in the street it was careful to express a balanced view. In contrast the PLO announced support for Saddam Hussein's stand against the West and for his attempt to link the occupation of Kuwait with Israeli occupation of the West Bank and Gaza Strip. By September 1990 clashes were being reported between Hamas and PLO supporters in the Tulkaram refugee camp and Jenin in the West Bank and in parts of the Gaza Strip. After intense arbitration between local Hamas and Fatah leaders a thirteen-point plan of co-operation was issued in late September 1990. The plan accorded Hamas full recognition in a number of committees organised to harness the uprising and co-operation was agreed in a number of other areas. Unfortunately commitment to the plan soon waned and at the end of September Hamas supporters in Nablus attacked a local nationalist figure, Dr Nihad al-Masri. Open antagonism towards one nationalist faction or another was increasingly expressed by Hamas as it sought to undermine UNLU in Nablus, the capital of nationalism in the West Bank.

The massacre of seventeen Palestinian worshippers and the wounding of over a hundred others at the al-Aqsa mosque in Jerusalem by the Israeli police on 8 October 1990 outraged the

Islamic world. Hamas militancy escalated in response and the Izz ad-Din al-Qassam Brigade retaliated with acts of political violence against Israeli soldiers and settlers in a battle they declared a 'war of the knives'. In one of their leaflets Hamas called for new attacks on the enemy: 'Point One: Every soldier and settler in Palestine is considered a target.'[24]

Further political activity by both Hamas and UNLU was limited in the last stages of the Gulf crisis as the Israeli authorities placed the whole of the occupied territories under a blanket curfew for the duration of the war. The months following the end of the war consolidated further the position of Hamas in the Gaza Strip. The PLO, on the other hand, was plunged into financial crisis by the withdrawal of its wealthy Gulf backers. In May 1991 it was reported that the US$ 28 million a month from Saudi Arabia that the PLO had routinely received before Gulf crisis was going to Hamas instead. Throughout 1991 and 1992 national institutions in both the Gaza Strip and the West Bank announced massive budget cuts and staff suffered the non-payment of wages. Hamas, meanwhile, continued to fund its large welfare network and, through the *zakat* committees, extended financial aid to needy individuals formerly subsidised by the PLO. The ability of, Hamas to meet the financial needs of the community and its leaders' reputation for honesty made a considerable impact on popular opinion; any tarnishing of its reputation during the war was quickly forgotten. In the competition for ascendancy between Hamas and the PLO it began to look as if Hamas might be the victors.

Internal Crisis on the Path to Peace

The idea of peace talks between the Palestinians and Israel, supported by the United States of America, led to the re-emergence of the public dispute between Hamas and Fatah and marked and continues to mark the most recent phase of the organisation's development after the Gulf War. Throughout the summer and early autumn of 1991 dispute raged between the nationalists and Islamists over proposals to hold a peace conference between Israel and the Palestinians. Hamas remained adamantly opposed to any negotiations with Israel and hoped Palestinian public opinion would support this stance. By September 1991 conflict between Hamas and Fatah in the Nablus area had reached crisis point. Dispute still centred on the peace process and the issue of Palestinian representation. By this time it had been agreed that Israeli and Palestinian representatives (although not the PLO which Israel refused to recognise) would meet along with other Arab parties in the Spanish capital of Madrid for peace talks. Just one month before the Madrid Conference in October 1991, a Hamas leaflet ordered a general strike to protest against the decision by the PLO's ruling body, the Palestine National Council (PNC), to support a Palestinian delegation from the West Bank and Gaza Strip. Hamas later went a step further issuing a *fatwa* condemning the Palestinian delegates to the Madrid conference. The Hamas stance was rejectionist, arguing that no part of Palestine should be ceded in exchange for peace with the Israelis.

The Madrid Conference, held on 31 October 1991 was convened with the following in attendance: Israel, a joint Palestinian–Jordanian delegation, and Syria. The process embarked on would consist of a series of bi-lateral and multi-lateral negotiations with the aim of achieving peace treaties between the Arab parties and Israel. From October 1991 to August 1993 Israel and the Palestinians engaged in eleven sessions of negotiations. However, the Madrid process, as it was popularly referred to, was riven with a number of problems which ultimately immobilised the movement towards peace. These included: continued settlement-building by the Israelis in the occupied territories, the public intransigence of then Israeli prime minister, Yitzhak Shamir, the public nature of the negotiating process and internal dissension within the Palestinian community over the peace process.

Hamas capitalised on difficulties in the peace negotiations and joined other groups, such as the Popular Front for the Liberation of Palestine (PFLP), rejecting the peace process. By spring 1992 a show-down between Hamas and the pro-peace Fatah faction of the PLO looked imminent. In Gaza, where there were armed disputes between the two groups, reconciliation became harder after each incident. With Palestinians increasingly frustrated by the lack of progress made at the negotiating table, Hamas gained popular support by stepping up the activities of the Izz ad-Din al-Qassam Brigade with a number of increasingly successful armed attacks against Israeli soldiers and settlers.

Throughout the summer and autumn of 1992 Hamas leaders protested against the peace process. The election of a Labour government headed by Yitzhak Rabin, apparently committed to peace, did not augur well for the organisation. While Rabin courted the PLO and pushed his agenda for negotiations with the Palestinians,

Hamas continued its attacks on Israeli soldiers and civilians. The stabbings and shootings by the Izz ad-Din al-Qassam Brigade became more frequent, alarming many Israelis who called on the government to take firm action against the Islamic threat. By this point the Izz ad-Din al-Qassam squads were heavily armed and completely committed to waging a war against Israel on two fronts: against Israeli citizens' soldiers, settlers or civilians who in 1992 were attacked with increasing frequency; and within the Palestinian community against those whom Hamas marked out as collaborators with Israel. As one leader of an Izz ad-Din al-Qassam Brigade remarked:

> Since our enemies are trying with all their might to obliterate our nation, co-operation with them is clearly a terrible crime. So our most important objective must be to put an end to the plague of collaboration.[25]

Collaborator killings by Hamas were linked to the organisation's attempts to assume some control over law and order in the Gaza Strip and West Bank. The execution of collaborators was viewed as a religious obligation and a means of protecting the religion in the face of Israel.

The issue of collaborators and the policy of Hamas and Islamic Jihad towards them would continue to engage the Islamist and nationalist movements for years to come.

Mass Expulsions or Transfer?

In December 1992, after two armed attacks on Israeli soldiers and the kidnapping and murder of an Israeli border policeman, an Israeli crackdown on Hamas activists severely weakened the organisation. The abduction of Sergeant-Major Nissim Toledano from the Israeli town of Lod on 12 December marked a new peak in Hamas ascendancy. The kidnapping was shocking in itself, but the accompanying ransom demand which called for the release of Sheikh Yassin in return for Toledano's freedom was unprecedented. The leaflet issued by the units of the Izz al-Din al-Qassam Brigade following the kidnap declared:

> We announce to the occupation authorities and the leadership of Israel to release Sheikh Ahmad Yassin in return for the release of this officer ... We pledge from our side to release the officer once the sheikh is released in a way we deem fit.[26]

Prime Minister Rabin responded immediately by saying that Israel would not give in to the kidnappers' demand. The Israeli government launched a widespread and intensive search operation and hundreds of roadblocks were erected throughout the country in a desperate attempt to find Sergeant Toledano. The operation failed and three days later Toledano's body was discovered by a Bedouin shepherd near the Jerusalem–Jericho highway.

On 17 December 1992 hundreds of Hamas leaders, members and supporters together with the remaining Islamic Jihad activists were arrested or removed from jail and put on buses heading for the Lebanese border. Altogether 408 individuals were expelled to Marj al-Zahour in Israeli-occupied south Lebanon. The expulsions breached the Fourth Geneva Convention and an international controversy was sparked. Within the Palestinian community there were real fears that the expulsions were part of a wider policy of transfer directed against the entire population and that if Israel was allowed to get away with this particular action a precedent would be set. Rabin's justification for the measure was made clear in a statement to the Knesset:

> This government will fight any manifestation of violence and terror, and will not permit, and will not allow either Hamas or the Islamic Jihad to harm citizens of the State of Israel and it will take all legal steps at its disposal, to battle murderous terrorist organisations.[27]

Rabin's speech was an unequivocal declaration of war against the Islamic movement, part of the 'battle to the end against terror ... to temporarily remove from the occupied territories Hamas and Islamic Jihad activists who nourish the flames of disturbance and terror.'[28]

In the occupied territories news of the expulsions was greeted with wholesale condemnation of Israel and a mini-Intifada erupted in Gaza as thousands took to the streets in protest. The entire future of the peace process looked bleak. The expulsions provoked an intense debate within the Palestinian community about the place of the Islamists in the political fabric of society. Their implications ran deep and led many to question the motives of the Israeli peace partners. The PLO, in particular, was forced to take a stand on the issue as its chief opponents, now subject to fierce repression, were demanding a response from the nationalist movement. The PLO could no longer ignore Hamas or the popular support the movement enjoyed among Palestinians in the West Bank and Gaza Strip. If the PLO were to act truly as representatives of the Palestinians then the Hamas case would have to be championed.

In early January 1993 Fatah and Hamas representatives, including Yasser Arafat, met in Khartoum to discuss attempts to co-ordinate protest efforts and increased co-operation between the two groups in the occupied territories, including work on joint committees and an end to the factional violence which had increasingly characterised relations. Hamas, weakened and debilitated organisationally, needed Fatah's support. Fatah refused to agree to Hamas' demand that the Palestinian delegation withdraw from the peace negotiations entirely, but agreed to delay returning to the talks until Israel had met certain Palestinian demands. The Khartoum meeting lasted for four days and was an important political coup for Arafat, signalling the strength of the nationalists in the face of the Israeli crackdown on Hamas.

The expulsions had other ramifications for the political and security situation in the occupied territories. While it was true that over 400 Hamas and Islamic Jihad leaders, members and supporters had been rounded up, an important element of the Islamists remained at large. The Israeli authorities had been unable to capture the majority of the members of the armed Izz ad-Din al-Qassam Brigade scattered throughout the Gaza Strip and West Bank. Leaderless and temporarily bereft of strong organisational support, the armed gangs posed a real threat to Israel's security. Far from acting as a deterrent to attacks against Israelis in the occupied territories or over the 1948 border, the expulsions in fact left the Israeli security apparatus vulnerable, exposing its inability to capture the Izz ad-Din al-Qassam guerrillas. By the end of January the Brigade was back in action, killing two Israeli soldiers in Gaza. Throughout the early spring of 1993 Hamas' armed brigade and individual supporters increased their attacks on Israeli targets, including the killing of soldiers, settlers and civilians.[29]

The stalling of the peace process, due to the expulsions, combined with the spiralling violence inside and outside the occupied territories, soon resulted in Rabin's decision to close the West Bank and Gaza Strip in March 1993, preventing Palestinians from either entering Israel or Jerusalem. Pressure mounted on the Palestinian delegation to return to the peace talks by April. The Palestinians eventually capitulated, returning to the talks, while the 400 expellees remained stuck in Lebanon's no-man's land. The expulsion of Hamas and Islamic Jihad leaders had backfired on the Israeli government, leading to a serious deterioration in the situation in the occupied territories and exposing the government to a barrage of international criticism and hostile press attention. Rabin and his political associates had miscalculated the effects of the expulsion. The Israeli public was alarmed, rather than reassured, by the Hamas expulsions and their implications while the international community condemned Israel.

By the summer of 1993 the Madrid process was in serious trouble and the momentum for peace appeared to have been lost. The Hamas expellees were still languishing in camps in southern Lebanon. Political violence against Israeli targets, including bus hijackings, stabbing and gun attacks, continued in the name of the Izz ad-Din al-Qassam Brigade. Most Israelis started actively to fear for their lives as acts of political violence multiplied and the Israeli authorities seemed powerless to prevent them. Popular support and sympathy for Hamas continued to grow, while the PLO endured its worst crisis for thirty years. The financial strain on the organisation, since losing its Gulf funds was having drastic effects in the occupied territories and consequently on popular confidence in the leadership, particularly in Yasser Arafat. By early August pressure on him was so great that there were unprecedented public calls for him to resign as chairperson of the organisation. But unknown to the Palestinian population at this time, Yasser Arafat had already authorised one of his closest aides, Ahmad Qrei, to attend a series of fourteen secret meetings in Oslo with Israeli government representatives. The meetings which had been taking place since January 1993 would prove decisive in brokering a peace process between Israel and the Palestinians.

Hamas, on the other hand, thought it was preparing itself for its moment of glory. Within its ranks it was believed that the imminent collapse of the PLO in the West Bank and Gaza Strip would provide the opportunity for which the organisation had been waiting. Hamas was prepared. In the Gaza Strip alone it could lay claim to over half of the 420 mosques in the camps, villages and poor urban neighbourhoods. It was also backed by a social infrastructure unrivalled by either the Israeli authorities or the PLO. The leadership felt it had proved its worth and its commitment to the Palestinian mass through the expulsions of December 1992 and it was poised to assume the mantle of the Palestinian struggle against Zionism. Secularism, Hamas believed, was soon to be vanquished and Islam would replenish the soul of the Palestinian nation.

Handshake in Washington

The failure of the Madrid peace process and the revelations, at the end of August 1993, of secret negotiations in Norway between the

PLO and Israel took the world, including the Islamic movement, by surprise. In many respects the subsequent plans for limited autonomy enshrined in the Declaration of Principles (DOP) signed on 13 September 1993 as part of the Oslo Accords signalled that the tide was turning against Hamas once and for all.[30] After months of secret negotiations a deal had been struck. The deal was based on a form of limited autonomy for the Palestinians in parts of the West Bank and Gaza Strip. Under this agreement the following arrangements were agreed for a five-year interim period, during which final status negotiations would be held on issues such as Jerusalem, Israeli settlements and the 1948 refugees. The IDF would withdraw its troops from Palestinian areas of the occupied territories and the Israeli civil administration would also relinquish its powers; in their place the Palestinians would deploy members of their own, newly established, Palestinian Police Force (PPF) to maintain public order and internal security. Under the newly established Palestinian National Authority (PNA) the Palestinians would have responsibility for taxation, welfare, health, education and tourism; elections to a Palestinian legislative council (with limited powers) would also be held.

In return for limited autonomy the Palestinian negotiators in Oslo, with Arafat's sanction, agreed to a number of important conditions including recognition of the right to Israel's existence, a halt to violence by nationalist groups against Israel and an end to the PLO's claim to sovereignty over Israel's 1948 borders. Both sides believed that significant compromises and gains had been made under the Oslo framework. Both sides would also encounter difficulties in persuading their domestic constituencies of the benefits of the deal. On the Palestinian side, the Oslo deal split the ranks of the PLO with Fatah and the communists on one side and the DFLP, PFLP and other smaller factions vehemently opposing the deal. In Israel the agreement resulted in a split within the political community with the Israeli right accusing Rabin of treachery. In November 1995 Rabin was assassinated by an Israeli opponent of the peace with the Palestinians.

The complete exclusion of Hamas from the negotiating process and the exile or imprisonment of its leadership implied that, despite popular support, it had certainly not attained legitimacy as a partner for peace in the eyes of either Israel or the international community. In spite of its efforts, Hamas was marginalised from the most significant political event in the conflict between the Palestinians and Israelis in more than twenty-five years. The leadership of the

PLO and in particular, Hamas' rival, Fatah, had made all the running with the Israelis and even excluded the Islamists from symbolic decision-making with regard to the accord.

The reaction of Hamas to the DOP was one of derision. Hamas has denounced the Oslo Accords and subsequent agreements between Israel and the PLO and condemns Palestinian 'capitulation' in the face of the 'Zionist entity'. Hamas leader, Dr Abd al-Aziz Rantisi, stated that no one had the right to sign away Palestine and that Muslims would not be obliged to observe the agreement.[31] The Hamas spokesman added that the organisation was still committed to the uprising against Israel. The literature and leaflets of the movement published since Oslo have been similarly consistent.[32] Hamas was concerned also with the agreement between Israel and the PLO for another reason. It believed that it had become the common enemy of both and it viewed the new era of co-operation as a sign that both sides had agreed to eliminate the impact of political Islam in the occupied territories. Hamas representative in Jordan, Mohammad Nazzal, declared in October 1993 that the movement was preparing itself for the attack in the new era of harmony between Israel and the PLO. He believed that there was a real possibility of Israeli and Palestinian security forces in combining to combat Hamas fighters.[33]

As part of its policy of opposing the Oslo Accords Hamas continued to play a part in the rejectionist alliance. In January 1994 Hamas, along with nine other Damascus-based rejectionist groups announced the formation of the Palestinian Forces Alliance (PFA), referred to colloquially as the Damascus Ten. The uncomfortable prospect of working with former political arch-rivals whose ideology was anathema to Hamas was assuaged by placing its relations with the other members of the Damascus Ten on a purely pragmatic rather than ideological level. In this way Hamas was able to front the Hamas–PFLP bloc in local elections without appearing to compromise on all that it stood for. Thus in the elections to the Student Council at Birzeit University in November 1993 Hamas student candidates were part of the same student bloc as the PFLP under the banner 'Jerusalem First' and ran against candidates from the Fatah organisation who ran under a similar banner: 'Jerusalem and the State'. Fatah was defeated.

Hamas was certainly not the only Islamic movement to condemn the Oslo Accords. Both Islamic Jihad and the Liberation Party issued leaflets opposing the peace plans. Islamic Jihad, in particular, the faction of the Damascus-based leaders Fathi Shqaqi and Sheikh Abd al-Aziz Auda declared that it was 'totally opposed and actively involved in defeating the accords'.[34] The Shqaqi–Auda faction aligned itself with the Damascus Ten but prepared to wage the jihad according to its own agenda. In the Gaza Strip leaders of the Shqaqi–Auda faction Hani Abed and Sheikh Abdullah Shami and their followers organised protests against the accords and concentrated on continuing their military strategy against Israel. An Islamic Jihad (Shqaqi–Auda faction) leaflet published shortly before the Oslo Accords were signed described the agreement between Israel and the PLO as a catastrophic step.

Hamas and Islamic Jihad announced that the DOP was a betrayal of the struggle for liberation and vowed to continue their jihad against Israel. Hamas, however, had to contend with the fact that public opinion was not with it on this issue. According to Palestinian opinion polls taken at the end of September, 73 per cent of Palestinians living in the occupied territories supported continued negotiations with Israel. Sixty per cent favoured the leadership of the PLO during this period compared to 17 per cent for Hamas and 22 per cent for other groups. There was a clear decline in the appeal of Hamas, with only 17–18 per cent of those polled believing that the Islamic forces could 'save' the political situation.[35]

The Political Position on Elections, Political Parties and Democracy

The nature of Hamas' opposition to the DOP has reflected and continues to reflect the lines of power and internal differences within the organisation. From his prison cell, Sheikh Yassin immediately advised his supporters and followers to proceed with caution. Initially it appeared that he was calling on the organisation to consider participation in scheduled elections for the proposed legislative council arguing a tactic of 'opposition from within'. In a series of letters published in the magazine *al-Wasat*[36] Yassin argued that Hamas' participation in local professional and municipal elections since the early 1990s had set a precedent for participation in PNA polls. Yassin's statement on elections surprised many; participation in elections to a body associated with the condition of limited Palestinian autonomy would imply recognition of the Oslo Accords after Hamas' absolute rejection of the Palestinian–Israeli agreement.

Sheikh Yassin's remarks were qualified, however, by a call for certain conditions to be met. Hamas' participation in elections would depend on the establishment of a framework in which a cease-fire (*hodna*) could be reached with the Zionist enemy. This truce, which would be temporary and agreed through the consensus opinion of religious leaders, would be like a conventional cease-fire in time of war. The cease-fire would be of fixed length, sufficient to allow the soldiers of the jihad to address other issues in their own society, but would not indicate the opening of dialogue or negotiations with the enemy. After the cease-fire was over the jihad would continue. During the period of cease-fire it would be conceivable for Hamas to participate in Palestinian elections.

Sheikh Yassin's sentiments were gradually reflected in the opinions of other Hamas leaders. Throughout the latter part of 1993 and during early 1994 a wide range of Hamas figures debated the issue of elections: participation and non-participation; conditions for co-operation; representation of the people, and whether or not the organisation should form a political party to represent its Palestinian constituency at the polls. Some Hamas leaders, however, opposed the idea of electoral participation. Bassam Jarrar, a West Bank leader and a former Marj al-Zahour expellee, made public his opposition to elections, which he perceived as bestowing legitimacy on the Oslo Accords and the PNA. He asked how Islamists could stand in self-rule elections when they were a product of the Oslo peace process: 'Participation in self-rule gives legitimacy to the peace process', he remarked.[37]

Hamas viewed Fatah's promotion of elections and democracy with suspicion, perceiving it as a political ruse to consolidate Arafat's power and weaken the forces of opposition, particularly in Gaza. Mahmoud Zahar expounded the view that Arafat's calls for quick elections were a sign of his weakness and the weakness of the PNA in the face of popular sentiment:

> The PNA demands the elections in order to achieve IDF redeployment in the West Bank! But Israel has no desire or interest in these elections. Israel will never move from its positions and it knows that current suffering on the Palestinian street will have a negative effect on its partner in the Oslo agreement.[38]

By the middle of 1995, however, the debate had gone full circle and the formation of a political party seemed unlikely. Many foresaw the possibility of the political wing of the movement outgrowing and even splitting away from the principle of armed struggle and resistance against the force of secularism and the Zionist entity. As the Gaza Islamist, Mohammad Hindi asked: 'Can the jihad continue when there is an Islamic political party, when the basic rights of Palestinians are ignored by their own representatives and no one is sure of the rules of the game?'[39] The Islamists feared the fate of such a political movement under the terms of the Palestinian–Israeli autonomy agreement. By late November 1995 Hamas had announced it would boycott any forthcoming elections for the presidency of the PNA or the 88-seat legislative council.

The election issue and the question of whether Hamas should form a political party were parts of a wider debate within the movement centring on the issue of democracy and the response of the Palestinian Islamists to increasing pressure for the establishment of a secular–democratic entity under the terms of the Oslo Accords. The Hamas leadership was charged with responding to the call for the complete democratisation of Palestinian society and to criticism of the organisation for its authoritarian rather than pluralistic structures. The debate was informed by examples from within and outside Palestinian society. Hamas was not the only Islamic group to face the democratic challenge; from Algeria to Saudi Arabia the democracy debate was making a huge impact.

For Hamas, however, a response was imperative in the post-Oslo era, forcing leaders like Sheikh Yassin, Abd al-Aziz Rantisi and Mahmoud Zahar to address the democracy debate. Their political opponents in Fatah had already declared their allegiance to the promotion of democracy in Palestinian society. PLO leader Yasser Arafat reiterated his apparent commitment to democracy in his homecoming speech when he returned to Gaza and addressed a rally on 1 July 1994: 'We all of us need to be as one man in order to achieve a free homeland. Yes, homeland ... a free and democratic homeland.'[40]

Hamas leaders faced a difficult task. How could Hamas reconcile its traditional rejection of democracy as a Western–secular notion with popular pressure to represent the Palestinian street? Its solution was the concept of *shura* (consultation) which its leaders now posed as an alternative to the Western notion of democracy. *Shura* allows Hamas to call for democratic activity within the ranks of its own organisation and the population at large. Hamas has positioned political Islam in parallel to democracy. Islam, they argue, was democratic in nature long before the articulation of a democracy doctrine in Western Europe. As Islamist Dr Khader Sawandek remarked at a

Palestinian conference on democracy: 'The political system of Islam is a divine system, democracy is a human system and therefore atheist. Is there a historical similarity? No, because Islam precedes democracy not vice versa.'[41] The solution, in Hamas' thinking, was to accept that the participation in activities linked to the promotion of democracy would be an interim measure, a necessary stage and means to achieve the real Islamic goal: the creation of an Islamic state in Palestine. If activities were not viewed as part of this interim stage, Hamas would boycott them.

The Military Option

It is clear that, in light of the political changes resulting from the DOP, Hamas reassessed its strategy. Despite the debates about elections, political parties and democracy, Hamas remained committed to a continued jihad against Israel, including revenge attacks. In the first sixteen months following the signing of the Oslo Accords, Hamas and Islamic Jihad were responsible for the death of approximately 120 Israelis; and their campaign of violence continued even after the redeployment, in May 1994, of Israeli troops in Jericho and Palestinian population centres in the Gaza Strip. The presence of a Palestinian authority backed by a local police force did not deter Hamas from launching attacks on Israeli targets; the organisation remained committed to its jihad against Israel.

Hamas military strategy was altered, however, by the Hebron factor – the massacre, on 25 February 1994, of twenty-nine Palestinian Muslim worshippers at the Ibrahimi mosque in Hebron. The massacre was perpetrated by an Israeli settler named Baruch Goldstein. A religious Jew from the settlement of Kiryat Arba in Hebron, he had entered the mosque and opened fire on the Muslim worshippers who were conducting dawn prayers. In the minutes and hours after the massacre more Palestinians were killed by Israeli soldiers in Hebron. This massacre of Muslim worshippers profoundly affected Hamas' position on the nature of its targets in Israel and the occupied territories. Hamas vowed to avenge the lives of the 'innocents of the Ibrahimi mosque'. In a leaflet entitled 'The Settlers will Pay for the Massacre with the Blood of their Hearts' issued by Hamas in the wake of the massacre, the Izz ad-Din al-Qassam Brigade vowed revenge for Hebron and to take a life for a life.[42]

Forty-one days after the massacre, following the traditional period of forty days mourning, Hamas took revenge. On 6 April 1994 in the town of Afula in the north of Israel, seven Israelis were killed when a Hamas suicide bomber detonated explosives near a bus stop in the town square. All the victims were unarmed, all of them civilians. The bomber, a nineteen-year-old youth from the West Bank village of Qabatia named Riad Zarkaneh died in the attack. Hamas spokesman in Jordan, Ibrahim Ghosheh, appeared on Israeli television that night stating that the attack, carried out by Zarkaneh in the name of the Izz ad-Din al-Qassam Brigade and the victims of Hebron, was in retaliation for the massacre. The ominous warnings issued by Hamas after Hebron had become a reality for the stunned Israeli public. The suicide bomb, in Israel and against unarmed civilians, shed an entirely different light on security considerations and public support for negotiations with the Palestine Liberation Organisation. In the immediate aftermath of the bomb the Rabin-led government ordered a crackdown on Hamas and the closure of the borders with the West Bank and Gaza Strip.

Afula marked a turning-point in Hamas strategy, but at this stage it was believed that the bombing was an isolated incident. The pundits were proved wrong seven days later. On 13 April a young mujahid set off another bomb. The target was an Israeli Egged bus in the northern coastal town of Hadera. Five Israelis and the bomber were killed in the explosion. Another twenty-eight people were wounded. The security crackdown and the closed borders between Israel and the Palestinians had not deterred Hamas from striking again. The bomber was identified as Ammar Armaneh, a twenty-two year old from the West Bank village of Yabad near Jenin.

Armaneh, writing in his will which was read out after his death, called on other young Palestinians to follow his example:

> The world is a Paradise for the infidel, but a prison for the believer. To you the lovers of Allah, I write with my blood. Follow the path of martyrdom. Be the best example of our Islamic nation, the martyr.[43]

The change in strategy signalled by the Afula and Hadera bombings and justified by Hamas in its publications alerted the Israelis to the most dangerous threat it faced in the post-Oslo era. The Israelis now had to admit that they faced a formidable enemy in Hamas. They also had to admit that they were unable to protect their citizens from these types of attack, since it was impossible to hermetically seal the borders with the West Bank and Gaza Strip. The suicide attacks in Afula and Hadera had proved the vulnerability of the population living inside the Green Line. The subsequent policy of imposing periodic closures of the West Bank and Gaza Strip from Israel and the arrest of illegal Palestinian workers in Israel was only a device to punish the Palestinian population and assuage Israeli public opinion about security. The bombings resulted in effective Israeli retaliation. By 21 April over 1,600 Islamists had been arrested in the West Bank and Gaza Strip. The government ordered the military and security services to hunt down the bomb-makers. They pressured the PNA and its security forces to capture the Islamists, gather intelligence on the movements of the armed brigades and assist with the battle to end the terrorist campaign against Israel. After initial reluctance to quell Hamas and Islamic Jihad, the PNA ordered the police and security forces to crack down on the Islamic movement. Prime Minister Rabin even turned to Jordan where he exerted pressure on King Hussein requesting he ban the activities of Hamas in Amman and arrest its leaders.

Hamas, for its part, met the news of the crackdown with its usual iron will. In a communiqué issued after the arrest campaign Hamas stated, 'The latest insane arrests will not affect Hamas' strength a bit. Rabin must understand, when he is able to make the sun rise in the West then and only then will he be able to affect the strength of Hamas.'[44] The same communiqué made a direct link between Hebron and the Afula and Hadera bombings. Hamas asserted its right to retaliate against Israel. The following are extracts from the post-Hadera leaflet:

> Compelled by its loyalty to the spilt blood of Hebron's recent martyrs, the Izz ad-Din al-Qassam Brigade decided to avenge this blood throughout the length and breadth of Occupied Palestine ... The outrageous criminal actions of the Zionists against the Palestinians ... in which Zionist soldiers did not discriminate between fighters and unarmed civilians, forced the al-Qassam Brigades to treat the Zionists in the same manner. Treating like with like is a universal principle ... .[45]

The Afula and Hadera bombings proved Hamas' military and technical capacity to undertake tactically complicated operations against Israel. Hamas' message was so powerful that it had been able to recruit young men willing to die in the name of the struggle to liberate the land. Hamas' military operations were so covert that the Israeli security services were unable to infiltrate the armed cells. Although the Israelis had identified the technician behind the bombings as Yahya Ayyash, 'The Engineer', they were unable to capture him, symbolising their weakness in this sphere.

Although many, from all levels of the Hamas movement, were imprisoned in the wake of the bombings, the attacks against Israelis continued and Israeli soldiers were shot and killed in Hamas ambushes in the Gaza Strip throughout July and August 1994. In early October the Izz ad-Din al-Qassam cells organised a gun attack in a pedestrian street in West Jerusalem which killed two civilians. On 9 October Hamas operatives kidnapped a twenty-year-old Israeli soldier. Hamas demanded the release of Islamic and other prisoners in return for his freedom. The soldier, Corporal Nashon Wachsman, appeared on a Hamas videotape played on Israel television asking for his freedom in return for the kidnappers' demands. Prime Minister Rabin stated he would not give in to the kidnappers' demands and blamed Yasser Arafat for sheltering the kidnappers in the Gaza Strip.

The deadline for Wachsman's kidnappers was pre-empted by an IDF attempt to free him. Acting on intelligence reports the IDF planned a rescue mission to rescue Wachsman from the village of Bir Nabala in the West Bank. The operation went badly wrong. As soldiers stormed the building, Wachsman was killed by his three Hamas captors who also killed another soldier, Captain Nir Poraz, in the ensuing gun-battle.

Five days after IDF's failed rescue attempt of Wachsman Hamas struck again. On 19 October a suicide bomber boarded a busy commuter bus in the heart of Tel Aviv carrying 20 kilograms of explosives in a bag. The bus blew up as it passed through Tel Aviv's main street, killing twenty-one Israelis, one Dutch national and the bomber and injuring fifty others. In a videotaped statement released after the bombing Hamas declared that the attack was revenge for the death of the three Qassam activists who had died during the Wachsman rescue attempt. The organisation identified the bomber as 27-year-old Salah Abdel Rahim Suwi. Suwi himself appeared on the Hamas video and declared 'We will continue our brave suicide operations. There are many young men who long to die for the sake of God.'[46]

The response of the Israeli government to the news of this latest atrocity seemed reactive and hastily thought out. Rabin ordered yet another crackdown on the movement, declared a full closure of the West Bank and Gaza Strip and pressured the PNA to take action against wanted Hamas activists in the Gaza Strip. The authority responded by arresting hundreds of Hamas leaders and activists. The West Bank was targeted by the IDF and arrest campaigns were orchestrated against Hamas and its supporters throughout October and November. In Nablus and in Hebron hundreds were rounded up and arrested in raids on homes, work-places and mosques.

By the end of 1994 the Izz ad-Din al-Qassam Brigade had been responsible for three suicide bombings in which a total of thirty-three Israelis, the majority of whom were civilians, had died. Hamas had shot and killed soldiers and settlers throughout the Gaza Strip and the West Bank, and individual Palestinians had carried out armed attacks on Israelis in the name of the organisation. For their part the Israeli authorities were only ever able to halt temporarily the armed campaign and they were increasingly dependent on the Palestinian Police Force (PPF) to assist them in their work. The closures and arrests were effective in the short-term but they had not prevented Hamas from continuing its jihad against the 'Zionist entity'. The Israeli intelligence services had foiled many attacks throughout 1994 but were powerless against the conviction of young men like Armaneh and his brothers-in-arms.

In 1995 Hamas pledged to continue its jihad – the bombings, revenge attacks, and continued targeting of the IDF and the settlers in the West Bank and Gaza Strip. Only political change within the ranks of Hamas would be likely to bring an end to the military campaign. By the end of 1995 such change was evident. Joint Israeli and Palestinian efforts to apprehend bombers, a lack of popular support for Hamas from the Palestinians and increasing popular support for Arafat's rule did not bode well for the proponents of the armed campaign.[47]

Into the Fray: Islamic Jihad

The other branches of political Islam had their own responses to the peace process. By the early 1990s a renaissance of Islamic Jihad activity had taken place in the Gaza Strip. From the Arab and Muslim capital cities of Tehran, Beirut, Amman, Damascus and Khartoum the exiled leadership of Islamic Jihad transmitted orders to continue the jihad against Israel. Islamic Jihad's lieutenants in the Gaza Strip maintained a discreet but potent presence while maintaining popular support for the organisation. The Islamic Jihad Shqaqi–Auda faction also suffered losses and changes to its leadership in the post Oslo era. In 1994 Gaza-based leader Hani Abed was killed in a car bomb, in November 1995 Fathi Shqaqi was assassinated in Malta, both killings were attributed to the Israeli intelligence services. Following

Shqaqi's death Ramadan Shallah became leader of the faction. Islamic Jihad also stepped up its military campaign in the wake of the 1993 Oslo Accords. Like Hamas it had vowed to continue the jihad against Israel irrespective of the nature of internal Palestinian rule in the Gaza Strip. By this point the Shqaqi–Auda faction was the dominant group representing Islamic Jihad. Other factions were weakened by a campaign of Israeli crackdowns throughout the 1990s or maintained a low profile as a result of close ties to the PLO during this period. In a statement issued in the Gaza Strip in the summer of 1994 and which quoted Jihad leader Fathi Shqaqi extensively, the faction announced that jihad was now the main strategy of the movement:

> The movement concluded that the only option open to our people is continuation of the jihad with all our strength and resolve … The Zionists harbour hate and a grudge against our people and a desire to kill and destroy.[48]

From September 1993 to February 1994 Islamic Jihad (Shqaqi–Auda faction) claimed responsibility for six attacks in which nearly thirty Israelis were killed. During the first year after Oslo the Shqaqi–Auda faction carried out four attacks, shooting IDF soldiers and stabbing an Israeli taxi driver. There was a marked increase in the frequency and, importantly, in the ferocity of attacks after it was alleged and widely believed that the Israelis had successfully planted a bomb under the car of the Shqaqi–Auda leader in Gaza, Hani Abed, who was killed on 2 November 1994. The Israelis did not deny the accusation that they were responsible for his death.

It seemed inevitable that Abed's death would be avenged and inconceivable that the Israelis had not imagined there would be repercussions after the assassination. Abed was a popular and widely respected Islamic figure throughout the Gaza Strip. His charismatic personality had attracted a devoted clique of devout religious students. His disciples were deeply attached to their leader and stunned by his death. At his funeral Islamic Jihad vowed to avenge his death and kill those responsible for the bomb. On 11 November the Shqaqi–Auda faction struck back. At the Netzarim check-point in Gaza, a bomber on a bicycle detonated explosives strapped to his body and killed three IDF officers. The IDF, shocked at the simplicity of the assault, complained that the nature of the peace accords with the Palestinians limited their ability to protect Israeli checkpoints throughout the Gaza Strip.

For Islamic Jihad the bombing was significant in a number of ways. First, the attack indicated that Islamic Jihad, like Hamas, had access to explosives and was now prepared to use them. Second, the Israeli policy of undermining Islamic Jihad had temporarily backfired; although organisationally small, Islamic Jihad had always been able to generate popular support in Gaza as was evident at the funeral and demonstrations following Hani Abed's death which was a catalyst for revenge in the faction's ranks. The attack also symbolised the growing level of support and co-operation between Islamic Jihad's and Hamas' military wings. Both groups shared technical knowledge and provided mutual assistance. In essence the Netzarim attack was the first step in the Islamic Jihad's new campaign of suicide-bombing against Israel.

Following an Israeli and Palestinian crackdown on its activities in both Gaza and the West Bank throughout December 1994, the group did not engage in any major attacks against Israeli targets. Minor incidents were reported throughout the month but the crackdown had the temporary effect of quelling the group's activities, until Sunday 22 January 1995. On that day as Israeli soldiers all over the country travelled back from weekend leave, two suicide bombers detonated explosives at a busy junction in Beit Lid near the coastal town of Netanya in the north of Israel. Excluding the bombers, the death toll at Beit Lid was twenty-two, all but one of whom were young Israeli soldiers. Once again, for days after the bombing a national outpouring of shock and grief was palpable, and the Israeli government announced the closure of the West Bank and Gaza Strip and barred Palestinians from Jerusalem and Israel. Rabin repeated his call, made following the Tel Aviv explosion, for a permanent separation between Palestinians and Israelis and it was announced that a committee would be formed to come up with proposals to that end. It was even suggested that the Israelis might literally fence off the Palestinian population from Jerusalem, Israel and areas of the occupied territories where Israeli settlements were based. There were certainly increased calls for an end to reliance on Palestinian labour in Israel. In the Israeli press the day after the bombing editorials and press comments called for an end to Israel's internal political disputes over the peace process with the Palestinians in the face of Islamic terror.

As with Hamas, the Israeli authorities have been unable seriously to limit the armed campaign organised by Islamic Jihad. Despite pressure on foreign governments to cut financial and other links to the group, Israel has not been able to combat the problem completely. Although the arrest campaigns (Israeli or PNA-ordered) that followed every attack and death have limited the scope of activities that the groups engaged in, Israel has failed to guarantee an end the armed campaign waged by the devotees of Izz ad-Din al-Qassam and Islamic Jihad.

The Politics of Change

The signing of the Oslo Accords heralded immense changes in the nature of politics in the Palestinian arena. The Islamic movement viewed the contents of the agreements as an attempted vindication of the secular–nationalist option in Palestine. The Accords also paved the way for Yasser Arafat's return to Palestine and the establishment of Fatah-dominated PLO rule in the autonomous areas. For the forces of political Islam the implications of these political changes (the Fatah decision to recognise Israel, talk about a final peace agreement, acceptance of limited self-rule in a small area of the West Bank and Gaza Strip, the holding of elections, the establishment of a programme for national economic reconstruction, calls for democracy and free elections, the prospect of hegemonic national secular rule) were immense. The leaderships of Hamas, Islamic Jihad and the Liberation Party (LP) were faced with a major political dilemma. How could these organisations respond to the rule of the PLO? What future could the Islamic movement expect under the national leadership of a figure like Arafat? What would the conditions for self-rule, such as the formation of a Palestinian police force and security apparatus, imply for the future of the armed wings of Hamas and Islamic Jihad.

There followed a period of debate and reflection throughout the ranks of political Islam. The leaderships of Islamic Jihad, Hamas and the Liberation Party were obliged to formulate a response to the changes which required a re-formulation of strategy, a revision of the current Islamic agenda and a re-evaluation of Palestinian public opinion on the issue of reaching peace with Israel. Finding a response to these challenges was easier for some than for others.

The Liberation Party leadership was initially reluctant to involve itself in any response at all. While the rank and file pressed it on the matter, the leadership abroad prevaricated over the issue, unable to agree on whether or not to respond officially from the LP perspect-ive. Eventually it was agreed that party members in the West Bank would be free to comment on the national debate and to take a position on specific issues. These positions, however, would be informed by the party's general perspective and would not deviate from the general goal of the organisation. Thus, since September 1993 the LP in Jerusalem has been responsible for issuing a series of leaflets addressing particular issues pertaining to the new political era. The leaflets have served as a commentary from the viewpoint of the Liberation Party. They have not called for direct action of any sort. The leaflets are a means of reminding the public at large of the role and presence of the LP in their midst. The party has, nevertheless, confined its activities to its traditional spheres of influence while its membership, which remains small and highly secretive, meets regularly to address specific themes or debates.

Hamas' Politics of Peace

In Hamas the debate about the prospect and potential nature of internal political change has been thorough and wide-ranging. The Oslo Accords have affected and continue to affect the organisation at almost every level of its activities in the West Bank and Gaza Strip. They have changed the nature of Hamas' relationship with the Palestinian population. The return of the PLO from exile, for example, has had major implications for Hamas and its position in local political, religious, charitable, education and welfare circles. The impact of foreign-donor funds in supporting the attempted regeneration of the Palestinian economy has empowered the nationalist forces and weakened Islamic opposition. The nationalist policy of normalisation in Gaza and the West Bank, including the re-opening of places of entertainment, relaxing of dress codes and re-secularisation of society, has won many supporters and cut into Hamas' position.

Hamas has formulated a position on all the issues relating to internal Palestinian politics since Oslo, amongst them: Israeli troop redeployment away from centres of population in Gaza and Jericho in May 1994; the establishment and arrival of the Palestinian police force and accompanying security apparatus; the return of hundreds of high-ranking PLO officials, including Yasser Arafat, in July 1994; the debate about disarmament; and the formation of the PNA with its ministries in Gaza, Jericho and other towns in the West Bank. It is difficult to assess if these positions reflect the views of the leadership alone or are a response to pressure from the rank and file for change.

Hamas responded initially to these internal changes by announcing that although it rejected and renounced the Oslo Accords it would not work to undermine the PNA or threaten national unity. The spectre of civic strife in the face of the Oslo Accords was a scenario that neither the Islamic or nationalist movement desired. The leadership of Hamas, often against the force of popular pressure in its own ranks, cautioned against open or direct confrontation with the PLO. The leadership was politically astute enough to recognise that political opposition was enough to maintain public support and resist the rise of secular rule. Hamas therefore committed itself to treaties of coexistence with the nationalists.

From September 1993 until the spring of 1994 it is fair to say that Hamas and Islamic Jihad committed themselves wholeheartedly to preserving national unity in Gaza as they watched the PLO establish the framework for self-rule there and in Jericho. The national unity issue stood at the heart of many of Hamas' statements throughout this period. In essence, it reserved the right to continue its attacks on Israel but would not bring arms to bear in Gaza and Jericho and would welcome the Palestinian police to the streets of Jericho, Rafah, Khan Yunis and Gaza city. As Hamas spokesman Mohammad Nazzal stated in July 1994, 'We will avoid a clash with any Palestinian side.'[49] It was even rumoured that Hamas was willing to curtail certain armed operations in order to avoid confrontation with the Palestinian police.

After the Honeymoon

Throughout 1994 and 1995 it became increasingly apparent that the honeymoon period between Hamas and the Fatah-dominated PLO was over. Increasingly negative relations emerged between the two forces. The advent of the PNA in Gaza changed Hamas' hitherto powerful position. The informal structures of governance that Hamas had created were being challenged and sometimes replaced by the formal establishment of institutions of limited self-rule. Social affairs, policing, religion, education, youth, employment, trade and industry now fell under the nationalist agenda of the PLO through its new ministries. Hamas' patience in the face of Yasser Arafat's increasingly authoritarian leadership wore thin over time however, and the facade of national unity began to crack. Relations with the new forces of the PNA, including the thousands of police and security operatives, soured and were exacerbated by the PNA's cavalier attitude to human rights, its creation of military courts and the countless arrest campaigns against Hamas and Islamic Jihad. Hamas and others in the opposition waged a campaign of protest against the PNA, accusing them of betraying the Palestinian cause, and co-operating with Israel to suppress any form of internal opposition.

Hamas and the Islamic Jihad were soon targeted by the PNA and asked to disarm, but the leadership of both groups maintained the right of activists to bear arms and even to kill collaborators. A Hamas spokesman was quoted thus:

> As far as we in Hamas, and the Palestinian people, are concerned, we will tell the self-rule authority to go to hell. We will not surrender or abandon our arms, because we are keeping them to carry out our jihad operations to fight the settlers and the Zionist enemy.[50]

Week after week, month after month, Hamas and Islamic Jihad activists staged protests and demonstrations outside police stations and prisons throughout the Gaza Strip to protest against the detention, normally without charge, of leading Islamic figures and clerics. In September 1994 Islamic Jihad threatened the PNA with retribution if the arrest campaign continued. From Damascus, Fathi Shqaqi warned that Yasser Arafat would be held responsible for Islamic Jihad arrests: 'We will respond to the arrest campaigns by escalating our political and popular moves against the self-rule authority and by carrying out more military activities against the occupation.'[51] The arrest campaign united the Islamic movement; Hamas made statements throughout the summer of 1994 in support of Islamic Jihad and against the PNA. Hamas spokesman Ibrahim Ghosheh declared, 'We share with the Islamic Jihad in their ordeal. All opposition factions should close ranks, in fact all Palestinian people should stand united against what Arafat is doing.'[52] In turn Islamic Jihad called for the freedom of Hamas members arrested by the Palestinian police. The arrest campaign against the Islamists continued throughout 1994 and 1995. After each Hamas or Islamic Jihad attack against Israeli targets the government of Yitzhak Rabin demanded that the PNA move against the Islamic movement; the PNA would respond, inviting Islamist accusations that the authority was collaborating with Israel.

By November 1995 relations between the Islamic organisations and the forces of the PNA had reached unprecedented levels of tension. In the year since the establishment of the authority the forces of political Islam had been weakened severely. Clashes between the Palestinian Police Force (PPF) and the Islamic groups, were symbolised in the Black Friday massacre when Palestinian policemen killed Palestinian Islamic activists.[53] Throughout 1995 the PNA ordered the arrest of hundreds of Hamas and Islamic Jihad activists. The apex of this humiliating scenario of Palestinians arresting Palestinians in response to Israeli pressure was reached when Hamas leader, Dr Mahmoud Zahar, had his beard shaved off while under PNA detention. The assassination of Islamic Jihad such leaders Hani Abed and Fathi Shqaqi also left the organisation in some disarray. Popular opinion grew in support of Arafat and declined for Hamas. The increasing likelihood of troop redeployment in the West Bank and elections in early 1996 further weakened the group's morale. The assassination of Israeli Prime Minister Yitzhak Rabin in November 1995 served only to strengthen the force for peace, championed by Yasser Arafat as the 'peace of the brave' and rejected by Hamas and Islamic Jihad as a 'peace of the weak'.

Hamas policy by this point began to show evidence of a vacillation between wanting to play a part in politics and rejecting the current political leadership of the Palestinian community. The organisation began to make a distinction between the PNA as an institution and Fatah as a political organisation, allowing it to find ways to co-operate with the PNA while at the same time criticising Fatah policies and Arafat's campaign against them. The tide, once again, had turned against Hamas. Its decision to boycott the poll held on 21 January 1996 for the President of the PNA and eighty-eight-member legislative council came as no surprise. The wisdom of this strategy has to be questioned. While it is true that the absence of the forces of political Islam have left the election process bereft of a credible opposition, the 85 per cent vote for Yasser Arafat has finally confirmed his, rather than Hamas', legitimacy and supports his claim to represent the Palestinian people.

Institutional Islam

The position of institutional Islam has also been affected by the political changes wrought by the Oslo Accords. During the Intifada the official Waqf in the West Bank remained under Jordanian control and the Jordanians used this situation to maintain its influence. There was some concern that new mosques were not Waqf-funded but while in part this was due to the policies of Hamas and Islamic Jihad to create their own centres of worship, the Waqf was in such a poor financial state and that it could not have funded a massive mosque-building programme even if it had wanted to. Most Waqf activity was ineffective in face of the growing forces of political Islam and Israeli pressure to reign in and control the Islamic organisations. The Jordanian-appointed Waqf officials were unable even to assert their authority over shrines like the al-Aqsa mosque, the Dome of the Rock and the Ibrahimi mosque in Hebron, which literally became battlegrounds of the Intifada. Sermons given in Waqf-run mosques were also subject to Israeli military censorship. Waqf revenue from rents and land declined during the Intifada, exerting further pressure on the poorly funded system. This can be contrasted against the increase in funding for the Islamists during this period. Thus, the force of institutional Islam, in the West Bank, remained firmly harnessed to a pro-Jordanian agenda.

In the Gaza Strip the *waqf* system was extremely weak. Sometimes it was a conduit of Israeli funding for mosque repairs, renovation and building but otherwise it remained marginalised and of minor interest to the Israeli authorities. Its revenues were small and could in no way sustain the type of programme essential at the time to meet the needs of Gaza's Muslim community.[54]

The establishment of the PNA and return of the PLO from exile, however, allowed the nationalist political leadership to harness the forces of institutional Islam to the state-building strategy. In December 1994 in a direct challenge to Jordanian influence in the West Bank and claims to custodianship of al-Aqsa and the Dome of the Rock, the PNA announced the creation of an alternative Palestinian Waqf organisation. This would also serve as a useful symbol for Palestinian claims to Jerusalem in future negotiations over the status of the city. The PLO's position that Jerusalem should be the capital of any future Palestinian state, and thus a Palestinian-controlled Waqf, implying control over the extensive *waqf* network in the city, is very important. Israel indicated that it preferred continued Jordanian control over Jerusalem's Islamic shrines and *waqfs* to Arafat's Palestinian challenge. Israel has been willing to exploit inter-Arab tensions over this issue to bolster its own claim to sovereignty over a unified Jerusalem as capital of the state.

In February 1995 the PLO challenged Jordanian hegemony over the *waqf* in Jerusalem when the Palestinian-appointed mufti, Akram Sabri, upstaged his Jordanian-appointed counterpart, by announcing the start of the Ramadan fast a day earlier. The PNA has also appointed its own personnel to the Shari'a courts and given posts to religious functionaries in areas such as religious legislation. Even in the Ministry of Justice a head of the Shari'a courts has been appointed along with religious personnel responsible for *fatwas* and legislation. The implications of these activities are very clear. The PNA, like Arab regimes in the region, is seeking to establish institutional Islam in order to sanction its own policies and activities no matter how un-Islamic they are. State-paid Muslim preachers will serve the interests of the ruling elite, as they have done in Jordan, Egypt, Iraq and Saudi Arabia. Dissent and opposition will not characterise this ulama-class. Islamic opposition to the state will remain the province of political Islam, once again repeating and reflecting the diverse political nature of this world religion.

Conclusion

The Intifada has precipitated the most significant change in Palestinian politics in more than twenty-five years. The unified action of the Palestinian people in protesting the Israeli occupation of the West Bank and Gaza Strip, combined with regional and global changes in the balance of power, have ensured that Israel's rule over the area would never endure through military occupation. Through the Intifada both secular and religious Palestinians proved to themselves and the rest of the world that they were capable of mass protest and a strategy of disengagement from their Israeli rulers that worked. Within this context the forces of political Islam waged their own bitter battle against the forces of both Zionism and secularism with Hamas and Islamic Jihad increasingly relying on political violence to broadcast their Islamic vision.

The gains of the Intifada, in the post-Oslo era, are tangible, the Israeli occupation of Palestinian land has been severely undermined both by the political force of the Intifada itself and the promises enshrined in the Oslo Accords. Troop redeployments in 1994 and 1995 and, more importantly, Palestinian self-rule are significant steps on the path to peace. While during the Intifada the strength of the political Islamists grew and won popular support, with the self-rule experiment, both Hamas and Islamic Jihad have found their strategy for liberation (jihad) of all Palestine, not only the West Bank and Gaza Strip, increasingly hard to sell to the Palestinian people. Religio-political violence is no longer winning the support it once did, while the PNA and Yasser Arafat, as president of the PNA, establish Palestinian rule in the West Bank and Gaza Strip for the first time this century. The extreme conditions which generate mass support for political violence or legitimacy for its representativeness have passed, and the forces of political Islam must address themselves to this new reality.

The goals of organisations like Hamas and Islamic Jihad can never be revised. Like their forebears in the Muslim Brotherhood, the Mujama, the Liberation Party and even the Qassamites, they share the same vision of a resurrected caliphate in Palestine and the restoration of the Islamic shrines to Muslim hands. What can change, however, is strategy and the means to achieve the ends. In this respect Hamas and Islamic Jihad are like any political organisation: they must respond to changes in the political climate and the environment around them because a failure to do so will result in the marginalisation of political Islam and even its demise. While its social role and input may never be undermined, the political future of Hamas is now under threat.

6

Islamic Palestinian Solutions

Political Islam in Palestine offers an alternative to the political ideal of the secular nation-state adopted by the nationalist movement. Hamas, the Liberation Party (LP) and Islamic Jihad all espouse an ideal which reflects that of current Islamist movements throughout the Middle East: the establishment of an Islamic state governed by *shari'a* law according to the prescriptions of the Qur'an, *hadith* and *sunna*. Political consensus on how to achieve that goal, however, is not evident; indeed each organisation has a different programme, reflecting the diversity characterising political Islam in Palestine.

Any discussion of the political programme of Islamist organisations in Palestine must take note of the paucity of original Palestinian sources or interpretation of the subject. The lack of a Palestinian tradition of *ijtihad* (interpretation) has led to a dependence on external Islamic ideologues. Modern-day Islamist ideologues in Hamas and Islamic Jihad rely mostly on Indian, Iranian, Egyptian and other sources for inspiration and guidance. Only the Liberation Party has attempted to articulate a distinct ideological position of its own. However, this position has not embraced a specifically Palestinian perspective since Taqi ad-Din an-Nabahani, the LP's ideologue, developed an ideology that was pan-Islamic not Palestinian.

Thus, the ideological position of political Islam in Palestine has inherently reflected the concerns and response of Islamists from other parts of the world. It also echoes the larger relationship between the Arab world and the West. The anti-colonial, anti-secular content of Hamas and Islamic Jihad ideology is central to the political viewpoint of each. These sentiments are fused with an anti-Zionist and anti-Jewish perspective that has been shaped both by doctrine drawn from the Qur'an and other Islamic sources as well as by Eurocentric anti-Semitic perspectives. The ideology of the movement has also evolved as a matter of necessity, expediency and realpolitik in response to rapidly changing political circumstances. This final point explains some of the more glaring contradictions within Palestinian Islamist political ideas and has often resulted in apparently hastily thought-out tenets, belying the importance of certain subjects.

The ideology of both Hamas and Islamic Jihad for the most part, reflects a Sunni Islamic agenda.[1] The ideological outlook of both organisations, particularly in the Intifada era, sheds light on the context in which these groups have arisen. It is important to identify and question the ideas expressed, the function of the arguments presented and why a particular form of logic is pursued. It is also important, in the light of the Islamic resurgence in Palestine and the acculturation debate, to assess the degree to which each organisation has been influenced by a dialogue with Western ideas and approaches, and whether specific viewpoints are rooted in other than Islamic trends. This endeavour will throw light on the extent to which the practice of political Islam in the West Bank and Gaza Strip, while embracing basic Islamist thought, also incorporates a strategy which reflects the effect on the internal political agenda of a number of other factors including those of a Zionist state and the secular movement.

The Ideology of Hamas: Era of Change

Hamas ideology was initially rooted in a modernist-reformist Islamic approach to political change. Drawing on al-Afghani, Abduh, Rida, al-Banna and Qutb, this element in Hamas thought addresses the crisis within Islam and the victory of the West over the Arab world. Hamas finds in the reformist approach a way to make sense of a foreign occupation, military subjugation and the Western domination of ideas over daily life. Israel is viewed as a Western puppet, an artificial entity, and its demise is premised on a return to Islam in Palestinian society, through religious practice and principle, preaching and education, and, as a last resort and act of defence, jihad. The organisation's ideology is populist; it does not portray itself as an elite vanguard, a gatekeeper of knowledge and thought. Rather, it seeks to influence the entire Muslim community of Palestine, to encourage the practice of Islamic mores and values and the preservation of a perceived Muslim tradition. It aims to reform the current political reality represented by the dominance of the modern secular nation-state and secular–nationalist strategies of change.

Hamas ideology is also built around a party-political approach to power and representation. It is presented as an agenda designed to win support from a particular constituency and as a programme of realisable political change posited from an Islamist–nationalist base. The realist element in Hamas ideology accounts for its popularity. While outsiders and external forces perceive Hamas ideology as threatening and extremist, most Palestinians do not see it, or its call for jihad, as a threat but rather as representing the aspirations of many Palestinians for a return to Islam in their society. Nor is Hamas ideology premised solely on political violence or the radical overthrow of the existing political order, although political violence has been incorporated as a strategy of the organisation. (This approach is in direct contrast to Islamic Jihad which is premised on political violence but justified in the guise of jihad.) A comprehensive reading of Hamas literature conveys an outlook based on the idea of Islamic reform and change. The literature does not explain why, however, in the current political context, wings of the Hamas movement have turned to political violence to convey the organisation's message.

Like Islamic Jihad, Hamas disseminates its ideas through books, pamphlets and leaflets (*bayanat*), which it promotes through book-shops, book-fairs, mosques, libraries, market-stalls and hawkers. Publications include magazines like *Falastin al-Muslima*, biographical works of Islamic leaders like Hassan al-Banna, Sayyid Qutb and Sheikh Yassin. Hamas cannot dominate other aspects of the media, it does not have its own newspaper in the occupied territories, air-time on television, or radio stations. The printed word is thus important to its work. More specifically, documents like the Hamas Covenant or constitution (*mithaq*), published in August 1988, can be identified as manifestos or ideological tracts. Much of the ideological material disseminated is designed specifically for popular consumption and presents ideological points through simple analogy or plain historical reference to past events of common knowledge. The message of political Islam promoted by organisations like Hamas and Islamic Jihad is, of course, broadcast also in the mosque, where Islamist preachers articulate the organisations' viewpoints.

Any reading of Hamas literature and propaganda brings to light a number of themes which distinguish the Hamas perspective on life and conflict in the occupied territories from that of other Palestinian political actors. The Hamas Covenant can be identified as the main ideological tract of the organisation which, along with supporting literature, delineates the distinction between its ideological stance and that of the nationalist-inspired PLO. Hamas claims that its ideology or way of thinking is Islam *per se*: 'It resorts to it [Islam] for judgement in all its conduct, and it is inspired by it for guidance of its steps.'[2]

Six themes, which explain basic arguments and in themselves reveal how a movement like Hamas fits into the Palestinian picture, are addressed in this chapter as follows: (i) the crisis within the Palestinian Muslim community; (ii) the Jew as foe; (iii) the strategy of holy struggle (jihad); (iv) Palestinian nationalism as an Islamic form; (v) the creation of an Islamic state, and (vi) the challenge of the opposition. I go into considerable details about the ideology of Hamas and much less about that of Islamic Jihad, because I consider Hamas to be the main player in the movement of political Islam at the present time and a grasp of its essential ideas to be fundamental to an understanding of current political developments in the occupied territories.

Crisis Within the Palestinian Muslim Community: Straying from the Straight Path

> If faith is lost, there is no security and there is no life for him who does not adhere to religion. He who accepts life without religion, has taken annihilation as his companion for life. [*Hamas Covenant*, Article 1]

The loss of faith and its implications is an important theme in Hamas ideology and Hamas explains the current predicament of the Palestinians in these terms. The unnatural hegemony of Israel over Palestinian lives is the result of the loss of faith in society. Israeli occupation is a form of punishment for bad Muslims, and can only be ended if Palestinians return to the practice of the faith and observation of its rules. As a Palestinian Islamist Bassam Jarrar points out, 'building the individual, reordering their basic ideas, and encouraging their strength through Islam is a priority of Hamas.'[3] The bitter history of Arab defeat at the hands of the Israeli army is viewed in this context as a crisis in faith. By the same token, Hamas views the State of Israel as a product of (Judaic) faith. Since Palestine can only be recovered as an Islamic state by Muslims who have returned to their religion, the secular-nationalist approach is doomed to failure. Hamas, then, is concerned with individuals, re-educating them, encouraging them back to Islam and using the individual as the starting-point for the re-Islamisation of society. In this respect Hamas reflects the reformist principles embraced by the Muslim Brotherhood and Sheikh Yassin in the decades before the Intifada. Hamas continues to recognise the importance of recovering the Muslim soul from the secular realm and relocating it in the Muslim heartland that is Palestine.

Hamas believes that by bringing people back to the mosques, to the ritual of prayer, to fasting and to the giving of alms it will revive Islamic society and thereby defeat the occupation. It thus aims to end secular practices, lifestyles and ways of thought, and to encourage Islamic dress, moral behaviour and social activities. This ideological mission is taken to serious lengths. Hamas has promoted the imposition of the *hijab* on women in Gaza,[4] closed down venues of popular entertainment, segregated the beach and, according to popular rumour, disconnected the electricity supply to parts of Gaza regularly on Friday afternoons to stop people watching popular Israeli-broadcast films. Through the regulation of society and the recreation of Muslim imperatives, argues Hamas, the Muslims of Palestine will rise again, strong and able to defeat the Jews, a people of great religious faith who have conquered in the name of their religion. This reflection is offered in the text of the Covenant when Hamas describes its objectives:

> The IRM [Hamas] found itself at a time when Islam had disappeared from life. Thus rules were broken, concepts were vilified, values changed and evil people took control; oppression and darkness prevailed, cowards became like tigers; homelands were invaded, people were scattered ... Thus, when Islam is absent from the arena, everything changes.[5]

The Jews as Foe: Echoes of 'The Protocols'

Each time Hamas addresses the Palestinian people or proffers a thesis, critique or argument it includes as a significant part of its reasoning its opposition to the existence of Jews in Palestine. Its hatred of the Jews is almost blind, extending well beyond the realm of religion, theology or ecumenical conflict. Some claims made by Hamas, even by its own religious terms of reference, stretch the limits of credibility and are clearly a symptom of racism rather than religious difference.

Hamas is distinguished from other groups also by its standpoint in relation to Israel. When it addresses the issue of Israel it does so in terms that deal with the current dispute in an entirely religious perspective. Israel is not viewed as a secular democratic state in which both Jews and Arabs live but rather as an exclusively Jewish homeland which discriminates on religious grounds against those citizens not of the Jewish faith. This differs from the nationalist view of the Israeli–Palestinian conflict, because for Hamas there is always the presence of the religious tension between Islam and Judaism. Hamas insists on recognising the religious nature of the state of Israel and believes that religious doctrine carries considerable political weight in Israeli decision-making. In this sense Hamas blames the Jews for turning the conflict with the Palestinians into a religious one, as Hamas leader Mahmoud Zahar argues:

> They [the Jews] made their religion their nation and state ... They have declared war on Islam, closed mosques and massacred defenceless worshippers at al-Aqsa and in Hebron. They are the Muslim-killers and under these circumstances we are obliged by our religion to defend ourselves.[6]

Ironically, for all its claims of rejection of Western domination, personified by the Israeli occupation, Hamas has borrowed heavily from Western sources to inform its view of the enemy. There are a number of assumptions which become apparent in the way in which Hamas ideologues have understood Judaism, Zionism and the Jewish people as a race. As well as reflecting influences from Qur'anic tales and sagas, the way in which the Jews are understood also reflects European anti-Semitism. For example, Hamas has consistently referred to the Israelis as 'the Nazi Jews' in its publications.[7]

For Hamas, it is the Jews conceived as a religious community rather than the Zionists who are the enemy. In this respect Hamas ideology is not necessarily so different from that of its Islamist counterparts in other countries. As the author Ron Nettler has pointed out: 'The Muslim community continues to suffer from the same Jewish machinations and double-dealing which discomforted the early Muslims.'[8] The Jews in this context are the Jews the Prophet challenges, who are portrayed in the pages of the Qur'an, the stories of the *hadith* and the *sunna*, a portrait derived from seventh-century Arabia. The Prophet offered to embrace the Jews into the new religion, yet condemns them as hypocrites appearing to accept the new religion yet really mocking it and its messenger. Passages from the Qur'an bear testimony to this interpretation, one of the most powerful examples being from the Sura of Repentance:

> And some of them [Jews] made covenant with God: If He gives us His bounty we will make offerings and be of the righteous. Nevertheless, when

He gave ... they were niggardly of it, and turned away, swerving aside. So as a consequence He put hypocrisy into their hearts ... and they were liars.[9]

Within the text of the same Sura Bedouins are also berated for their hypocrisy and 'tarrying', exactly the same traits as the Jews. Yet Hamas does not interpret this as a call to arms against the Bedouin.

The 'problem with the Jews' is compounded, in Hamas literature, by the battles that took place between the Prophet and his companions and the Jews. The most famous case in the Battle of Khaybar, which is often cited by Hamas in its leaflets, articles and other publications.[10] The historical reference to past relationships between the Muslims and the Jews, however, is also explained in paternalistic terms in which Muslim states protected a Jewish minority. As Bassam Jarrar argues: 'Historically, there are few examples of conflict between the Muslims and the Jews. This contrasts against the eras of Christian–Jewish conflict which is centuries old and full of pain. The *shari'a* enshrines the principle of respect for minorities in Islam.'[11] Thus the constant reference to past relationships between Jews and Muslims by Hamas is predicated on what Nettler describes as 'the notion of Islam's past trials and present tribulations with the Jews'.[12] In Islam's past the Muslims defeated the Jews. The tribulation of the present, for Hamas, is that the Jews have defeated the Muslims. An explanation must be developed and articulated to explain this phenomenon.

In one respect, Hamas also reflects a trend prevalent in the thought of Muslim writers in the twentieth century who have addressed the creation of the State of Israel and the presence of a Jewish nation in the Muslim heartland. Writers including Sayyid Qutb, and Abu A'la al-Mawdudi, an Indian Islamist, have made a considerable contribution to this subject. For example, when explaining Muslim failure and weakness in terms of a lack of faith Qutb, would cite the Jews as an example of the power of devotion. Hamas subscribes to this way of thinking. It believes that the power of religious devotion helped the Jews to military victory and that if Muslims are as devoted to their religion Islam will be restored to its rightful place.

This attitude, which is often displayed in the writings published by or in the name of Hamas, is, however, only a partial reflection of the relationship that grew up between the Muslims and the Jews. Yet this conception dominates the perspective of Hamas. The first page of the Hamas Covenant overflows with prejudice:

> They [the Jews] are smitten with vileness wheresoever they are found; unless they obtain security by entering into a treaty with Allah, and a treaty with men and they draw on themselves indignation from Allah, and they are afflicted with poverty. This they suffer, because they disbelieved the signs of Allah.[13]

Later in the text of the Covenant, and in other literature, the call to jihad is justified because the battle is about killing the Jew, who was the enemy of the Prophet. A famous *hadith* is cited as a fundamental reason for this obligation upon Muslims:

> Allah's messenger [the prophet Mohammad] already spoke of a time when the Muslim would fight the Jews and kill them – and the Jew would hide behind rocks and trees. The rocks and trees would say, O, Muslim, servant of Allah, this Jew is hiding behind me, come and kill him. Only one bush – the wild orache – is an exception to this rule because this is a Jewish bush.[14]

As noted, the Hamas view of the Jewish people is not drawn solely from the pages of the Qur'an and *hadith*. Its myopia is also the product of Western anti-Semitic influences. While Hamas, like other modern-day Islamists, has developed its argument on the Jewish question by relying on Qur'anic and other Islamic sources, it also, as Nettler notes, makes it 'modern by appropriate commentary, and supplemented by felicitous borrowing from such classical Western anti-Semitic sources as *The Protocols of the Elders of Zion*'.[15] Such opinions are influenced by the most bizarre form of Gentile paranoid conspiracy theory. For example, one article in the Hamas covenant declares:

> They [the Jews] were behind the French Revolution, the Communist Revolution and World War I, when they were able to destroy the Islamic Caliphate, making financial gains and controlling resources.[16]

The assertion that the Jewish people are to blame for conflict on a global scale is also prominent in the text of *The Protocols*: 'Remember the French Revolution, which we call the "Great", the secrets of its preparatory organisation are well known to us, being the work of our hands. From that time onwards we have led nations from one disappointment to another … .'[17]

The authors of Hamas publications are apparently convinced that Zionism and Israel are part of a Jewish conspiracy to conquer the world. Indeed Zionism, Israel and the Jews are to them interchangeable words. For Hamas the idea of a Jewish anti-Zionist is impossible; all Jews are Zionists.

Time and again Hamas refers to *The Protocols* as a source on the Jewish character. It is as if the hand or hands that wrote the Covenant had the pages of *The Protocols* open. That the themes in the Hamas Covenant which demonise the Jews in Islamic terms are bolstered by Western anti-Semitic sources is ironic given that the organisation is dedicated to offering an Islamic rather than Western, secular-inspired solution to the conflict with Israel. There is no Islamic basis to the Hamas claim that the Jews 'With their money ... formed secret societies, such as the Freemasons, Rotary Clubs, the Lions and others in different parts of the world for the purpose of sabotaging societies and achieving Zionist interest.'[18] The source of this claim is clear. In the introduction to *The Protocols* it is asserted that *The Protocols* (a work of complete fiction) were procured 'by a woman from one of the most influential and most highly initiated leaders of Freemasonry ... in France, that nest of Jewish Masonic conspiracy'.[19] The text goes on to illustrate alleged Jewish control of such societies: 'Until the time we attain power we will try to create and multiply lodges of freemasons in all parts of the world ... We will centralise all these lodges under one management, known to us alone, and which will consist of our learned men.'[20]

When Hamas rails against alleged Jewish control of the media ('With their money they took control of the world media, news agencies, the press, publishing houses, broadcasting stations and others,' the organisation states in its Covenant) again it echoes arguments presented in *The Protocols* outlining a Jewish plan to control the 'future of the press'.[21] Hamas appears to have conveniently forgotten that *The Protocols of the Elders of Zion* is a forgery. By failing to acknowledge this and by repeating the arguments in the name of its own cause the ideologues of Hamas do themselves and their struggle an immense disservice. Misinformation and anti-Jewish propaganda produced in the West does nothing to support the arguments of an Islamic organisation working in the territories occupied by Israel in 1967.

Hamas' methods of characterising the 'enemy' and the nature of the conflict with Israel stand in marked contrast to the viewpoint generated in Palestinian nationalist ideology. The PLO Charter, which the Hamas Covenant seeks to replace, makes no such reference to the Jews; the enemy is Zionism. The charter declares that:

> Zionism is a political movement organically associated with international imperialism ... The liberation of Palestine, from an Arab viewpoint, is a national duty and it attempts to repel the Zionist and imperialist aggression

against the Arab homeland, and aims at the elimination of Zionism in Palestine.[22]

Only one reference is made to the religious dimension of the conflict:

> The liberation of Palestine, from a spiritual point of view, will provide the Holy Land with an atmosphere of safety and tranquillity, which in turn will safeguard the country's religious sanctuaries and guarantee freedom of worship and of visit to all.[23]

Yet for Hamas the conflict remains a Muslim–Jewish one, a stance that can be seen as part of an overall strategy of response and challenge not just to Judaism but to the secular ideology of the Palestinian nationalist movement. Hamas, in this sense, is offering an alternative to the PLO in the battle to win the hearts and minds of the people. Its explanation, therefore, for the root of the current conflict is simple and relatively un-constructed.

From an ideological perspective then, there are a number of reasons why Hamas cannot reconcile itself to the idea of a Jewish state in Palestine. In practice, however, the relationship between Hamas and the Israeli government has not always been governed by such ideological rhetoric. Aside from ideology, Hamas and the Israelis have in the past had a pragmatic relationship, both parties exploiting their antipathy towards the PLO and its Palestinian nationalist forces. However, as illustrated in the preceding chapter, a change in Hamas' strategy triggered a turning-point in this relationship causing deepening hostility between the two sides.

The Strategy of Holy Struggle

> Raise the banner of jihad in the face of the oppressors, so that they would rid the land and the people of their uncleanness, vileness and evils. [*Hamas Covenant*: Article 12]

In direct contrast to the ideological call of the Mujama, Hamas literature constantly emphasises the importance of jihad.[24] In the text of the Covenant alone there are a large number of references to jihad: 'There is no solution to the Palestinian problem except through jihad ... In the struggle against the theft of Palestine by the Jews there is no alternative to raising the banner of jihad ... the IRM [Islamic Resistance Movement] is a link in the chain of jihad against the Zionist invasion.'[25] The call for jihad in this context must be viewed as a maximalist solution to the current hostilities with the

Israelis.[26] In this sense the Hamas call to jihad is different from that of others because firstly it declares it incumbent on every Palestinian Muslim and secondly participation in jihad can be carried out by anyone by many methods. As Islamicist Bassam Jarrar explains: 'Jihad, then, is the duty of every Muslim, but in practical terms jihad is waged at many levels and in many forms.'[27]

More importantly, the call to holy struggle by Hamas is linked inextricably to the liberation of Palestine (rather than for the resurrection of the caliphate in all Muslim countries) from Israeli (Jewish) rule. It is a rallying-call to the Muslim population of the occupied territories. As Zahar asserts, 'This is our land, historically, morally, religiously; it is *waqf* promised to the Muslims'. Jihad, he argues is incumbent of every Muslim 'it is a commitment on Palestinian Muslims.'[28] While the path may be steep, the rewards are great; should the mujahid lose his or her life in the service of the struggle, a place in paradise is assured: 'Whosoever fights in the way of God and is slain or conquers, We shall bring him a mighty wage.'[29] The mantle of martyrdom then, is assumed with a commitment to wage an armed battle against Israel. The Qur'anic promise of life in the hereafter is rich in reward for those who die in the course of the jihad: 'And besides these shall be two gardens – green pastures, therein two fountains gushing water, therein fruits and palm-trees and pomegranates – therein maidens good and comely.'[30]

This promise of paradise cannot be made by the PLO. Only Hamas and Islamic Jihad offer a true 'martyrs' reward. Yet using the call to jihad to liberate the land from Israeli rule is a complex matter. On the one hand the call meets the rules of religious prescription for an act of this nature. It is a defensive act against aggressive oppressors occupying the land. It is a war of last resort, the exception to the rule. In the absence of a government, argues Hamas, the people have to turn to acts of aggression as a means of defending the Muslims of Palestine from foreign occupation. However, the call to jihad is also cast in nationalist hues and is customised to the specificity of the Palestinian milieu. Hamas writing on the subject then reveals a view of jihad that is particularly Palestinian.

Hamas presents jihad as the only path for the struggle against Israel: 'There is no solution for the Palestinian question except through jihad.'[31]. It rejects the PLO's dialogue and negotiations with Israel and is highly suspicious of the role played by the international community in facilitating the negotiation process. Hamas does not believe that its goal can be realised through a process which it condemns as a betrayal of the Islamic nature of Palestine, a status that does not permit the land to be the subject of negotiation with Israel: 'Palestine is an Islamic *waqf* … This being so, who could claim to have the right to represent Muslim generations till Judgement Day?'[32] Initiatives, and so-called peaceful solutions and international conferences are also expressly condemned:

> The IRM does not consider these conferences capable of realising the demands, restoring the rights or doing justice to the oppressed. These conferences are only ways of setting the infidels in the land of Moslems as arbitrators. When did the infidels do justice to the believers?[33]

Hamas leaders argue that the basis for such negotiations denies Palestinian rights and is an expression of weakness. As the leader Dr Abd al-Aziz Rantisi argues: 'The Islamic movement rejects this current peace process, based on its belief that the militarily weak is weak in negotiations, and the militarily strong is strong in negotiations.'[34] The justification for the armed struggle is made clear by Hamas in this context. A leaflet disseminated in November 1991 objecting to the first round of the Madrid peace talks between Israel and the Palestinians outlined Hamas' objections: 'One of the reasons for prosecuting holy war is repelling oppressive tyranny. Making peace interrupts the religious duty of jihad … which must continue until it achieves its aims … .'[35]

This call to religio-political violence is inspired both by the Qur'an and other Islamic sources, in particular the writer Sayyid Qutb. Nevertheless the translation of such sources into Hamas literature is not necessarily rigid. Hamas often presents a vague concept of jihad that means many things, from a war against the enemy fought through armed struggle to the notion of jihad as striving and individual contribution through areas like education, art or literature. Thus jihad becomes all things to all people.

In his famous book *Milestones* Sayyid Qutb states that: 'Those who say that Islamic jihad was merely for the defence of the "homeland of Islam" diminish the greatness of the Islamic way of life and consider it less important than their "homeland".'[36] Qutb further declares that 'The jihad of Islam is to secure complete freedom for every man throughout the world by releasing him from servitude to other human beings so that he may serve his God.'[37] Yet Hamas argues for the method of jihad for the liberation of the homeland and the homeland alone: 'Palestine is Islamic *waqf* assigned to Muslims until the end of time … the homeland must be restored and they (Muslims) must fight their jihad in order to raise the banner of Allah over the homeland.'[38] Hamas argues that jihad is the way to regain the Muslim homeland after its theft by the Jews.

Through such a departure from the traditional calls of the Muslim Brotherhood (of which Hamas claims to be a wing), Hamas has 'Palestinianised' and 'nationalised' Islamic issues. It is using ideas that are widely held among the Palestinian community and adding to them a perspective that is allegedly Islamic. This perspective does not require the community to learn new sets of ideas or concepts. The call to armed struggle is perceived solely as a means of getting rid of the 'Jews or Zionists'.

Hamas is expressing a line which before the Intifada its predecessor the Mujama had always opposed. The Mujama had always preferred a gradualist, reformist approach. Only Palestinian elements such as the forces of secularism or the left were subject to political violence in the name of Islam. The defence of the community through jihad was waged from within and the forces of Israeli occupation were largely ignored. The call to jihad, which during the Intifada has become the dominant theme of Hamas, was previously never made.

The Marriage of Palestinian Nationalism and Islam

There is and has been a general perception that nationalism and Islam are incompatible. Nationalism implies a separation of state and religion and a secular society. This assumption is based on the Western generation of theories of nationalism which are inherently Eurocentric, and is premised on the notion of religion as marginal to the political and socio-economic aspects of society. However, Hamas presents the case of a political movement in which there has been an attempt, clumsy though it may be, to marry Islam and nationalism. The motives for and nature of this attempt provide an insight into the political battle for power which Hamas has waged with the Palestinian national movement in the occupied territories since the outbreak of the Palestinian uprising in 1987.

At the level of articulating nationalist sentiment, identity and ideology Hamas must compete with an already existing Palestinian nationalist movement. Palestinian nationalism, which predicates itself on the notions of self-determination, independence and democracy, has harnessed nationalist aspirations without articulating a religious agenda. The PLO proudly declares that it is 'secular, non-sectarian'.

It acknowledges religion and promises freedom of worship to all but does not base its political call on it. The emergence of Hamas and the Islamic alternative challenges the notions of nation and nationalism previously held in secular Palestinian politics. Hamas will only accept the PLO on Islamic terms, declaring, 'The day the PLO adopts Islam as its way of life, we will become its soldiers, and fuel for its fire that will burn the enemies.'[39] For the PLO, nationalism has been a response to the violation of 'nationalist sentiment'. As Ernest Gellner noted, 'There is one particular form of violation of the nationalist principle to which nationalist sentiment is quite particularly sensitive: if the rulers of the political unit belong to a nation other than that of the majority of the ruled ... .'[40]

The objective of the Palestinian nationalist movement has been to replace this foreign rule. The problem with this form of nationalism, a product of specific processes of development and modernisation, is it increasingly reflects an elite-based view of society and is open to the accusation that it ignores what Hobsbawm refers to as 'the view from below i.e. the nation as seen not by governments and the spokespersons and activists of nationalist movements, but by the ordinary persons who are the objects of their action and propaganda ... .'[41]

It is the 'view from below' which Hamas claims to articulate. This view may be increasingly Islamic, yet it is inextricably linked to secular, nationalist influences through the irrevocable process of acculturation that affects present-day Islamist movements. Hamas claims to speak as a national movement but with an Islamic-nationalist rather than secular-nationalist agenda. The organisation also makes it clear that it can never align itself to a Eurocentric viewpoint of the nation 'intensified through orientalists, missionaries and imperialists' and its end-product, the secular state. Hamas is unequivocal: 'Secularism completely contradicts religious ideology. Attitudes, conduct and decisions stem from ideologies.'[42]

The concept of nationalism (*wataniyya*), however, is a major theme running through Hamas ideology: 'Nationalism in the eyes of the IRM is part of religious faith ... nationalism is a religious precept ... .'[43] This argument is developed with a rationale that asserts that a nationalist is a Muslim who seeks to eject trespassers or enemies from Muslim land. Dr Mahmoud Zahar a high-ranking leader of Hamas, makes a clear connection between the Muslim and the nationalist, 'the most honest *watani* (nationalist) in the world is a Muslim, he considers the land as holy land ... .'[44] Nationalism, as expressed through Islam is not derived, as one Islamic leader Sheikh Abu Jibna; argued, 'from the jingoistic Western sense of the word', but from a struggle which pre-dates the Israeli occupation and addresses the question of political rule over Palestine.[45] This Islamic nationalism is shaped by the 'Palestinian experience'. As Sheikh Abu Jibna asserts, 'The Islamic movement in Palestine has experienced, much more over the years than other movements elsewhere, the quagmire of these other ideologies and they have seen the failure of all these "isms".'[46] Having established this concept of nationalism, the love of the land of Palestine with its special position because of its holiness, Hamas goes on to argue that because the land is occupied by an enemy it must be liberated through jihad. For Hamas all of Palestine from the Mediterranean to the River Jordan must be liberated as a nationalist and Islamic duty.

Hamas criticises the 'Arab army' and the nationalists for their 'conspiracy in ceding the coastline of the Palestinian people to the Jews'.[47] The organisation argues that there is no earthly power that thus has the authority to negotiate for the future of this territory. Hamas condemns any Palestinian who cedes any part of Palestine, and for this reason accuses the PLO of 'capitalising on the fruits and successes of the Intifada', and warning that, 'All Palestine is the right of the Muslim, past, present and future ... No Palestinian has the right to give up the land soaked in the martyrs' blood.'[48] Nationalism, then, is not about territorial compromise, but about territorial acquisition of all land that is deemed Islamic or holy for the Muslim faith. On closer examination, however, the Hamas concept of nationalism falls into no one particular category but seeks to straddle Arab nationalist rhetoric with Islamic sentiments all encased in a particularly unique Palestinian perspective.

The Creation of an Islamic State

Hamas ideology, a Palestinian Islamic nationalism in response to a people without a state, is severely at odds with prevailing radical Islamist ideology on the issue of nationalism. The work of Sayyid Qutb again illustrates this point. In *Milestones* Qutb relates the experiences of the Prophet Mohammad to illustrate his views on modern nationalism. The Prophet in the battle of Medina seeks to point out that some bonds (family, soil and property) are irrelevant to the true Muslim: 'The Muslims' country has not been a piece of land but the homeland of Islam (*dar al-Islam*).'[49] This homeland is symbolised not by borders from the Mediterranean to the River Jordan but by a community that accepts *shari'a* law as the law of the state. Qutb notes that the *dar al-Islam* is also not a government, a flag or a family and that war for any of these things is not a worthy war. 'Nationality means belief and a way of life', he concludes.

Ideologues of the Hamas movement do not perceive the struggle in the manner of Qutb. As is clear from many of their leaflets they call for a state, a government, a people and a flag. An Islamic state is the eventual goal of the current struggle. The Palestinian element is constantly referred to by Hamas as an exclusively Palestinian movement within the territory of Palestine and its boundaries. Notable by its absence from the ideological literature is the argument that the liberation of Palestine is the first step towards the creation of a *dar al-Islam* irrespective of borders and boundaries.

The Challenge of the Opposition

It is clear that the overriding motive in producing ideological tracts like the Hamas Covenant is to respond to the threat posed, first, by the Palestinian nationalist movement and other Palestinian groups, specifically Islamic Jihad, and, second, by the Israeli occupation. This essentially political adaptation to circumstances and realpolitik has led to a number of ideological quirks. For example, Hamas displays many characteristics of the very aspects of political life and struggle which it, as a force for political Islam, seeks to destroy and replace. The concept of Palestinianism has become so ingrained in a people nurtured by political movements like the PLO that Hamas has the unenviable task of reorienting the Palestinian sense of identity to become Muslim first and Palestinian second. At present very few in the occupied territories would describe themselves as Muslim Palestinians as opposed to Palestinian and Muslim.

Whether Hamas is able successfully to marry the notions of nationalism and Islam is debatable but it is not unusual for political Islam to create a synthesis with nationalism.[50] Nor is it rare for nationalism to embrace religion to legitimate certain political perspectives and arguments. There are many examples throughout the world of this relationship: Japan and Shintoism, America and the Christian fundamentalists, the BJP in India and Hinduism, Tibet and Buddhism. Yet Hamas is different because it synthesises a particularly Palestinian brand of Islam with a particularly Palestinian brand of nationalism. At an ideological level Hamas raises particular objections to its Palestinian opponents in the national movement, including the various wings of the PLO. Ideological consistency of argument has been maintained by Hamas but has not always been reflected in relations between the two groupings, which have been dogged by fierce rivalry. They espouse diametrically opposed positions over a number of important issues and the possibility for real reconciliation of ideas and objectives between them is inconceivable without fundamental compromise.

Hamas has always rejected PLO overtures inviting it into the nationalist fold. It has demanded more of the PLO than it can ever give, thus making it impossible for a permanent alliance to be reached. For example, it demanded that the PLO allocate to it 40 per cent of the seats of the Palestine National Council (PNC) in return for its co-operation. It sees no ideological link between itself and groups like the leftist PFLP or the communists. This stand has not in practice, however, prevented a relationship developing between Hamas and the Palestinian left. Hamas has joined with the PFLP and DFLP in a tactical alliance against Fatah to protest against the current peace negotiations with Israel and has formed a number of local alliances with PFLP activists where disputes with Fatah have broken out.

The Hamas leadership believes that it can stand as a meaningful alternative to the Palestine Liberation Organisation. In response, the PLO has not sought to aggravate that challenge. Both sides have sought to preserve Palestinian unity under the auspices of the Intifada against the Israeli occupation authorities although sometimes this unity has broken down and clashes have resulted. There have been minor concessions and attempts at reconciliation but these have either failed or been short-lived. The ideological dichotomy between the two organisations was exacerbated by the Declaration of Principles signed between Israel and the PLO on 13 September 1993 which Hamas rejected completely. Hamas repudiates the claim to sole leadership of the Palestinian people made by the PLO and offers an alternative in every respect. The Hamas Covenant therefore, despite considerable conceptual overlap with the Charter of the PLO stands as a direct challenge to the latter. The Covenant is, in many ways, representative of everything that is opposite to the world-view presented by the PLO.

Hamas ideology, as described in this chapter, is in many respects still being formulated. Hamas has developed a working agenda which embraces the principal elements of contemporary Islamic thought on issues such as the Israeli state, the struggle against Israel and relations with other political actors. What is strikingly absent from Hamas thinking is the formulation of a policy on economy, state politics, democratisation and legal rights. Hamas responds to such criticism by pointing to the 'Islamic state system' as its model. But which Islamic state system does it mean – the system of the Prophet Mohammad, or Omar or Salah ad-Din? As many other Islamic movements which proffer maximalist solutions have discovered, broad models based on the past cannot always satisfy contemporary conditions and problems. This dilemma reflects the noticeable absence of intellectual cadres formulating the position of Hamas.

Islamic Jihad – a Muslim Alternative

The outbreak of the Palestinian uprising provided an opportunity for the Islamic Jihad movement to consolidate its own ideological objectives with a strategy for attaining them. It was through its attempts to fulfil these objectives that the organisation was exposed to the full wrath of the Israeli military and political establishment.

In identifying what is specific in the ideology of Islamic Jihad the most fundamental factor to bear in mind is that the movement's thinkers and ideologues have sought to take the tenets of their religion and, through translation, use them actively to end the Israeli occupation of the West Bank and Gaza Strip. This change has always been envisaged as radical rather than reformist, militant rather than passive. Thinkers identified with Islamic Jihad recognise that Palestinian society is in a state known as *jahiliyya*, a pre-Islamic or non-Islamic situation in which the religion is abandoned and society experiences deep disturbance. Sayyid Qutb is a great source of inspiration on this issue. Qutb notes: '*Jahiliyya* wants to find an excuse to reject the Divine system and to perpetuate the slavery of one man to another.'[51] The slavery of Palestinian Muslims, according to Islamic Jihad, is linked to their suppression under the yoke of Israeli, or more specifically, Jewish rule. This disturbance of the Palestinian Muslim identity results in dislocation and a loss of identity. In contradiction to its Islamic counterparts in the occupied territories Islamic Jihad has always advocated armed struggle (jihad) as the principal means by which the move from *jahiliyya* to Islamic state can be made.

Islamic Jihad ideologues are seeking to formulate an Islamic solution that starts with Palestine and ends with contemporary

Muslim society. The organisation itself was formed in response to a perception of a Palestinian–Islamic struggle that places the conflict with Israel at the centre of Islamic thinking and now excludes the external and secular Arab contribution. The pan-Arab nationalist contribution is excluded because Islamic Jihad thinkers recognise that its past record is littered with failure. Therefore, they argue, liberation of the land can be successful only if it is Islamic.

Throughout the Intifada, the ideology of Islamic Jihad, like that of other political actors, was expressed through the a variety of publications: locally-issued leaflets, communiqués from an exiled leadership, and magazines such as *Islam wa Falastin*, *al-Tali'a al-Islamiyya*, and *al-Mukhtar al-Islami*. According to Shaul Mishal, 'Islamic Jihad has published the fewest leaflets … [it] says it is not eager to issue leaflets because according to its view the whole Palestinian public is the leadership of the uprising.'[52] While it may be true that Islamic Jihad has published least, this does not imply that it is reluctant to engage in this form of communication. The format of the locally-issued leaflets, for example, is the same as those issued by Hamas or the United National Leadership of the Uprising (UNLU). Each has a particular theme, an issue, an anniversary or an event to which it dedicates its main text. For example, a leaflet issued in the name of Islamic Jihad and dated 15 August 1989 was concerned solely with education and the return of Palestinian children to school after a two-year absence. Another issued in September 1989 commemorated the 1982 massacres of Sabra and Shatilla in Lebanon. The leaflets are not, then, exclusively religious in theme although they are sometimes dedicated to religious events or celebrations such as the birthday of the Prophet Mohammad, Ramadan, Jihad or feast celebrations. The leaflets contain the same types of calls and directives found in Hamas or UNLU documents:

> Point 7: We ask our masses and all the strike forces to pursue and wipe out all the traitors and hirelings because both the Islamic law and the people have permitted their killing. We did them no wrong but they have wronged only themselves.[53]

Throughout the Intifada Islamic Jihad sought to communicate its message to the Palestinian public. It wanted to win its sympathy and support. The Islamic Jihad leaflets helped maintain a link with the uprising, and reiterated the broad ideological thrust of the organisation: liberation and Islamic statehood through military jihad against Israel.

Formative Influences

Islamic Jihad thinkers have sought to reassert a specifically Palestinian perspective with regard to the conflict with Israel and a host of other issues. If in the 1950s the work of Sheikh Taki ad-Din an-Nabahani represented the first attempt at an indigenous Palestinian–Islamic response to problems and issues, then in many respects the thinkers identified with the Islamic Jihad can be identified as attempting to resurrect a revolutionary Islamic intelligentsia that had been largely absent from the Palestinian arena.

Islamic Jihad has been influenced by the ideas of other Islamists but these outside influences have been viewed from an explicitly Palestinian perspective. A number of authors, including Israeli and Palestinian academics, Elie Rekhess and Ziad Abu Amr, identify a set of core influences, or personalities, which have influenced Islamic Jihad thinking. Abu Amr cites Hassan al-Banna, Sayyid Qutb and Sheikh Izz ad-Din al-Qassam as the three 'Islamic personalities' influencing the ideas and ideology of Islamic Jihad. He notes also that the example of the Iranian revolution and Ayatollah Khomeini are 'of great importance'.[54] Rekhess in addition identifies and places great emphasis on the impact of the Iranian revolution and aspects of Shi'ism on Islamic Jihad ideology, asserting that Islamic Jihad is 'a militant Sunni group, steeped in Sunni notions and traditions, yet inspired and emboldened by the Shi'i revolution in Iran'.[55]

It is true that an examination of the ideology of Islamic Jihad highlights the influences of external factors. There is a clear familiarity with Western secular concepts such as nationalism which reveal the secular education of many of these thinkers. However, they differ from those in Hamas in that they use their understanding to argue against what they regard as the pernicious hold of these ideologies in the contemporary Middle East. Writing in an edition of *Islam wa Falastin* an Islamist author, after running through the history of the development of the nation-state, identifies the positive features of the Islamic state *vis-à-vis* the nation-state: 'The state in the Islamic world … is not based on the domination of a certain elite race and language group. It is the state where the law of Allah prevails.'[56]

Religious War

During the first weeks and months of the Palestinian Intifada the Islamic Jihad groups in the Gaza Strip and West Bank distributed a number of leaflets addressing the Palestinians masses. On more than one occasion they began with the following sura: 'But those who struggle in Our cause, surely We shall guide them in Our ways; and God is with the good-doers.'[57] This verse enshrines the concept of jihad or struggle promoted by the group, placing the act of struggle on the side of good. The sura also illustrates the importance of religious guidance and the support of God promised to the mujahidin (the strugglers). An act of striving, whether violent or otherwise, is condoned as an act of resistance against attack.

The single most important and so, not surprisingly, most consistent theme in the ideology of Islamic Jihad is the need for struggle as a form of liberation from unjust and un-Islamic rule for the entire Muslim community (*umma*). A leaflet published in 1988 makes this clear:

> What is now taking place in the Holy Land is not just a battle [jihad] for the Palestinian people alone. It is a battle for the future of the entire Umma. It is a battle against the foreign arrogance – against colonial hegemony over our world.[58]

It must be remembered that the inspiration for the concept of jihad is divine. The Qur'an and Muslim tradition provide countless examples of the execution of jihad in the name of Islam. The Qur'an outlines specific circumstances under which the jihad is waged. It is supported by a long tradition of jihad in the Muslim faith contributing tales of brave mujahidin. Jihad, in this context, is viewed as a necessary virtue and is linked specifically to the notion of a vanguard leading the jihad on behalf of the Muslim masses. This vanguardism typifies the ideas of many Muslim ideologues who have written on the subject. In this context the meaning of jihad has a wider focus than armed struggle although armed struggle, for the Palestinian movement, remains the fundamental strategy. The jihad, as illustrated above, is about liberation from subjugation. Islamic Jihad advocates jihad to release all Muslims from tyranny and ignorance and to conquer the hegemonic forces of colonialism. As ideologue Fathi Shqaqi declared following his deportation from the Gaza Strip in 1988, the jihad against Israel, 'is not an isolated event ... but a continuation of the battle against Judaic–Christian expansionism in the region.'[59] In this respect the revolutionary call of Islamic Jihad is not so different from that of other revolutionary radicals.

While the Qur'an and the *hadith* are fundamental terms of reference for the movement, other more contemporary ideologues are acknowledged widely as being influential in the concept of jihad. The three figures most often cited in the organisation's literature itself and by authors writing about the movement are Sayyid Qutb, Sheikh Izz-ad-Din al-Qassam and the Syrian Islamist Sa'id Hawa.

The Islamist groups of the contemporary era cannot claim a monopoly on the notion of jihad. Secular–nationalist Arab leaders have also claimed that their battles are part of the jihad to liberate the Arab world from Western domination. Yasser Arafat claimed the mantle of jihad during the Israeli invasion of Lebanon and the routing of PLO forces in 1982:

> It was us that gave jihad a meaning in the present time after it has been absent for so long. In the siege of Beirut we lost 72,000 dead and wounded. We advance for martyrdom and ask whoever wants to follow. And I ask you, did I prevent anyone from using whatever method he chose to liberate Palestine? [60]

Arafat's notion of jihad, however, is very different from the notion formulated by Islamic ideologues like Sayyid Qutb, practised by figures like Sheikh Izz ad-Din al-Qassam and embraced by the Palestinian Islamic Jihad cells led by Fathi Shqaqi and Sheikh Abd al-Aziz Auda. Qutb and his followers enunciate a more complex notion of jihad based on a response to the current status of the contemporary Arab world and its relation to the international order.[61]

Sayyid Qutb's life and writing is a striking example of the influence of such writers on the Palestinian notion of jihad.[62] Qutb advocates a return to Islam and the urgent need for Muslims to seize power in the name of Islam to promote divine sovereignty. In 1966, after spending more than ten years in prison, Qutb was sentenced to death for allegedly leading a secret Islamic movement which plotted to overthrow Nasser. He was executed on 29 August 1966. Qutb's martyrdom for Islam became a symbol for future generations. He had advocated jihad in the pages of his many books and had died striving (a *mujahid*) against Nasser's Arab nationalist regime.

Qutb was a prolific author, writing during a turbulent period in Egypt's history characterised by revolutionary change: a radical transformation from a traditional political order to a new dawn in Arab nationalist and secular politics. Qutb's writings have made a major contribution to contemporary Islamic thinking and have inspired a number of region-wide Islamic groups. They fuelled an important change in the direction of contemporary Islamic politics, propelling it into a activist revolutionary realm based on the politics of change. As Ayubi notes: 'Qutbian discourse ... tends to influence people's thought and actions in a psychologically tense way that creates in the individual not the ability to reconstruct reality but rather the dream of breaking with that reality.'[63]

Qutb's analysis of Egyptian Muslim society was based on the premise of a decline in values and the state of *jahiliyya*. His notion of *jahiliyya* is inherently linked to the obligation of jihad. Jihad becomes the method of release from pagan rule; it is the key to the door of a true Islamic society based on Divine sovereignty in God. Qutb identifies the nature of *jahili* society in the contemporary era as foreign, at odds with the Islamic system of belief, posited on false value systems, economics, politics and education. He calls for liberation:

> We should remove ourselves from all influences of the *jahiliyya* in which we live and from which we derive benefits ... we must also free ourselves from the clothes of *jahili* society, *jahili* concepts, *jahili* traditions and *jahili* leadership ... Our aim is first to change ourselves so that we may later change the society.[64]

Qutb's call, then, reflected a change in the philosophy of political Islam. Unlike Hassan al-Banna who argued for gradual change from within and the reform of society, Qutb called for complete disengagement from the prevailing political order and that order's dissolution. Following Qutb's logic this is the only option open to Muslims who recognise the domination of the *jahili* system of rule over their lives. Change, according to Qutb, is best achieved through struggle or striving:

> The truth of the faith is not fully established until a struggle is undertaken on its behalf among the people. A struggle against their unwillingness and their resistance, a struggle to remove them from this state [*jahiliyya*] to that of Islam and truth. A struggle by word of mouth, by propagation, by exposition, by refuting the false and baseless ... A struggle physically to remove obstacles from the path of right guidance when it is infested by brute force and open violence.[65]

Qutb's call for Islamic liberation from all forms of other political rule has inspired the Palestinian Islamic Jihad. As Yvonne Haddad notes, ' ... the jihad is crucial if the *dawah* ("call" to Islam) is to proceed unimpeded.'[66] Qutb's call is echoed in the words of Islamic Jihad leaders like Fathi Shqaqi: 'We are defending the minimum of the usurped rights inside Palestine. We are determined to practise our armed jihad wherever there is an Israeli soldier in Palestine.'[67]

Qutb's call for liberation through jihad has, however, been popularly interpreted by many of the contemporary Islamic groups, including Islamic Jihad, as a call to arms. The Qutbian vision of *jahiliyya* society and its all-pervasive impact on the Muslim world appears to necessitate a violent and radical break away from the existing order, followed by revolution. As Palestinian Jihad leader Sheikh Abdullah ash-Shammi has remarked, the only option for Muslims is jihad: 'The real alternative is to keep the conflict with the occupation authorities open. Although we are weak today, we will be strong in future and the balance of power will tilt in our favour.'[68] In the context of the Palestinian Islamic Jihad it should be remembered that by embracing the Qutbian maxim of rejection of all things *jahiliyya*, the Islamic Jihad, ideologically speaking, also considers its Palestinian counterparts in the national–secular movement as enemies of Islam. While the practical relationship has been ambiguous, ideologically Islamic Jihad views the nationalists as seeking to replace Israeli occupation with a Western-inspired secular order which contradicts the Islamic values and state system to which the jihadists aspire. A leaflet issued by Islamic Jihad in October 1989 which was critical of nationalist activity (the PLO had just engaged in contacts with the American government) bears testimony to the anti-secular foundation to their political philosophy:

> The National Leadership ... [is] incapable today of understanding the historical and ideological dimensions of our struggle. These are the same people who only months before the Intifada were calling for total annexation of the West Bank and Gaza so that we would be able to make our political and parliamentary struggle for our rights.[69]

Sheikh Abd al-Aziz Auda reiterates the view that all other Palestinian ideologies of liberation will ultimately fail because they are premised on political viewpoints promoting not destroying *jahili* society. He intones the liberation theology of Islam that is inspired by a Qutbian approach to the contemporary order:

> We, the Islamic people, believe that the road to salvation is the road of Islam, not only for spiritual and emotional reasons but also for historical and objective reasons. Through the ages, Islam has been the path of a nation's rise from defeat ... Islam represents the main and central opposition to the Western assault and its symbols, particularly Zionism, in the region.[70]

As Qutb himself put it:

There is only one way to reach God; all other ways do not lead to Him. 'This is my straight path. Then follow it, and do not follow other ways which will scatter you from His path' (The Qur'an: Sura 6 v.153) For human life, there is only one true system, and that is Islam; all other systems are *jahiliyya*.[71]

The example of Qutb's own life, through his activities in the Egyptian Islamic movement and his martyrdom at the hands of the Nasser's Arab nationalist regime, is an inspiration to the Palestinian movement. His writing helps the Palestinian members and leaders of Islamic Jihad articulate a call to arms that includes a complete break with the existing order and promotes the resurrection of an Islamic utopian ideal. In this case, as Ayubi points out with reference to Egyptian neo-fundamentalists, the Islamic Jihad group in Palestine, through its Qutbian viewpoint, has

> ... thus completed the circle. From calling for an Islamic order, they proceed to condemn the existing society and its rulers for not being purely Islamic, and then conclude that the only way out is to establish an Islamic state through military struggle. The politicisation of religion has now been made complete.[72]

The impact of Sheikh Izz ad-Din al-Qassam on the ideological orientation of Islamic Jihad is different from that of Qutb. While Qutb's writings are an important source of inspiration the same cannot be said of al-Qassam. Al-Qassam has inspired Islamic Jihad by action alone. Given the evidence of al-Qassam's own role in the Palestinian struggle against Zionism and colonialism, described in Chapter One of this book, it is easy to see why he is so important. As Abu Amr remarks, 'The Islamic Jihad's supporters have elevated him to almost saintly status.'[73] Al-Qassam was responsible for raising the call to jihad in Palestine and it is his advocacy of jihad as an act of resistance and attack that appeals most to the current-day organisation.

Vanguardism – Discourse of Struggle and Martyrdom

Islamic Jihad does not conceive of itself as a populist movement; it is not dedicated to winning the Muslim masses to a broad and general call for reform in Islamic society. Instead it adopts a specifically vanguardist approach to its political doctrine as well as to its organisation. This vanguard role is influenced by the examples

of Qutb, Sheikh Izz ad Din al-Qassam and even the Lebanese and
Iranian Shi'i revolutionary movements.

The idea of Islamic vanguardism is addressed in the ultimate
Muslim source of reference, the Qur'an, which encourages the strong
who are able to represent the weak:

> Fight in the cause of God those who fight you; do not transgress limits;
> for God loves not transgressors ... And why should you not fight in the
> cause of God and of those who, being weak, are ill-treated (and oppressed)
> men, women and children, whose cry is 'Our Lord, rescue us from this
> town whose people are oppressors, and raise us from Thee, one who will
> protect and raise for us from Thee one who will help.'[74]

This notion of a vanguard, in the Leninist rather than military sense
of the word, is evident in the promotion of jihad. Jihad under these
conditions is not a universal act in which all Muslims must rise up
in arms against the enemy but an armed struggle waged by a few in
the name of the many. So defined, jihad is the representation of the
vanguardist tendencies of Islamic Jihad. The Islamic Jihad vanguard,
however, not only directs the revolution using its skills and knowledge
but also plays an active part in the act of revolution (jihad) itself.
Religio-political violence is sanctioned by the vanguard as a method
for liberation. Nevertheless, the Islamic vanguard is dependent on
the community around it for support and co-operation which is why
its message must be disseminated widely.

The Jews and Islamic Jihad

> I tell the Zionists in Palestine and everywhere, we will fight you child,
> woman and old man. This is because an eye is for an eye, a tooth for
> a tooth and he who begins injustice is the more heinous villain. We
> will not forget the massacres perpetrated against us. We will not forget
> Shatilla, Qafr Qassam, Qibyah or Dawayimah ... You kill one and we
> will kill 1,000. There will be no peace negotiations with you, so do
> whatever you like. God is with us. [Islamic Jihad leaflet, 7 February
> 1990]

The above statement was made by an Islamic Jihad member responsible for an armed attack on a bus carrying Israeli tourists in Egypt
in February 1990. Eight Israelis were killed in the attack whose
motive was blatant: to kill Jews who are perceived as the usurpers
of Muslim rights to Palestine. Islamic Jihad, like Hamas, articulates
an ideology that justifies and calls for the destruction of the state

of Israel because it is a Jewish state, a state that has taken Muslim land by force and promotes religious, political and other values which are at odds with Islam. The Jewish nation is perceived as an anathema, a representation of the Western conspiracy to defeat Islam. The state of Israel as a territorial entity is perceived by Islamic Jihad as a direct challenge to restore the land of Palestine to its rightful owners, the Muslims. The Jews have no place. They are traditional enemies and must be defeated. Sheikh Abd al-Aziz Auda defines the nature of the confrontation:

> Palestine is the battlefield in the confrontation with the Jews and Zionism. What is the problem that faces the Arabs and Muslims? It is the Western challenge and its spearhead [Israel] in Palestine. Palestine is a major Islamic goal as Israel is the embodiment of Western civilisation.[75]

Islamic Jihad doctrine views Israel through two parallel lenses. The first is religious. The Jews, a people of the Book, are nevertheless seen from the particular kind of religious perspective embraced by Jihad as traditional enemies of Islam. The second perspective portrays the Zionist movement as a political movement acting on behalf of Western interests in the Muslim world. Thus the state of Israel (a separate territorial entity and nation-state) is not and cannot be recognised as legitimate by Islamic Jihad. For Islamic Jihad the state of Israel was created through force and violence, land was stolen from the Palestinians and Zionism advocated this theft. An example of this viewpoint can be found in one of the first leaflets issued by Islamic Jihad during the Palestinian uprising:

> The enemy are Zionist invaders and they are *kufr* [infidel] and they are agents of the American leadership and collaborators. They are Zionist-fascists and we call on you good people – the sons of Salah ad-Din, Izz ad-Din al-Qassam and the Mujahidin – to raise the flag of jihad over our land to destroy the Zionist invaders.[76]

All this means that Islamic Jihad does not have much room for political manoeuvre. It has never advocated negotiation with the government of Israel. The dialectic and hostile relationship of enemies prevents the organisation from entering into any political relationship with its enemy. Islamic Jihad works on the premise that Israel represents the forces of evil, of *jahiliyya*, or the world of war (*dar al-harb*) which can only be defeated through jihad. Jihad is the only way to restore Palestine to Islam, to the world of Islam, where other religions have a place but not over Islam.

This viewpoint has, again, clearly been influenced by local figures such as Sheikh Izz ad-Din al-Qassam who had advocated armed struggle in the attempt to halt Zionist immigration into Palestine, as well as Sayyid Qutb and leading Islamic figures in Iran and Lebanon who have addressed the issue of Zionism and Palestine. Islamic Jihad has determined the nature of conflict with Israel through its rigidly theological and ideological view of the Jews and the Zionists. This notion of the Jews is similar to that held by many in the ranks of the Hamas movement.

Islamic Jihad countenances no settlement to the Arab–Israeli, Muslim–Israeli, Muslim–Jewish conflict in the region other than the complete destruction of the Zionist entity. This refusal of a political solution, including the offer of land for peace, highlights the intractable nature of the conflict on this level. The position is summed up in an Islamic Jihad leaflet which is also critical of the national movement for its strategy towards Israel:

> If there is a national liberation struggle it is in reality an illusion, throwing sand in the eyes of the people. We are not part of this so-called liberation, we are working for real liberation. Thus, we call on the Palestinian people to continue the jihad and condemn normalisation with the enemy because the concessions of the Palestinian leadership strengthen the enemy.[77]

Islamic Jihad remains, by choice, an advocate of a zero-sum game in which the declared objective is the destruction of Israel. Here religio-political violence (jihad) is an external force against Israel. Contrary to many of its counterparts in countries like Egypt or Algeria, Islamic Jihad has not yet advocated a strategy of jihad from within against the secular forces in the Palestinian population. Under these circumstances the ideological justification for jihad would be questioned.

Conclusion

The constituent organisations of political Islam in Palestine have formulated a number of political programmes and addressed themselves to some major issues affecting the lives of the Palestinians of the West Bank and Gaza Strip. There are, however, some areas where all organisations have failed to present a comprehensive position. Neither Hamas or Islamic Jihad, for example, addresses itself directly to the realities, hopes and political aspirations of the Palestinian diaspora though it is true that both movements enjoy support from sectors of that diaspora. The diaspora community is, however, addressed only through indirect reference to the rest of the Muslim community and the need for the latter's support in creating an Islamic state. Present-day Palestinian Islamic discourse also lacks a detailed programme of economic change.[78] Islamist activists will broadly advocate the adoption of Islamic economic principles but, with the exception of the *zakat* committee system, there is little evidence of a detailed Islamic economic programme for the development of Palestinian society. There are, on the other hand, other areas of social and political discourse where both movements have presented a comprehensive strategy.

The development of a Palestinian Islamic and quasi-nationalist viewpoint has occurred slowly and will continue for the foreseeable future. The ideology of each of these organisations, while claiming to eschew the Western cultural and intellectual dominance of the region, is itself a victim of this process of colonialism. The acculturation of Islamic thought and ideology is present in the views expounded by both Hamas and Islamic Jihad in the 1990s. Although the ideologies of both organisations call openly for a return to some seventh-century Islamic tradition, that so-called tradition is itself often part of an invented past constructed by the Islamists as a response to contemporary political problems. Palestinian Islamists have also consciously accepted certain Western constructs and have incorporated them into their respective ideologies. (The debate within Hamas about democracy and political parties, discussed in Chapter Five, is an excellent example of this.) In reality, the political survival of Islamic groups like Hamas and Islamic Jihad is dependent precisely on their ability to absorb Western liberal traditions and re-articulate them as part of an Islamic dialogue with the Palestinian community. Static and rigid ideological approaches, as we have seen with the Liberation Party, do not allow Islamists to survive the Palestinian political climate.

However, Islamist incorporation of Western ideas, political philosophy and models has also led into dangerous territory. Unlike the modernisers symbolised by al-Afghani, Abduh and Rida, who argued for the incorporation of Western change if it was beneficial to Islam, the ideologues of movements like Hamas are guilty of rejecting the values, activities and political philosophies of the West while at the same time hypocritically integrating some of the worst aspects of Western political thought into their own political system of belief. The slavish Islamisation of Western anti-Semitic thought by organisations like Hamas and Islamic Jihad is just one example.

It is, however, sometimes this simplistic portrayal of complex political situations that has won groups like Hamas so many supporters. Their pragmatic approach to ideology, their flexibility with complex political concepts, has helped them win considerable support within the Palestinian community in the Gaza Strip and West Bank. Palestinian Islamists have developed ideological positions reflecting the current concerns of the Palestinian community; in addition they have succeeded in appropriating many of the slogans, concepts and symbols of nationalism and re-articulating them in the voice of political Islam. The inherent danger in this path lies, however, in the over-assimilation and confusion of ideas and identity that flexibility could eventually reflect. Will there come a point where, for example, it is increasingly difficult to discern the Islamist nature of Hamas ideology as it parrots, re-appropriates and repeats the slogans of nationalism, secularism, anti-Semitism and other non-Islamic ideologies?

Epilogue

Here is your free and proud Intifada entering its eighth year, resisting the plots and campaign by some among us to the Zionist enemy and the world to ignore us and our struggle. Let all these plots which support the enemy, and are shameful, fail. Let the resistance and struggle and jihad continue until our liberation and freedom and independence. [Hamas Communiqué, 'The Seventh Anniversary of the Intifada', 6 December 1994]

The Palestinian Islamic movement has had a marked impact on the politics of Palestinian liberation. For more than seventy-five years political Islam in one form or another, and with greater or lesser degrees of success, has attempted to provide an alternative to a secular-nationalist resolution of the conflict with the Zionists and the state of Israel. The often fervent and messianic outlook of the followers of political Islam is compelling and sometimes irresistible. Convinced of their mission, the leaderships of groups like Hamas and Islamic Jihad now preside over a movement that has raised its own new generation of disciples. The boys who were eight to ten years old in 1987 and were taught in the mosques when their schools were closed are, at the time of writing, young adults. Many have dedicated their lives to the Islamic struggle, they truly are the 'children of the Hamas generation'. They have spent their childhood and adolescence throwing stones for Hamas, writing graffiti, hoisting green flags decorated with the Muslim confession of faith and praying for Islamic liberation of a land under Israeli occupation. For many of these young men Hamas is Islam and Islam is Hamas; a good Muslim is a Muslim who supports Hamas and a bad Muslim is a Muslim who supports other political alternatives. This is a generation raised on popular revolt against Israeli rule and faced with the prospect of a Palestinian rule not of its choosing; a generation of activists who have missed years of schooling, have no job prospects, but have instead the belief in Allah and the power of the Qur'an to guide them.

Both the Israeli and the Palestinian opponents of Hamas and Islamic Jihad need to recognise that political Islam in the West Bank and Gaza Strip can no longer be eradicated through miltary crackdowns, deportations, arrest campaigns or assassinations alone. Both the Israeli and Palestinian authorities will have to accept the need to use political as well as military methods of dealing with the influence of political Islam. These methods should be as democratic and as open as possible and should not always be dependent on accompanying strategies of coercion and control. The force of political Islam has sunk its roots deep into the fabric of Palestinian society. Indeed if the goal of the forces of political Islam had simply been the Islamisation of Palestinian society it could be argued that by the middle of the 1990s they had met with some success. In the Gaza Strip, for example, the forces of political Islam have had a considerable input in the areas of Palestinian education and health. They administer their own university, their own dental and health clinics, welfare programmes and kindergartens. As a result of the Intifada, however, the social goals of the Islamic movement have been somewhat overshadowed by the pressing political agenda the movement faces.

Although the Intifada could on one level be viewed as simply another chapter in the annals of the protracted Arab–Israeli conflict, on another level it can be seen as a radical departure from the pattern of politics that in the past characterised that conflict. For the Palestinians took their fate into their own hands and demanded both an end to the Israeli occupation and the creation of a Palestinian state. In the face of this political agenda the forces of political Islam were compelled to articulate a political response and an ideological viewpoint that not only embraced an Islamic perspective but also acknowledged and included the rich heritage of Palestinian nationalist politics.

In the post-Oslo era the prospects for achieving Islamist goals such as the liberation of all Palestine, the establishment of an Islamic state and the complete revival of Islam are complicated further by the presence of the nationalist forces under the framework of the Palestinian National Authority (PNA) and by the peace process with Israel. These are likely to be important factors in determining the future impact of the Islamic movement in the West Bank and Gaza Strip. There are, in fact, a number of scenarios over the next decade which the forces of political Islam are likely to face.

Internal Palestinian Politics:
Out in the Cold

Since the signing of the Oslo Accords and agreement for self-rule reached between the PLO and Israel the forces of political Islam have struggled to maintain their powerful hold over the popular mass in Palestinian society. Following Yasser Arafat's return to Gaza in July 1994, the popularity of the Fatah leader has continued to rise while that of Hamas has dropped. Hamas and Islamic Jihad face a double dilemma: how to wage their campaign against Israel when some sections of the Palestinian people have agreed to recognition of the State of Israel and peace, and how to articulate the message of political Islam under the Palestinian nationalist rule of the Palestinian National Authority (PNA).

The Islamic movement can continue to reject the current peace process. In this case it will remain in opposition to the nationalist forces of the PLO and specifically to Fatah. Along with their leftist allies in the PFLP and DFLP it can continue to deny legitimacy to the PNA. The forces of political Islam argue that they will tolerate the PNA only so long as its activities do not infringe on Islamic spheres of influence and power in Gaza. This is a forlorn hope; it is inevitable that the PNA through its ministries for education, health and religious affairs will trespass on to political turf long regarded as an important preserve of the Islamic movement. When this happens Hamas and Islamic Jihad will be faced with the difficulty of reconciling their need to preserve their bases of political power and the challenge of maintaining a commitment to national unity and avoiding civil conflict.

At present Arafat's authoritarian rule is strangling hopes for the establishment of a fully democratic system of rule. Since the re-deployment of Israeli troops in April 1994, and again in November–December 1995, the arrival of more than 14,000 Palestinian police and security agents and the return of Arafat himself in July 1994, the politics of the Gaza Strip and West Bank have become increasingly praetorian. One-party (Fatah) rule is on the rise and was recently legitimated in the Palestinian presidential and legislative council elections. The predominance of Fatah rule, supported by Israel and other external forces, relegates other political parties and organisations to the margins of Palestinian society.

State-building and the institutionalisation of Palestinian society under the PNA so far exhibit rigid top-down decision-making which ignores the pluralism of politics in contemporary Palestinian society. A number of factors indicate a negative political dawn under the Oslo framework: the absence of real democratic structures in those areas of authority bestowed on the PNA; the suppression of the press; the restriction of the right to free public assembly; the creation of military security courts; the official harassment of human rights' workers; and the considerable powers of arrest and detention without trial placed in the hands of the police and security services. Arafat's dependence on the armed loyalists of the Palestinian police, his own elite bodyguard unit, and various security services, create a perception among the Palestinian community of the West Bank and Gaza that it is witnessing the emergence of a Palestinian police state.

If, however, political stability is achieved and maintained through this system of Palestinian self-government then no matter how undemocratic it is it will endure. The monopoly of rule promoted by Yasser Arafat will be supported by both the PNA's Israeli and Jordanian neighbours as well as other regional and international backers of the self-rule experiment. Important financial backing will be maintained and the economic regeneration of the area will be designed to maximise capital at the expense of political rights to the whole community.

Under these conditions the forces of political Islam will be subject to continued threat, repression and dissolution. The voice of Hamas and Islamic Jihad will be marginalised. The PNA will pay token respect to Islam through its own waqf structures and loyal ulama while Islamicists will be branded as dangerous hotheads undermining political stability and peace in the area. Thus Hamas and Islamic Jihad have more to fear from Arafat and his supporters than from the Israeli authorities. Through his security apparatus Arafat now has the power to emasculate the force of political Islam, depriving it of its kudos and charisma and relegating its constituent organisations to the margins of society. Arafat, in this respect, would not be unlike Nasser in the 1960s when the Egyptian leader turned against political Islam in his relentless quest for hegemony in Egypt.

However, an alternative scenario may emerge as a reaction to authoritarian rule and the evaporation of Palestinian national aspirations under the rule of Arafat and the PNA. In this scenario the forces of democracy will benefit all political opponents of the current peace process and self-rule experiment.

Revolt and Islamic Rule

If Arafat chooses to adopt the authoritarian pattern of government that has characterised the regimes of Syria and Iraq then popular revolt supported by the Islamicists is a real prospect. If economic initiatives fail to provide much-promised jobs for the hundreds of thousands of unemployed Palestinians of the West Bank and Gaza Strip, and the peace economy benefits only capital and the entrepreneurial class, then popular discontent will rise. Economic hardship will not be tolerated if political rights are also suppressed; Palestinians will perceive Palestinian self-rule as one form of occupation replacing another. Under these circumstances Hamas and Islamic Jihad could well become the major representatives of a disenchanted and disenfranchised Palestinian underclass in a Palestinian police state. Their close relations and support in the refugee community and with the poor will allow them to spearhead a revolt against Israeli-supported Palestinian authoritarian rule.

There have already been indications that this type of scenario could emerge, and if the PNA wants to avoid this it must ensure that there is never a repeat of the November 1994 Black Friday massacre of thirteen Muslim activists by the Palestinian Police Force (PPF). This type of internal strife – use of unrestrained coercion by representatives of state rule against unarmed members of the community – will not be tolerated by the closely knit political community of the Gaza Strip. PNA rule through state coercion will only deepen already existing cleavages in society, heightening the differences between nationalists and the forces of political Islam, Fatah and Hamas, the PLO from Tunis and the leadership of the Palestinian community in the territories, the haves and the have-nots, the poor and uneducated, the rich and educated.

Thus, if the deterioration of the economic situation triggers popular dissatisfaction with the PNA and if there is a community-based revolt against Arafat's rule in Gaza then Hamas and Islamic Jihad will be ready to step into the political breech. At present the leadership of the Islamic movement in the Gaza Strip knows that it lacks the majority support needed to govern alone. In a crisis that immobilises the nationalist bloc, however, the Islamic movement might garner a sizeable increase in popular support. Hamas in particular will not hesitate to shoulder the political mantle under the slogan of 'serving the people'.

Hamas supporters argue that the leadership of the movement is already preparing for this scenario: 'The present system will not last long ... because the seeds of failure are in the [peace] treaty itself. We have faith in the future, the future is for the Islamic movement.'[1] Hamas and Islamic Jihad could forge a working alliance with the rejectionist front headed by the PFLP and DFLP. In this context Hamas or the Islamists in general could well stake a claim to be the sole representative of the Palestinian people.

Islamic rule in the Gaza Strip and West Bank under these conditions, however, would be doomed and short-lived. Israel would not tolerate an Islamic political entity of this sort under any circumstances and reoccupation would be inevitable. Regionally and internationally there would be no support for a Palestinian Islamic political entity. Its pariah status would stifle any hope for economic regeneration and the rise of the crescent over Palestine would end in further bloodshed and instability.

Loyal to a Jordanian Confederation?

Bookmakers might offer long odds on the prospect of an end to Yasser Arafat's rule and the ascension of King Abdullah to power over Gaza and the West Bank but possible confederation should not be ruled out. Hashemite claims to Jerusalem notwithstanding, Jordan, which concluded its own peace treaty with Israel in November 1994, has a vested interest in the continued political stability of the West Bank. If Arafat were to meet some untimely end, like his former negotiating partner Yitzhak Rabin, then the Jordanian option might be considered. Although King Abdullah might relinquish his claim to the West Bank in 1988 he might easily be persuaded to respond to a ground-swell of Palestinian popular opinion calling for a renewal of his sovereignty over the area. As William Quandt noted recently: 'A surprising number of Palestinians who used to be harsh critics of the Hashemites are now favourably comparing Jordan's emerging political norms with the political chaos that seems to characterise the PLO.'[2] The increasing number of analysts making this comparison are also concluding that the Jordanian option could have some value if it were to rescue the Palestinians from an Israeli reoccupation of the autonomous zones.

While direct Jordanian rule over the West Bank and Gaza Strip is unimaginable, what may be viable is a Palestinian–Jordanian confederation with Palestinian politicians relegated to symbolic leadership while the Hashemites assume real political power. Hamas leaders who address themselves to the possibility of such a scenario view it more positively than Arafat's rule over Gaza and the West Bank. There are a number of factors which support this proposition:

1. The Palestinian forces of political Islam (including the Muslim Brotherhood, Hamas and Islamic Jihad) have always enjoyed a more positive political relationship with the Jordanian regime than with the PLO.
2. Despite intermittent pressure from the Israelis, King Hussein permitted his capital to be used as an alternative headquarters for the Hamas movement, particularly for fund-raising, training and propaganda. It is often claimed that Iran and Sudan are the major external bases of support for Hamas, but this is a rather disingenuous assertion designed to discredit those countries and underplay Jordan's linch-pin role.
3. The example of the Muslim Brotherhood in Jordan has shown the Palestinian forces of political Islam, with the exception of the Liberation Party, that the Islamic trend can achieve a greater degree of political representation in the Jordanian political system than it ever could under the current Palestinian leadership. Jordan has proved one of the most tolerant and accommodating Arab regimes for the contemporary Islamist trend, which King Hussein successfully co-opted into the system through the resurrection of limited parliamentary rule. This does not mean that the Islamic movement in Jordan is completely free but rather that it has a degree of freedom other Islamic groups in the region do not enjoy. Under a Palestine–Jordan confederal model the moderates represented in Hamas know their future would be considerably safer than it would be under Fatah; furthermore, the Muslim Brotherhood which flourishes in Jordan is a natural ally and supporter of Hamas with which it has extremely close links.

Keeping up Pressure on Israel

The current era of negotiation between former enemies could also alter the nature of relations between the force of political Islam, in particular Hamas, and Israel. At present the Palestinians' relationship with Israel is regulated by the decision to nominate the PLO as partners for peace. Because of the armed campaign conducted by Hamas and Islamic Jihad against Israel and continued Israeli repression of the Islamic movement, Islamic–Israeli relations are at

Israeli relations are at an all-time low. However, Israel, by its own admission, cannot fully defeat the Islamic movement politically or militarily. It faces some of the same formidable obstacles as did the British mandate authorities in the 1930s when the latter tried to crush the nascent force of political Islam.

If Israel recognises that it will not defeat the Palestinian Islamic movement militarily, then what strategy can it pursue in the future? Israeli strategy has and always will be influenced by security considerations. If it is able to limit the impact of the armed campaign waged by the forces of political Islam inside the Green Line there will be more room to manoeuvre politically. Islamic Jihad, however, will never succumb to Israel, but it must be remembered that there was a time, before it resorted to armed struggle, when Hamas enjoyed a special relationship with the Israelis. If the political leadership of Hamas can persuade their armed units to end attacks on Israel then there could be room for some sort of political concessions in return.

It is not too far-fetched, then, to suggest that if Yasser Arafat could be persuaded by Israel to co-opt Hamas, and if Hamas were to accept a cease-fire (*hodna*), then some sort of political compromise between these forces could be achieved. After all, Hamas, under the condition of *hodna* suggested by Sheikh Yassin in spring 1994, requires only the withdrawal of Israeli forces, the release of prisoners, the dismantlement of settlements and an agenda for peace negotiations. These conditions are not so different from those suggested by the PLO before it agreed to negotiate with Israel; and, as we have seen, it has been easy for Israel to frustrate progress even in these areas if it considers it necessary.

Hamas is in theory a radical Islamic organisation intent on the liberation of Palestine. In practice it is willing to make intermediate political decisions that may appear to contradict the principle or the spirit of the movement. Like the secularists in the Palestinian national movement, Hamas will be able to argue that making short-term concessions to Israel when in a position of weakness will allow the movement to regroup and strengthen itself for the attainment of the ultimate goal: Islamic liberation of Palestine. Until that time Hamas leaders can, and have, argued that the forces of political Islam can make political concessions to Israel if this is in the interests of its ultimate Islamic objective.

Israel has an interest in eliminating or at least neutralising the Islamic movement and Hamas is the obvious target for such a policy. Although there is room for accommodation with Hamas, Israel will never be able to eliminate Islamic Jihad or find common ground with it. Islamic Jihad will never agree to a cease-fire (*hodna*) or halt its armed campaign; it will remain the most militant Islamic force in the Palestinian–Israeli arena. Hamas, however, can transform itself and through its Islamic political agenda carry the public will in a situation where the nationalists are vanquished.

Israeli policymakers will encounter most opposition to this strategy of containment not from the Palestinians but from the Israeli public. The trauma of peace-making with the Palestinians and its impact on Israeli society cannot be underestimated. Since the signing of the Oslo Accords more than 150 Israeli lives have been lost to Islamic violence, with more than 60 deaths in a seven-day period in February–March 1996 alone. Peace with the PLO has already resulted in the emergence of deep divisions. The fabric of Israeli society is under great pressure and unity under such circumstances has been very hard to maintain. If, however, political compromise with Hamas carries security guarantees then a majority of the Israeli public might be persuaded to travel this path.

The Past to the Present

Political Islam in Palestine remains central to Palestinian politics, and it is essential to take account of it in any resolution of the Palestinian–Israeli conflict. Peace processes, negotiations, agendas or frameworks which ignore it will fail ultimately to deliver security and stability to the area. The policy of quelling political Islam is not feasible in the foreseeable future. Palestinian, Israeli, American, European, Muslim, and non-Muslim policy-makers must reassess their views of the movement among the Palestinian people.

The most fundamental point is that the Islamic movement consisting of Islamic Jihad and its constituent factions, Hamas and its many wings, and the Liberation Party will remain a key political and military player in both Palestinian politics and the conflict with Israel. Whatever scenario emerges it is important, as we reach the end of the twentieth century, to take a realistic attitude to the Islamic movement. An alarmist response to the challenge posed by Palestinian–Islamic forces will create a vicious circle of violence and exacerbate the tensions that lie behind the facade of national unity in the post-Oslo era.

I set out in this book to debunk a number of myths and present a new account of the impact of political Islam in Palestine. The material I have gathered and analysed has, I hope, conveyed a picture of the heterogeneity of political Islam in Palestine, showing that its past portrayal as a monolithic phenomenon is misguided. Political Islam in Palestine has promoted an important and diverse vision which has sustained generations of Palestinians. Sheikh Izz ad-Din al-Qassam and Haj Amin al-Husseini, the Muslim Brotherhood, the Mujama, the Liberation Party, Hamas and Islamic Jihad all testify to the heterogeneous nature – and the enduring presence of political Islam in Palestinian society. Islam has been a factor in Palestinian politics for seventy-five years and a phenomenon contemporaneous with Palestinian nationalism. It has been sustained through a variety of ways and means. These have included social education and welfare programmes, the promotion of elite interests, mainstream politics, and military action. Furthermore, from the very first, political Islam encompassed both gradualist social reform and political violence and for much of its history has been neither an essentially terrorist nor fundamentalist threat. Thus the resonant call to jihad first raised by al-Qassam is present in the 1990s, while the caution and political pragmatism of leaders like Haj Amin al-Husseini is echoed by elements of the political leadership of Hamas. The dichotomy between institutional and activist Islam is, meanwhile, as strong today as it was in the 1930s under the British mandate and can be seen in the Waqf co-opted institutions of the PNA and Hamas of the present. The diversity of Islam, its reflective political nature has ensured its endurance in the past and will help it in the future whatever may happen.

This book has also dispelled the myth of the decline of secularism and the concurrent rise of political Islam in the occupied territories. As Chapters Four, Five and Six illustrate, the so-called resurgence of Islam among the Palestinians did not take place because of the crisis of secularism. Rather, the forces of political Islam were promoted as a counterweight to Palestinian nationalism. Yet Palestinian allegiance to the nationalist cause was ultimately too strong for Hamas, the LP or Islamic Jihad to break. The final assumption about political Islam – namely that the strategy of present-day Islamist groups has been solely dedicated to armed struggle, has been hard to argue with. While I do not attempt to deny the violence that has been carried out in the name of Hamas and Islamic Jihad, I hope that my account has thrown some light on the logic of political violence. My explanation of the violent tactics of these groups is not a justification for their acts but a way of understanding the violence in its context in a deeply divided society. A dedication to political violence does not characterise the entire Islamic movement and the task ahead must be to find a way of dissuading Islamists away from disorder and to finding peaceful means of resolving their conflict with Israel and the Palestinian nationalist movement in the West Bank and Gaza Strip.

Chronology of Islamic Politics in Palestine

1920   Britain awarded a mandate for Palestine by the League
                of Nations

1921   Sheikh Izz ad-Din al-Qassam arrives in Haifa, Palestine
                Haj Amin al-Husseini appointed Mufti of Jerusalem by
                   the British
                British establish the Supreme Muslim Council in
                   Jerusalem

1935   Izz ad-Din al-Qassam killed by British police at Sheikh
                Zeid near Jenin

1936   Palestinian revolt

1937   Haj Amin al-Husseini flees Palestine to Lebanon
                British order the arrest of Haj Amin al-Husseini

1939   The Palestinian revolt ends

1945–6   First branches of the Muslim Brotherhood opened in
                Palestine

1947   British relinquish mandate for Palestine
                United Nation Partition Plan to divide Palestine into
                   two states, one for the Jews and the other for the
                   Palestinians

1948   Israel declares independence
                First Arab–Israel War

1950   Jordan annexes the West Bank

1952 Taqi ad-Din an-Nabahani founds the Liberation Party (Hizb Tahrir)

1954 President Gamal Abdel Nasser of Egypt orders crackdown on activities of the Muslim Brotherhood in the Gaza Strip

1956–7 Israel occupies the Gaza Strip for six months

1964 Nasser orders further crackdown on the Muslim Brotherhood in the Gaza Strip

1967 Six Day War, Israel occupies the West Bank and Gaza Strip
Liberation Party announces cessation of activities in Palestine

1967–71 Fedayeen struggle in the Gaza Strip

1973 Sheikh Ahmad Yassin forms the Mujama organisation

1978 Mujama formally registered with the Israeli authorities as a charity. Israel has policy of encouraging forces of political Islam as foil to the nationalist movement

1980 Clashes in the Gaza Strip between Mujama and the nationalists.

1981 First cells of Islamic Jihad established in the Gaza Strip

1982 Israel invades Lebanon.
PLO ousted from Lebanon to Tunis, crisis within the national movement

1984 Israeli authorities arrest Sheikh Yassin and five of his colleagues. Imprisoned on the charge of possession of arms, membership of an illegal organisation and receiving funds

1985 Sheikh Yassin released from prison in PFLP–GC prisoner exchange

1987   Palestinian uprising

1988   Hamas is established
         Hamas Covenant published
         Leadership of Islamic Jihad deported by the Israeli
             authorities

1989   Israeli authorities outlaw Hamas

1990   Gulf Crisis

1991   Madrid Peace Talks between the Palestinians and Israel
         Hamas and Islamic Jihad join rejectionist alliance

1992   Following increase in armed attacks against Israelis
             more than 400 Hamas and Islamic Jihad leaders and
             members are deported to Marj al-Zahour in
             Lebanon on the orders of the Israeli government.

1993   Oslo Accords signed in Washington by PLO leader
             Yasser Arafat and Israeli Prime Minister Yitzhak
             Rabin
         Hamas and Islamic Jihad reject Oslo, step up military
             campaign against Israel and join rejectionist front
             Damascus Ten

1994   Palestinian National Authority (PNA) established in the
             Gaza Strip and Jericho
         Israeli troops withdraw from the Gaza Strip and Jericho
         Hamas and Islamic Jihad embark on campaign of
             suicide bombing
         Arafat returns to Gaza for the first time in more than
             twenty-five years
         'Black Friday' Palestinian police kill thirteen Islamic
             demonstrators in Gaza city

1995   Israeli authorities in the West Bank conducts arrest
             campaign against Hamas and Islamic Jihad
         PNA conducts arrest campaign against Hamas and
             Islamic Jihad in the Gaza Strip and Jericho

Israeli troops withdraw from most major Palestinian
    towns in the West Bank

1996   First Palestinian elections for Legislative Council and
            post of President to the PNA
        Hamas and Islamic Jihad embark on suicide bombing
            campaign in Israel

1997   PNA launches major crackdown on Islamists

1998   Wye accord between Israel and the PLO

Notes

Introduction

1. Aziz al-Azmeh, *Islams and Modernities* (London, 1993), p. 23.
2. John Esposito, *The Islamic Threat: Myth or Reality?* (Oxford, 1992), p. 72.
3. Yousef Choueri, 'Neo-Orientalism', *Review of Middle East Studies*, 4 (1988), pp. 52–68.
4. Interview with Mr Bassam al-Jamal, London, 10 January 1989.
5. Hilal Dessouki, *Islamic Resurgence in the Arab World* (New York, 1982), p. 4.
6. Bassam Tibi, 'The Renewed Role of Islam in the Political and Social Development of the Middle East', *Middle East Journal*, no. 6 (Summer 1978), pp. 53–68.
7. Esposito: *The Islamic Threat*, p. 14.
8. Interview with Dr Ahmad Saati, Gaza city, 14 September 1994.

Chapter One

1. For more on Sheikh Izz ad-Din al-Qassam see: S. A. Schleifer, 'The Life and Thought of Izz ad-Din al-Qassam', *Islamic Quarterly*, vol. 23 no. 2 (1979), pp. 61–81, and N. Johnson, *Islam and the Politics of Palestinian Nationalism* (London, 1982).
2. The author is grateful to S. A. Schleifer for his advice on this section.
3. Hassan Yacoubi, *They Killed You!* (Islamic University of Gaza) [966] 25 November 1935.
4. *al-Jami'a al-Islamiyya*, 25 November 1935, p. 1.
5. For more on these thinkers see: A. N. Busool, 'Shaykh Mohammad Rashid Rida's Relations with Jamal al-Din al-Afghani and Mohammad Abduh', *The Muslim World* vol. 66 no. 4 (1976), pp. 272–86, N. Keddie, *Sayyid Jamal ad-Din al-Afghani: A Political Biography* (Los Angeles, 1972) and M. H. Kerr, *Islamic Reform: The Political and Legal Theories of Mohammad Abduh and Rashid Rida* (Los Angeles, 1966).
6. See: Y. Seferta, 'The Concept of Religious Authority According to Mohammad Abduh and Rashid Rida', *Islamic Quarterly*, vol. 30 no. 3 (1986), pp. 159–64.

7. J. Esposito, *Islam – The Straight Path* (Oxford, 1994), p. 127.

8. Johnson: *The Politics of Palestinian Nationalism*, p. 39.

9. Schleifer: 'The Life and Thought', pp. 63–4.

10. PRO file CO733/257/12, Situation in Palestine 1935.

11. Tegart Papers, Box 1, File 3c, from report on 'Terrorism 1936–37', p. 7 (MEC, Oxford).

12. Tegart Papers, Box 1, File 3c, from report on 'Terrorism 1936–37', p. 7 (MEC, Oxford).

13. Schleifer: 'The Life and Thought', p. 75.

14. Ahmad Sheikh Saad, a member of al-Qassam's group donated the considerable sum of P£400 for arms purchases.

15. *Palestine Post*, 21 November 1935, p. 1.

16. See: Subhi Yassin, *al-Thawra al-Arabiyya al-Kubra fi Falastin* (Damascus, 1959) for a full account of events leading to al-Qassam's death.

17. 'Large Crowds at Burial of Three Arab Terrorists', *Palestine Post*, 22 November 1935, p. 1.

18. PRO file CO 75156/4/35, Report from Sir Arthur Wauchope on Situation in Palestine.

19. Johnson: *The Politics of Palestinian Nationalism*, p. 14.

20. P. Mattar, 'The Mufti of Jerusalem and the Politics of Palestine', *Middle East Journal* 42 (1989), p. 228.

21. J. Esposito, *Islam and Politics* (Syracuse, 1984), p. 66.

22. T. Jbara, *Palestinian Leader, Haj Amin al-Husayni, Mufti of Jerusalem* (New Jersey, 1985), p. 9.

23. J. Migdal, *Palestinian Society and Politics* (Princeton, 1979), p. 21.

24. U. Kupferschmidt, *The Supreme Muslim Council: Islam Under the British Mandate for Palestine* (Leiden, 1987), p. 82.

25. Kupferschmidt: *The Supreme Muslim Council*, p. 28.

26. *al-Hayat*, 8 September 1980.

27. PRO file CO733/257/12, Report from Palestine & file CP (34) Memo by Secretary of State for the Colonies.

28. Mattar: 'The Mufti of Jerusalem', p. 231.

29. A. W. Kayyali, *Palestine: A Modern History* (London, 1972), pp. 165–6.

30. 'A Speech by Haj Amin al-Husseini in Jerusalem', *al-Jami'a al-Islamiyya*, 25 January 1935.

31. 'Fatwa from Ulama', *al-Jami'a al-Arabiyya*, 28 January 1935.

32. PRO file CO733/278/13, 'Letter from Wauchope', 30 April 1935.

33. Y. Porath, *The Palestinian Arab National Movement 1929-1939: From Riots to Rebellion* (London, 1977), p. 132.

34. Jbara: *Palestinian Leader*, p. 142.

35. Ibid.

36. B. Kalkas, 'The Revolt of 1936: A Chronicle of Events', in I. Abu Lughod (ed.), *The Transformation of Palestine* (Evanston, 1970), p. 241.

37. *Palestine Post*, 23 June 1936, p. 5.

38. K. Stein, 'Rural Change and Peasant Destitution: Contributing Causes to the Arab Revolt in Palestine 1936–1939', in F. Kazemi and J. Waterbury (eds), *Peasants and Politics in the Modern Middle East* (Florida, 1991), p. 165.

39. T. Mayer, 'The Military Force of Islam, The Society of Muslim Brethren and the Palestine Question, 1945–1948', in E. Kedourie and S. Haim (eds), *Zionism and Arabism in Palestine and Israel* (London, 1982), p. 103.

40. Ibid. p. 104.

41. See: R. P. Mitchell, *The Society of Muslim Brothers* (Oxford, 1969), p. 56.

Chapter Two

1. See: B. Morris, *The Birth of the Palestinian Refugee Problem 1947–1949* (Cambridge, 1987) and B. Morris, *1948 and After, Israel and the Palestinians* (Oxford, 1994).

2. See: M. Dumper, 'Forty Years Without Slumbering: Waqf Politics and Administration in the Gaza Strip, 1948–1987', *British Journal of Middle Eastern Studies*, 20/3 (1993), pp. 174–90.

3. The Gaza district contained 1,368,900 dunums (4 dunums = 1 acre) of land. The majority of this land, however, was desert. After 1948 only 325,000 dunums remained in Arab hands and this area became known as the Gaza Strip.

4. Ziad Abu Amr, 'The Gaza Economy: 1948–1984', in G. Abed, *The Palestine Economy* (London & New York, 1988), p. 101.

5. PRO File CO733/398/10, Report no. 14, 15 July 1939.

6. Ibrahim Sqeiq, *Gaza: al-Tarikh* (n. p., 1976), p. 116.

7. Ibid., p. 117.

8. Interview with Mr Mohammad al-Radwan a.k.a. Abu Zaki, Gaza city, 13 November 1989.

9. Interview with Dr Haider Abdel Shaffi, Gaza city, 14 November 1989.

10. See: J. Hilal, 'West Bank and Gaza Strip Social Formation Under Jordanian and Egyptian Rule (1948–1967)', *Review of Middle East Studies* 5 (1992), pp. 33–74 or Z. Abu Amr, 'The Gaza Economy: 1948–1967', in G. Abed, *The Palestine Economy* (London & New York, 1988), p. 101.

11. See: J. Baster, 'Economic Aspects of the Settlement of the Palestine Refugees', *Middle East Journal* 18/1 (1954), pp. 54–68.

12. Dumper: *Forty Years without Slumbering*, pp. 174–90.

13. Alan Hart, *Arafat: Terrorist or Peacemaker?* (London, 1984), p. 33–4.

14. Interview with Mr Mohammad Habash, Nussierat camp, Gaza, 5 September 1993.

15. Ibid.

16. Interview with Mr Mohammad al-Radwan Gaza city, 10 November 1989.

17. Interview with Abu Mohammad, Nussierat camp, Gaza, 5 September 1993.

18. Ibid.

19. Interview with Mr Mohammad Habash, Nussierat camp, Gaza, 5 September 1993.

20. Interview with Abu Mohammad, Nussierat camp, Gaza, 5 September 1993.

21. Mitchell: *The Society of Muslim Brothers*, p. 107.

22. *Middle Eastern Affairs*, (March 1954), pp. 94–100.

23. Mitchell: *The Society of Muslim Brothers*, p. 141.

24. R. Stephens, *Nasser* (London, 1971), p. 136.

25. Zvi Kaplinsky, 'The Muslim Brotherhood', *Middle Eastern Affairs*, (December 1954), pp. 377–85.

26. Interview with Mr Assad Saftawi, Gaza city, 20 December 1989.

27. A. Idwan, *Shaykh Ahmad Yassin, Hayatah wa Jihad* (Gaza, n. d.), p. 21.

28. 'Watchful Atmosphere', *The London Times*, 2 August 1955.

29. Ibid.

30. M. Basisou, *Descent Into Water* (Illinois, 1980), p. 36.

31. Ibid, p. 15.

32. Interview with Mr Mohammad al-Radwan a. k. a. Abu Zaki, Gaza city, 30 October 1989.

33. 'Trouble in the Gaza Strip', *Middle East Journal*, no. 9 (Spring 1955), p. 66.

34. *Jerusalem Post*, 3 March 1955, p. 1.

35. Basisou: *Descent Into Water*, p. 16.

36. P. Cossali and C. Robson, *Stateless in Gaza* (London, 1986), p. 14.

37. Interview with Mr Mohammad Radwan a. k. a. Abu Zaki, Gaza city, 30 October 1989.

38. BBC, *SWB Middle East MS* no. 79, 2 November 1956.

39. Arlette Tessier, *Gaza* (Beirut, 1971), p. 26.

40. Interview with Dr Rabbah Muhanna, Gaza city, 28 November 1989.

41. Interview with Dr Haider Abdel Shaffi, Gaza city, 14 November 1989.

42. Cossali and Robson: *Stateless in Gaza*, p. 18.

43. Interview with Dr Haider Abdel Shaffi, Gaza city, 14 November 1989.

44. Interview with Dr Mahmoud Zahar, Gaza city, 29 November 1989.

45. Mustafa Hala, 'The Islamic Tendency in the Occupied Territories', *al-Mustaqbal al-Arabi*, 113 (July 1988), p. 80.

46. Idwan: *Sheikh Yassin*, p. 36.

47. See: Michael Dumper, 'Muslim Institutions and the Israeli State, Muslim Religious Endowments (Waqf) in Israel and the Occupied Territories, 1948–1987', Ph.D. University of Exeter, Devon, 1991.

48. See: Avi Schlaim, 'The All Palestine Government', *Journal of Palestine Studies*, vol. 21 no. 4 (Summer 1991), pp. 37–53.

49. P. A. Smith, *Palestine and the Palestinians 1876–1983* (London, 1987), p. 189.

50. Ibid. p. 188.

51. A. Abidi, *Jordan: A Political Study 1948–1957* (London, 1965), p. 195.

52. Ibid., p. 197.

53. Amnon Cohen, *Political Parties in the West Bank Under the Jordanian Regime 1949–1967* (London, 1982), p. 149.

54. Interview with Dr Yousef al-Athm, Amman, 20 June 1989. A former head of the movement, Dr al-Athm noted that the brotherhood organised marches, strikes and demonstrations against British influence in the country and region more generally.

55. See: Kamal Salibi, *The Modern History of Jordan* (London, 1993).

56. Interview with Mr Subhi Anabtawi, Nablus, 12 August 1989.

57. For example, in 1953 the Muslim Brotherhood published a small pamphlet entitled 'The Muslim Brotherhood and the Palestine Problem'.

58. Interview with Sheikh Said, Nablus, 12 August 1989.

59. The Jordanian intelligence files were seized by the Israelis during the 1967 war and are now held by the Israel State Archives, Talpiot, West Jerusalem. The files, however, have been closed and are not open for inspection. The only source on these files is Cohen: *Political Parties in the West Bank*, p. 149.

60. Abidi: *Jordan: A Political Study*, p. 197.

61. Y. Oron (ed.), *Middle East Record* (Tel Aviv, 1960), p. 321.

62. Interview with Abu Islam, Nablus, 12 August 1989.

63. Interview with Mr Subhi Anabtawi, Nablus, 12 August 1989.

64. Ibid.

65. See: Suha Taji-Farouqi, *The Islamic Liberation Party*, Ph.D. Exeter University, Devon, 1993 and D. Commins, 'Taqi ad-Din al-Nabahani', *Muslim World*, vol. 81 nos. 3–4 (1991), pp. 195–211.

66. Cohen: *Political Parties in the West Bank*, p. 209.

67. Interview with Abu Ali, Bourqa village, 18 August 1993.

68. Ibid.

69. Cohen: *Political Parties in the West Bank*, p. 213.

70. n. a. *The Road to Victory*, pamphlet attributed to the Liberation Party. n. d.

71. Taqi ad-Din an-Nabahani, *Nizam al-Islam* (Jerusalem, 1953), pp. 1–66.

72. *al-Jihad* newspaper, 2 August; '9 October 1960 in Oron', *Middle East*, p. 320.

73. *The Road to Victory*, p. 26.

74. Cohen: *Political Parties in the West Bank*, p. 209.

75. Ibid., p. 229.

76. D. Dishon (ed.), *Middle East Record*, (Tel Aviv, 1967), p. 408.

Chapter Three

1. John Esposito, *Islam and Politics* (Syracuse, 1984), p. 154.

2. Gilles Kepel, *The Revenge of God, The Resurgence of Islam, Christianity and Judaism in the Modern World* (Cambridge, 1994), p. 21.

3. Fouad Ajami, *The Arab Predicament* (Cambridge, 1992), p. 47.

4. John J. Donohue, 'Islam and the Search for Identity in the Arab World', in J. Esposito (ed.), *Voices of Resurgent Islam* (New York, 1983), p. 48.

5. Interview with Dr Mahmoud Zahar, Gaza city, 29 November 1989.

6. See: E. Sivan, *Radical Islam – Medieval Theology and Modern Politics* (Yale, 1985), pp. 16–21.

7. P. Cossali and C. Robson: *Stateless in Gaza* (London, 1986), p. 22.

8. Interview with Mr Bashir Barghouti, Ramallah, 14 October 1989.

9. A. Gresh and D. Vidal, *A-Z of the Middle East* (London, 1990), p. 208.

10. *Al Ahram*, 6 June 1967, p. 1–3.

11. D. Holden, and R. Johns, *The House of Saud* (London, 1982), p. 252.

12. Ibid., p. 253.

13. This summit did not take place until 1969 and was held after Muslim outrage at an arson attack of the al-Aqsa mosque earlier that year.

14. See: M. Heller, 'Political and Social Change in the West Bank since 1967', in J. Migdal (ed.), *Palestinian Society* (Princeton, 1980), pp. 185–211; or S. Tamari, 'The Palestinians in the West Bank and Gaza, the Sociology of Dependency', in K. Nakleh and E. Zureik (eds), *The Sociology of the Palestinians* (London, 1980), pp. 84–111.

15. Interview with Mr Assad Saftawi, Gaza city, 20 December 1989.

16. Interview with Dr Ali Sharabat, Hebron, 18 October 1989.

17. Ibrahim Dakkak, 'Back to Square One: A Study in the Re-emergence of Palestinian Identity in the West Bank', in Alexander Scholch (ed.), *Palestinians Over the Green Line: Studies on the Relations Between Palestinians on Both Sides of the 1949 Armistice Line since 1967* (London, 1983), p. 70.

18. Dakkak: 'Back to Square One', p. 79.

19. J. Metzger, M. Orth, C. Sterzing, *This Land is Our Land, The West Bank Under Israeli Occupation* (London, 1983), p. 141.

20. For a full list of Sheikh's activities in this period see: n. a., *The Resistance of the Western Bank of Jordan to Israeli Occupation* (Beirut, 1967), pp. 73–4.

21. M. Dumper, *Islam and Israel: Muslim Religious Endowments and the Jewish State* (Washington, 1995), p. 272.

22. J. Metzger, M. Orth and C. Sterzing: *This Land is Our Land*, pp. 82–113.

23. Nissim Rejwan, 'The Checkered Career of Ghassan Hamzawi', *Midstream*, February 1969, p. 11.

24. Interview with Dr Ziad Abu Ghanameh, Senior Officer in the Muslim Brotherhood, Amman, 27 June 1989.

25. Interview with Sheikh Said, Nablus, 12 August 1989.

26. Interview with Sheikh Ibrahim, Hebron, 25 August 1989.

27. Interview with Sheikh Said, Nablus, 12 August 1989.

28. Ibid.

29. Interview with Sheikh Ibrahim, Hebron, 25 August 1989.

30. Interview with Dr Ali Sharabat, Hebron, 18 October 1989.

31. Interview with Mr Khalid Mohammad Suleiman Amayreh, Hebron, 7 August 1989.

32. Interview with Mr Ziad Abu Ghanameh, Amman, 27 June 1989.

33. Interview with Mr Subhi Anabtawi, Nablus, 14 August 1989.

34. Interview with Abu Othman, PFLP leader, Khan Yunis camp, Gaza Strip, 14 November 1989.

35. Interview with Mr Assad Saftawi, Gaza city, 20 December 1989.

36. Interview with Dr Mahmoud Zahar, Gaza city, 1 December 1989.

37. Interview with Mr Assad Saftawi, Gaza city, 20 December 1989.

38. Interview with Sheikh Abdel Hakim, Gaza city, 24 December 1989.

39. Interview with Mr Assad Saftawi, Gaza city, 20 December 1989.

40. Emile Sayliyeh, *In Search of Leadership: West Bank Politics Since 1967* (Washington, 1988), p. 137.

41. Ann Mosely-Lesch, *The Gaza Strip: Heading Towards a Dead End* (Washington, 1984), p. 6.

42. The Islamic Conference held in October 1968 in Amman, at which the Islamic leaders of over thirty countries were present, announced that Palestinians killed in the fight against Israel would be accorded the rights of martyrs killed in jihad.

43. A. Schleifer, 'The Emergence of Fatah', in *The Arab World*, May 1969, p. 20.

44. Interview with Abu Othman, Khan Yunis camp, 14 November 1989.

45. Interview with Dr Mahmoud Zahar, Gaza city, 1 December 1989.

46. Interview with Dr Haider Abdel Shaffi, Gaza city, 14 November 1989.

47. Notes from the following newspaper reports: *The Guardian*, 16 July and 18 August 1971, *The Observer*, 1 August 1971, and *The London Times*, 3 September 1971.

48. Interview with Dr Haider Abdel Shaffi, Gaza city, 14 November 1989.

49. Interview with Dr Majd Yassin, Belfast, 12 November 1993.

50. For accounts of Sheikh Yassin's activities during this period see: A. Idwan, *Al-Shaykh Ahmad Yassin, Hayatah wa Jihad* (Gaza, n. d.), pp. 6–20.

51. On the principles of *tabligh wa da'wa* see: M. W. Khan, *Tabligh Movement* (New Delhi, 1986).

52. Idwan: *al-Shaykh Yassin, Hayatah wa Jihad*, pp. 40–3.

53. Interview with Dr Mahmoud Zahar, Gaza city, 30 November 1989.

54. Idwan: *Al-Shaykh Yassin, Hayatah wa Jihad*, p. 40.

55. Press Release, *International Committee for the Defence of Sheikh Yassin*, 1990.

56. Kepel: *The Revenge of God*, p. 24.

Chapter Four

1. Interview with Dr Haider Abdel Shaffi, Gaza city, 14 November 1989.

2. Ibid.

3. Mr Assad Saftawi was assassinated on 21 October 1993. Although he had long-standing links with the Islamic movement he had become a senior Fatah figure in the Gaza Strip. His assailants remain unknown.

4. S. Cohen, 'Khomeinism in Gaza', *New Outlook*, March 1980, p. 7.

5. Interview with Mr Abdel Karim, Khan Yunis, 15 November 1989.

6. Cohen: 'Khomeinism in Gaza', p. 6.

7. Statement issued by the Red Crescent Society, Gaza Strip, January 1980.

8. Cohen: 'Khomeinism in Gaza', p. 8.

9. Interview with Dr Haider Abdel Shaffi, Gaza city, 14 November 1989.

10. Interview with Dr Mohammad Nairab, Gaza city, 10 October 1989.

11. *al-Fajr*, 16–22 August 1981, p. 9.

12. *al-Fajr*, 'Islamic Bloc Enlist Thugs to Break Employee Strike at Islamic University', 3 June 1983, p. 3.

13. 'Muslim Fanatics Attack Bir Zeit and Gaza University', *al-Fajr*, 10 June 1983, and interview with Dr Rabbah Muhanna, Gaza city, 20 November 1989.

14. Similar reactions to the teaching of Darwin's Theory of Evolution were recorded among Islamists at Bir Zeit University. See: W. Claiborne, 'Brotherhood Blooms on the West Bank', *Washington Post*, 15 March 1982.

15. Interview with Dr Rabbah Muhanna, Gaza city, 20 November 1989.

16. 'Anti-nationalist Cell Sentenced in Gaza', *al-Fajr*, 14 December 1984, and 'Gazans Charged with Planning Holy War', *The Jerusalem Post*, 23 October 1984.

17. Interview with Dr Rabbah Muhanna, Gaza city, 20 November 1989.

18. Ian Black, 'Israelis Alarmed as Islamic Fundamentalism Tightens its Hold on Occupied Gaza Strip', *The Guardian*, 26 October 1987.

19. M. Sella, 'Islamic Terrorism in the Gaza Strip', *Koteret Rashit*, 21 October 1987.

20. Leaflet published in the name of The Islamic Jihad movement in Occupied Palestine, 8 March 1988, p. 2.

21. Interview with Dr Mohammad Nairab, Gaza city, 16 October 1989.

22. Leaflet published in the name of The Islamic Jihad movement in Occupied Palestine, 8 March 1988, p. 2.

23. Interview with Sheikh Abd al-Aziz Auda, 'The Wound in Palestine is a Wound to the Heart', *al-Fajr*, 23 August 1987.

24. Interview with Ismaen Fagawi, Khan Yunis camp, 19 October 1989.

25. Among the known associates at this stage were: Ahmad Muhanna, Ramadan Shallah, and Faiz al-Aswad a. k. a. al-Aswar. Following the assassination of Shiqaqi in Malta in November 1995 Ramadan Shallah was appointed head of the Islamic Jihad movement based in Damascus.

26. Interview with Ismaen Fagawi, Khan Yunis camp, 19 October 1989.

27. Interview with Dr Mohammad Nairab, Gaza city, 16 October 1989.

28. This figure is based on Israeli arrests in 1986 and 1987 when the group was most active. The author is also grateful to Ramadan Shallah for his assistance and guidance on this section.

29. Ziad Abu Amr, *al-Harakat al-Islamia fi Gaza wa Difa Gharbiyeh* (Acre, 1988), p. 42.

30. Abu Amr: *al-Harakat al-Islamia*, p. 42.

31. Interview with Mr Fadeel Yunis, Amman, 20 June 1989.

32. Interview with Dr Ramadan Shallah, London, 15 November 1990.

33. See: Bradley Burston, 'Gaza Tense as Terrorist Trial Opens', *The Jerusalem Post*, 13 May 1987, p. 2.

34. M. Sella, 'Islamic Terrorism in the Gaza Strip', *Koteret Rashit*, 21 October 1987.

35. Ze'ev Schiff and Ehud Ya'ari, *Intifada, The Palestinian Uprising – Israel's Third Front* (New York, 1989), pp. 72–4.

36. Schiff and Ya'ari: *Intifada, The Palestinian Uprising*, p. 225.

37. Ziad Abu Amr, 'Hamas: A Historical and Political Background', *Journal of Palestine Studies*, vol. 22 no. 4, (Summer 1993), pp. 5–20.

38. n. a., 'Gazans Charged with Planning Holy War', *The Jerusalem Post*, 23 October 1987.

39. Interview with Dr Yousef al-Athm, Amman, 20 June 1989.

40. Interview with Dr Mohammad Nairab, Gaza city, 16 June 1989.

41. Interview with Dr Mohammad Saqr, Amman, 27 June 1989.

42. D. Shipler, 'Clashing Loyalties Heighten Gaza Tensions', *International Herald Tribune*, 1 April 1981.

43. M. Sella, 'Islamic Terrorism in the Gaza Strip', *Koteret Rashit*, 21 October 1987.

44. M. Sella, 'Resistance is a Moslem Duty', *The Jerusalem Post*, 25 May 1989, p. 5.

45. Salim Tamari, 'The Transformation of Palestinian Society: Fragmentation and Occupation', in M. Heiberg and G. Ovensen (eds), *Palestinian Society in Gaza, West Bank and Arab Jerusalem: A Survey of Living Conditions* (Oslo, 1993), p. 25.

46. L. Taraki, 'The Development of Political Consciousness Among Palestinians in the Occupied Territories 1967–1987', in J. Nassar and R. Heacock (eds), *Intifada: Palestine at the Crossroads* (New York, 1991), p. 66.

47. Claiborne: 'Brotherhood Blooms', p. 12.

48. Interview with Mr Sadiq Anabtawi, Nablus, 2 September 1989.

49. Iyyad Barghouti, 'Religion and Politics Among the Students of Najah National University', *Middle Eastern Studies*, vol. 27, no. 2, (April 1991), p. 207.

50. Interview with Dr Jihad, Nablus, 13 March 1990.

51. D. Richardson, 'Flourishing Fundamentalism', *The Jerusalem Post*, 20 January 1982.

52. In February 1984, clashes between student supporters of the Muslim

Brotherhood and the Communists flared again. See: *International Herald Tribune*, 21 February 1984.

53. Interview with Dr Abu Dajani, Nablus, 14 March 1990.

54. Source: Student Council Records, Najah University, Nablus.

55. Interview with Student Council Member, Nablus, 15 March 1990.

56. Interview with Dr Salim and Dr Abu Dajani, Nablus, 13 March 1990.

57. Interview with Mr Marwan Barghouti, Amman, 17 June 1989.

58. Munir Fasheh, 'Political Islam in the West Bank', *Middle East Report*, no. 103, 1988, pp. 5–13.

59. 'Islamic Rioters Exonerated by Supreme Islamic Council Enquiry', *Al-Fajr*, 28 October 1983, p. 4.

60. Interview with Mr Bashir Barghouti, Ramallah, 26 March 1990.

61. R. Rosenberg, 'Police Hold 43 after al-Aqsa Riot', *The Jerusalem Post*, 10 July 1983.

62. Rekhess: 'Islamic Fundamentalism', p. 2.

63. S. Nour, 'Jihad Alternative for Palestine', *Arabia*, December 1986, p. 5.

64. Y. Gazit, 'Three Held for Dung Gate Attack', *The Jerusalem Post*, 20 October 1986.

65. S. Ghazali, 'Interview with Sheikh Abd al-Aziz Auda', *Islam and Palestine*, vol. 2, no. 14, (May 1989), p. 16.

66. J. McManus, 'Islam Drives Old Enemies Together', *The Guardian*, 17 March 1982, p. 7.

67. McManus: 'Islam Drives Old Enemies Together', p. 7.

68. n. a., 'Terror Cell Smashed, 7 Fanatics Held', *The Jerusalem Post*, 13 February 1981.

Chapter Five

1. See: Palestine Human Rights Centre (PHRIC), 'Database on Palestinian Human Rights', 5 & 21 September and 31 October 1988.

2. PHRIC: notes, 'The main mosque in Breijj camp has now been closed for over three months.' 12 March 1988. Also, n. a. 'Soldiers Use Koran as Toilet Paper', *Israeli Mirror*, 29 May 1989.

3. The small committees were organised around factional interests as well as medical and health issues. They addressed urgent issues like first-aid for the injured and provision of food supplies to areas under Israeli imposed curfew.

4. Ze'ev Schiff and Ehud Ya'ari, *Intifada, The Palestinian Uprising – Israel's Third Front* (New York, 1989), p. 220.

5. *The Covenant of the Islamic Resistance Movement (Hamas)*, (Jerusalem, 1988), Article 1.

6. Interview with Abu Othman, Khan Yunis camp, 14 November 1989.

7. Hamas leaflet, 'In Memory of the Massacres of Qibyah and Qufr Qassam', 5 October 1988.

8. Nationalists often used mosques for organising activities and recruiting.

9. For more on Hamas' fund-raising and alleged activities abroad see: S. Emerson, 'The Other Fundamentalists', *The New Republic*, 12 June 1995, pp. 21–9 and K. Abu Toameh, 'In the Money', *Jerusalem Report*, 23 May 1991, p. 36.

10. Consult Chapter One for details of Sheikh Izz ad-Din al-Qassam's impact on Islamic politics in Palestine.

11. Israel Government Press Office, 'IDF announces #21 Press Bulletin', 22 December 1989.

12. Following the expulsion of over 400 Hamas supporters in December 1992 the Israeli authorities admitted that they were still unable to capture the members of Hamas armed cells.

13. Hamas leaflet, 'In Memory of the Massacres of Qibyah and Qufr Qassam', 5 October 1988.

14. 'News Reports', *Crescent International*, September 1988, pp. 5–6.

15. See: UNLU leaflets, 'Appeal for the Martyrs of Massacres', 6 September 1988 and 'Appeal on the Feast of Independence', 20 November 1988.

16. Estimated that support for Hamas at this time was around 30–40 per cent.

17. Until the passing of new legislation in January 1993 meetings between the PLO and Israelis were prohibited by law.

18. For example, Dr Zahar attended a meeting at the Israeli Ministry of Defence in May 1989 just two weeks before the Sasportas–Sa'don kidnapping.

19. Interview with Mr Bashir Barghouti, Ramallah, 26 March 1990.

20. See: O. Nir & D. Sagir, 'Background on Hamas Arrests', *Ha'aretz*, 10 May 1989, p. 2.

21. 'Hamas Activists Arrested by IDF' *Middle East Mirror*, 22 May 1989, p. 18.

22. 'Marxists and Moslem Fundamentalists in Areas Join in Move Against Fatah', *Jerusalem Post*, 2 April 1990, p. 1.

23. J. F. Legrain, 'A Defining Moment: Palestinian Islamic Fundamentalism', in J. Piscatori (ed.), *Islamic Fundamentalism and the Gulf Crisis* (Chicago, 1991), p. 81.

24. Hamas Leaflet, 'The Appeal of the al-Aqsa Massacre', 9 October 1990.

25. n. a. 'Videotape Transcript – Killing Collaborators: A Hamas How-To', *Harpers Magazine*, May 1993, pp. 10–13.

26. Hamas leaflet, 'Toledano Kidnap', 12 December 1992.

27. Yitzhak Rabin, 'Speech to the Knesset', *Israel Government Press Office*, 21 December 1992.

28. Rabin: 'Speech to the Knesset', p. 3.

29. See: D. Kuttab, 'The Cycle of Violence', *Middle East International*, 19 March 1993, p. 5.

30. For more on the Oslo process see: J. Corbin, *Gaza First–The Secret Norway Channel to Peace Between Israel and the PLO* (London, 1994).

31. See: Hamas leaflets, 'Negotiations – Like It or Not', 1 July 1993 and 'Congratulations to You Dark-Eyed Beauties of Paradise for the Martyrs of Islam and Muslims', 3 July 1993.

32. See: 'Hamas Rejects Accord', *al-Quds*, 2 September 1993.

33. 'Hamas is Planning to Inherit the PLO', *al-Wasat*, 5 October 1993, pp. 3–4.

34. Islamic Jihad leaflet, 'The Oslo Treason', November 1993.

35. See: JMCC, 'Opinion Poll', 23 September 1993.

36. 'Letters from Sheikh Yassin', *al-Wasat*, 6 November 1993.

37. G. Usher, Peace in Autonomy – An Interview with Bassam Jarrar', *Middle East Report*, July–August 1994, pp. 28–9.

38. Interview with Dr Mahmoud Zahar, Gaza city, 29 May 1995.

39. M. Hindi, 'The Islamists and Oslo', *al-Quds*, 11 July 1994, p. 2.

40. 'Arafat's Speech', *Palestine Report*, 4 July 1994, p. 3.

41. Lecture by Dr Khader Sawandek, Birzeit University, 3 September 1993.

42. Hamas leaflet, 'The Settlers Will Pay', February 1994.

43. Reuters News Report, 'Palestinian Suicide Bomber', *Palestine-Net*, 14 April 1994. and Associated Press Report, 'Suicide Bombing Funeral', *Palestine-Net*, 16 April 1994.

44. Hamas leaflet, 'Rabin's Attempt to Cover Up His Failing Criminal Policies', 16 April 1994.

45. Hamas leaflet, 'Rabin's Attempt to Cover Up His Failing Criminal Policies', 16 April 1994.

46. See: *Palestine Report*, 23 October 1994, p. 1.

47. For further debate about the suicide bombing strategy see: B. Milton-Edwards, 'Factors Behind the Hamas Bombings', *Middle East International*, August 1995, pp. 18–19.

48. *FBIS-NES-94-152*, 8 August 1994, p. 15.

49. *FBIS-NES-94-132*, 'Hamas' Nazzal Comments' 11 July 1994, p. 18.

50. See: *al-Sharq al-Awsat*, 16 August 1994, p. 4.

51. *FBIS-NES-94-130*, 7 July 1994, p. 21.

52. *FBIS-NES-94-177*, 13 September, p. 9.

53. For more on the events surrounding the events of November 18, 1994 known as 'Black Friday' see: E. Silver and K. Abu Toameh, 'An Iron Fist Against Hamas', *The Jerusalem Report*, December 15, 1994, pp. 26–8.

54. See: M. Dumper, 'Forty Years Without Slumbering: Waqf Politics and Administration in the Gaza Strip, 1948–1987', *British Journal Middle Eastern Studies*, vol. 20 no. 2 (1992) pp. 174–190.

Chapter Six

1. It is argued that Islamic Jihad has been influenced ideologically by aspects of Shi'i thinking.

2. *The Covenant of the Islamic Resistance Movement – Hamas* (Jerusalem, 1988), Article 1.

3. *The Covenant*: Article 6.

4. Interview with Bassam Jarrar, al-Bireh, 22 May 1995.

5. See: Rema Hammami, 'Women, the Hijab and the Intifada', *MERIP*, May–August 1990, pp. 24–7.

6. *The Covenant*: Article 9.

7. Interview with Mahmoud Zahar, Gaza city, 29 May 1995.

8. See for example, Hamas Leaflet, 'The Massacres Committed by the Nazi Jews – Continuing Down the Road of Deir Yassin', 7 April 1988.

9. R. Nettler, *Past Trials and Present Tribulations: A Muslim Fundamentalists View of the Jews* (Oxford, 1987), p. 72.

10. *The Koran*, [Translated with an Introduction by A. J. Arberry], (Oxford, 1982) 7:75.

11. See Hamas leaflet, 'The Anniversary of Khaybar' in which the example of the battle of Khaybar, where the Prophet defeated the Jews, is used as an example to encourage Palestinians with the uprising. Hamas issues the order that the day of the anniversary of Khaybar should be 'a day of defiance and resistance ... We must redouble our efforts against the Jews ...', 5 September 1988.

12. Interview with Bassam Jarrar, al-Bireh, 22 May 1995.

13. *The Covenant*: Preface.

14. *The Covenant*: Article 7.

15. Nettler: *Past Trials and Present Tribulations*, p. 21; see also: *The Jewish Peril–Protocols of the Elders of Zion*, (London, 1920).

16. *The Covenant*: Article 22.

17. *The Jewish Peril–Protocols*, p. 15.

18. *The Covenant*: Article 22.

19. *The Jewish Peril–Protocols*, p. iii.

20. *The Jewish Peril –Protocols*, pp. 50–3.

21. *The Jewish Peril –Protocols*, pp. 41–8.

22. *Charter of the Palestine Liberation Organisation* (London, n. d.), Articles 22 & 15.

23. *Charter of the PLO*: Article 22.

24. Jihad is meant both as spiritual and physical striving as well as holy struggle. See: R. Peters, *Islam and Colonialism: The Doctrine of Jihad in Modern History* (The Hague, 1979).

25. *The Covenant*: Article 12.

26. For further debate, see: B. Milton-Edwards, 'The Concept of Jihad and the Palestinian Islamic Movement: A Comparison of Ideas and Techniques', *British Journal of Middle Eastern Studies*, vol. 19 no. 1, (1992), pp. 48–54, and Ibrahim Malik, 'Jihad – Its Development and Relevance', *Palestine and Israel Journal* 2, (Spring 1994), pp. 26–35.

27. Interview with Bassam Jarrar, al-Bireh, 22 May 1995.

28. Interview with Dr Mahmoud Zahar, Gaza city, 29 May 1995.

29. *The Koran*: 4:75.

30. *The Koran*: 55:65.

31. *The Covenant*: Article 13.

32. *The Covenant*: Article 11.

33. *The Covenant*: Article 12.

34. 'No Peace Without Securing Palestinian Rights', *Al-Fajr*, 3 August 1992.

35. 'Only Truce, No Permanent Peace', *The Jerusalem Post*, 29 November 1991.

36. Sayyid Qutb, *Milestones* (Beirut, 1978), p. 130.

37. Qutb: *Milestones*, p. 128.

38. *The Covenant*: Article 1.

39. *The Covenant*: Article 27.

40. Ernest Gellner, *Nations and Nationalisms* (Oxford, 1983), p. 1.

41. E. J. Hobsbawm, *Nations and Nationalism since 1780 Programme, Myth, Reality* (Cambridge, 1990), p. 11.

42. *The Covenant*: Article 27.

43. *The Covenant*: Articles 9 and 13.

44. Interview with Dr Mahmoud Zahar, Gaza city, 1 September 1992.

45. Interview with Sheikh Abu Jibna, Hebron, 25 August 1989.

46. Interview with Sheikh Abu Jibna, Hebron, 25 August 1989.

47. Hamas Leaflet No 28, 1 September 1988.

48. Hamas Leaflet No 28, 1 September 1988.

49. Qutb: *Milestones*, p. 236.

50. See: Hakan Yavuz, 'Nationalism and Islam: Yusuf Akura and Uc Tarz-i Siyaset', *Journal of Islamic Studies*, vol. 4 no. 2, 1993, pp. 175–207 for an example of other cases.

51. Qutb: *Milestones*, p. 75.

52. Shaul Mishal, 'Paper War – Words Behind Stones: The Intifada Leaflets', *The Jerusalem Quarterly* no. 51, 1989, p. 27.

53. *BBC SWB Middle East*, 'Islamic Jihad Organisation Statement', 8 May 1989.

54. Ziad Abu Amr, *al-Harakat al-Islami fi Gaza wa Difa Gharbiyeh* (Acre, 1988), p. 27.

55. Elie Rekhess, 'Iranian Impact on the Islamic Jihad Movement in the Gaza Strip', (Tel Aviv, 1988).

56. *Islam wa Falastin*, vol. 1 no. 9 (November 1988), pp. 2–4.

57. *The Koran*: 29:69.

58. Islamic Jihad leaflet, 'Anniversary of Isra and Miraj', 8 March 1988.

59. 'Speech by Shqaqi', *Islam wa Falastin*, vol. 1 no. 8 (October 1988) pp. 2–4.

60. 'Special Report on Palestine', *Arabia*, July 1986, p. 21.

61. See: Z. Abu Amr, *Islamic Fundamentalism in the West Bank and Gaza Strip* (Indiana, 1994), J. F. Legrain, 'Islamistes et lutte nationale Palestinienne dans

les territoires occupes par Israel', *Revue Française de Science Politique*, vol. 26 no. 6 (April 1986) and H. Mustafa, 'al-Jihad al-Islami fi al-Ard al-Muhtalla', *Qadaya Fiqruyya*, no. 6, (April 1987).

62. S. Qutb: *Milestones*, p. 236.

63. N. Ayubi, *Political Islam – Religion and Politics in the Arab World* (London, 1991), p. 141.

64. S. Qutb: *Milestones*, pp. 32–4.

65. S. Qutb, *The Religion of Islam* (Kuwait, 1988), pp. 8–9, and pp. 32–4.

66. Y. Haddad, 'Sayyid Qutb: Ideologue of Islamic Revival' in J. Esposito (ed.), *Voices of Resurgent Islam* (New York, 1983), p. 82.

67. *FBIS-NES-94-177*, 13 September 1994, p. 9.

68. Interview with Sheikh Abdullah al-Shammi, *al-Hayat*, 13 August 1994, p. 5.

69. Islamic Jihad Leaflet, 12 October 1989.

70. S. Ghazali, 'Interview with Sheikh Abd al-Aziz Auda', *Crescent International*, 16 October 1987, p. 6.

71. S. Qutb: *Milestones*, p. 220.

72. Ayubi: *Political Islam*, p. 145.

73. Z. Abu Amr, *Islamic Fundamentalism in the West Bank and Gaza Strip* (Indiana, 1994), p. 98.

74. *The Koran*: 2:190 & 16:75.

75. S. Ghazali: 'Interview with Sheikh Abd al-Aziz Auda', p. 6.

76. Islamic Jihad Brigade Leaflet, 'A Call to Jihad', 29 January 1988.

77. Islamic Jihad Leaflet, 'Why We Won't Join the United Leadership', October 1988.

78. Sheikh Taqi ad-Din an-Nabahani is the only Palestinian Islamist to consistently address economic issues in his many publications.

Epilogue

1. Interview with Mr Ahmad Saati, Gaza city, 22 September 1994.

2. W. Quandt, 'The Urge for Democracy', *Foreign Affairs*, (Summer 1994), pp. 2–7.

Select Bibliography

Primary Sources

Formal Interviews (alphabetical order)

Mr Abdel Karim, Khan Yunis, 15 November 1989.

Abu Ali, Bourqa village West Bank, 18 August 1993.

Dr Abu Dajani, Nablus, 14 March 1990.

Dr Ziad Abu Ghanameh, Amman, 27 June 1989.

Abu Islam, Nablus, 12 August 1989.

Abu Mohammad, Nussierat camp, Gaza, 5 September 1993.

Abu Othman, PFLP leader, Khan Yunis camp, Gaza Strip, 14 November 1989.

Mr Khalid Mohammad Suleiman Amayreh, Hebron, 7 August 1989. Mr Sadiq Anabtawi, Nablus, 2 September 1989.

Mr Subhi Anabtawi, Nablus, 12 August 1989.

Dr Yusuf al-Athm, Amman, 20 June 1989.

Mr Bashir Barghouti, Ramallah, 14 October 1989.

Mr Marwan Barghouti, Amman, 17 June 1989.

Ismaen Fagawi, Khan Yunis, 19 October 1989.

Mr Mohammad Habash, Nussierat camp, Gaza, 5 September 1993.

Mr Bassam al-Jamal, London, 10 January 1989.

Mr Bassam Jarrar, al-Bireh, 22 May 1995.

Dr Jihad, Nablus, 13 March 1990.

Dr Rabbah Muhanna, Gaza city, 28 November 1989.

Dr Mohammad Nairab, Gaza city, 10 October 1989.

Mr Mohammad al-Radwan a.k.a. Abu Zaki, Gaza city, 13 November 1989.

Mr Assad Saftawi, Gaza city, 20 December 1989.

Dr Mohammad Saqr, Amman, 27 June 1989.

Dr Ahmad Sa'ti, Gaza city, 14 September 1994.

Dr Haider Abdel Shaffi, Gaza city, 14 November 1989.

Dr Ramadan Shallah, London, 15 April 1991.

Dr Ali Sharabat, Hebron, 18 October 1989.

Sheikh Abdel Hakim, Gaza city, 24 December 1989.

Sheikh Abu Jibna, Hebron, 25 August 1989.

Sheikh Ibrahimi, Hebron, 25 August 1989.

Sheikh Said, Nablus, 12 August 1989.

Dr Majd Yassin, Belfast, 12 November 1993.

Mr Fadeel Yunis, Amman, 20 June 1989.

Dr Mahmoud Zahar, Gaza city, 29 November and 1 December 1989, 1 September 1992 and 29 May 1995.

Leaflets, Documents, Papers

Leaflet published in the name of The Islamic Jihad movement in Occupied Palestine, 8 March 1988.

Hamas leaflet, 'Islamic Resistance – A Call for a General Strike', 11 March 1988.

Hamas Leaflet, 'The Massacres Committed by the Nazi Jews – Continuing Down the Road of Deir Yassin', 7 April 1988.

Hamas leaflet, 'The Anniversary of Khaybar', 5 September 1988.

Hamas leaflet, 'In Memory of the Martyrs of Qibia and Qufr Qassem', 5 October 1988.

Hamas Leaflet, 'The Appeal of the al-Aqsa Massacre', 9 October 1990.

Hamas leaflet, 'Toledano Kidnap', 12 December 1992.

Hamas leaflet, 'Negotiations – Like It or Not', 1 July 1993.

Hamas leaflet, 'Congratulations to You Dark-Eyed Beauties of Paradise for the Martyrs of Islam and Muslims', 3 July 1993.

Hamas leaflet, 'The Settlers Will Pay', February 1994.

Hamas leaflet, 'Rabin's Attempt to Cover Up His Failing Criminal Policies', 16 April 1994.

Hassan Yacoubi, *They Killed You!* (Islamic University of Gaza) [966] 25 November 1935.

Islamic Jihad Brigade Leaflet, 'A Call to Jihad', 29 January 1988.

Islamic Jihad leaflet, 'Anniversary of Isra and Miraj', 8 March 1988.

Islamic Jihad Leaflet, 'Why We Won't Join the United Leadership', October 1988.

Islamic Jihad leaflet, 'The Oslo Treason', November 1993.

UNLU leaflets, 'Appeal for the Martyrs of Massacres', 6 September 1988 and 'Appeal on the Feast of Independence', 20 November 1988.

PRO file CO733/142, Arab Political Activities, June 1927.

PRO file CO733/157/57202, Holy Place in Palestine, 1928.

PRO file CO733/161/57560, Supreme Muslim Council, Petition of Citizens, 1928.

PRO file CO733/163/67013, Wailing Wall, 1929.

PRO file CO733/178/67500, Supreme Muslim Council, Jamal al-Husseini, 1929.

PRO file CO733/204/87153, Situation in Palestine: Arab Unrest and Incitement to Violence, 1931.

PRO file CO733/257/12, Situation in Palestine 1935.
PRO file CO733/278/75156 (2), Political Situation in Palestine, 1935.
PRO file CO 75156/4/35, Report from Sir Arthur Wauchope on situation in Palestine, 1935.
PRO file CO733/257/12, Report from Palestine & file CP (34) Memo by Secretary of State for the Colonies, 1935.
PRO file CO733/278/13, 'Letter from Wauchope', 30 April 1935.
PRO File CO733/398/10, Report no. 14, 15 July 1939.
Tegart Papers, Box 1, File 3c, from report on 'Terrorism 1936–37', p. 7. (MEC, Oxford).
FBIS–NES.
BBC SWB Middle East MS.
The Covenant of the Islamic Resistance Movement (Hamas), (Jerusalem, 1988).
The Jewish Peril – Protocols of the Elders of Zion, (London, 1920).
Charter of the Palestine Liberation Organisation (London, n. d.).

Secondary Sources

Books, Monographs, Edited Works, Pamphlets

Abidi, A., *Jordan: A Political Study 1948–1957* (London, 1965).
Abu Amr, Z., *al-Harakat al-Islamia fi Gaza wa Difa Gharbiyeh* (Acre, 1988).
—— *Islamic Fundamentalism in the West Bank and Gaza Strip* (Indiana, 1994).
Ajami, Fouad, *The Arab Predicament* (Cambridge, 1992).
Ayubi, Nazih, *Political Islam – Religion and Politics in the Arab world.* (London, 1991).
al-Azmeh, Aziz, *Islams and Modernities* (London, 1993).
Basisou, M., *Descent Into Water* (Illinois, 1980).
Cohen, Amnon, *Political Parties in the West Bank Under the Jordanian Regime 1949–1967* (London, 1982).
Corbin, J., *Gaza First–The Secret Norway Channel to Peace Between Israel and the PLO* (London, 1994).
Cossali, P. and C. Robson, *Stateless in Gaza* (London, 1986).
Dessouki, Hilal, *Islamic Resurgence in the Arab World* (New York, 1982).
Dishon, D. (ed.), *Middle East Record*, (Tel Aviv, 1967).
Dumper, M., *Islam and Israel: Muslim Religious Endowments and the Jewish State* (Washington, 1995).
Esposito, John, *Islam and Politics* (Syracus, 1984).
—— *The Islamic Threat: Myth or Reality?* (Oxford, 1992).
Gellner, Ernest, *Nations and Nationalisms* (Oxford, 1983).
Green, D. F., *Arab Theologians on Jews and Israel* (Geneva, 1976).
Gresh, A. and D. Vidal, *A–Z of the Middle East* (London, 1990).
Hart, A., *Arafat: Terrorist or Peacemaker?* (London, 1984).

Hobsbawm, E. J., *Nations and Nationalism since 1780 Programme, Myth, Reality* (Cambridge, 1990).

Holden, D. and R. Johns, *The House of Saud* (London, 1982).

Idwan, A., *Shaykh Ahmad Yassin, Hayatah wa Jihad* (Gaza, n. d.).

Jbara, T., *Palestinian Leader, Haj Amin al-Husayni, Mufti of Jerusalem* (New Jersey, 1985).

Johnson, Nils, *Islam and the Politics of Palestinian Nationalism* (London, 1982).

Kayyali, A. W., *Palestine: A Modern History* (London, 1972).

Kepel, G., *The Revenge of God, The Resurgence of Islam, Christianity and Judaism in the Modern World* (Cambridge, 1994).

Keddie, N., *Sayyid Jamal ad-Din al-Afghani: A Political Biography* (Los Angeles, 1972).

Kerr, M. H., *Islamic Reform: The Political and Legal Theories of Mohammad Abduh and Rashid Rida* (Los Angeles, 1966).

Kupferschmidt, U., *The Supreme Muslim Council: Islam Under the British Mandate for Palestine* (Leiden, 1987).

Metzger, J., M. Orth and C. Sterzing, *This Land is Our Land, The West Bank Under Israeli Occupation* (London, 1983).

Migdal, J., *Palestinian Society and Politics* (Princeton, 1979).

Mitchell, R. P., *The Society of Muslim Brothers* (Oxford, 1969).

Morris, B., *The Birth of the Palestinian Refugee Problem 1947–1949* (Cambridge, 1987).

——*1948 and After, Israel and the Palestinians* (Oxford, 1994).

Mosely-Lesch, Anne *The Gaza Strip: Heading Towards a Dead End* (Washington, 1984).

Qutb, Sayyid, *Milestones* (Beirut, 1978).

—— *The Religion of Islam* (Kuwait, 1988).

an-Nabahani, Taqi ad-Din, *Nizam al-Islam* (Jerusalem, 1953).

Nettler, R., *Past Trials and Present Tribulations: A Muslim Fundamentalist's View of the Jews* (Oxford, 1987).

Oron, Y., (ed.), *Middle East Record* (Tel Aviv, 1960).

Peters, R., *Islam and Colonialism: The Doctrine of Jihad in Modern History* (The Hague, 1979).

Porath, Y., *The Palestinian Arab National Movement 1929–1939: From Riots to Rebellion* (London, 1977).

Salibi, Kamal, *The Modern History of Jordan* (London, 1993).

Sayliyeh, Eimile, *In Search of Leadership: West Bank Politics Since 1967* (Washington, 1988).

Schiff, Ze'ev and Ehud Ya'ari, *Intifada, The Palestinian Uprising – Israel's Third Front* (New York, 1989).

Sivan, E., *Radical Islam – Medieval Theology and Modern Politics* (Yale, 1985).

Smith, P. A., *Palestine and the Palestinians 1876–1983* (London, 1987).

Sqeiq, Ibrahim, *Gaza: al-Tarikh* (n. p., 1976).

Stephens, R., *Nasser* (London, 1971).

Yassin, Subhi, *al-Thawra al-Arabiyya al-Kubra fi Falastin* (Damascus, 1959).

Articles

Abu Amr, Ziad, 'Hamas: A Historical and Political Background', *Journal of Palestine Studies*, vol. 22 no. 4, (Summer 1993), pp. 5–20.

Barghouti, Iyad, 'Religion and Politics Among the Students of Najah National University', *Middle Eastern Studies*, vol. 27, no. 2, (April 1991), pp. 203–17.

Baster, J., 'Economic Aspects of the Settlement of the Palestine Refugees', *Middle East Journal* 18/1 (1954), pp. 54–68.

Busool, A. N., 'Shaykh Mohammad Rashid Rida's Relations with Jamal al-Din al-Afghani and Mohammad Abduh', *The Muslim World* vol. 66 no. 4 (1976), pp. 272–86.

Choueri, Youssef, 'Neo-Orientalism', *Review of Middle East Studies*, 4 (1988), pp. 52–68.

Commins, D., 'Taqi al-Din al-Nabahani', *Muslim World*, vol. 81 no. 3–4 (1991), pp. 195–211.

Dumper, M., 'Forty Years Without Slumbering: Waqf Politics and Administration in the Gaza Strip, 1948–1987', *British Journal of Middle Eastern Studies* 20/3 (1993), pp. 174–90.

Fasheh, Munir, 'Political Islam in the West Bank', *Middle East Report*, no. 103, (1988), pp. 5–13.

Hala, Mustafa, 'The Islamic Tendency in the Occupied Territories', *al-Mustaqbal al-Arabi*, no. 113 (July 1988), p. 80–4.

Hammami, Rema, 'Women, the Hijab and the Intifada', *MERIP*, (May–August 1990), pp. 24–7.

Hilal, J., 'West Bank and Gaza Strip Social Formation Under Jordanian and Egyptian Rule (1948–1967)', *Review of Middle East Studies* 5 (1992), pp. 33–74.

Kaplinsky, Zvi, 'The Muslim Brotherhood', *Middle Eastern Affairs*, (December 1954), pp. 377–85.

Malik, Ibrahim, 'Jihad – Its Development and Relevance', *Palestine and Israel Journal* 2, (Spring 1994), pp. 26–35.

Mattar, P., 'The Mufti of Jerusalem and the Politics of Palestine', *Middle East Journal* 42 (1989), pp. 227–40.

Milton-Edwards, B., 'The Concept of Jihad and the Palestinian Islamic Movement: A Comparison of Ideas and Techniques', *British Journal of Middle Eastern Studies*, vol. 19 no. 1, (1992), pp. 48–53.

Quandt, W., 'The Urge for Democracy', *Foreign Affairs*, (Summer 1994), pp. 2–7.

Schlaim, Avi, 'The All Palestine Government', *Journal of Palestine Studies* vol. 21 no. 4 (Summer 1991), pp. 37–53.

Schleifer, S. A., 'The Life and Thought of Izz ad-din al-Qassam', *Islamic Quarterly*, vol. 23 no. 2 (1979), pp. 60–81.

Seferta, Y., 'The Concept of Religious Authority According to Mohammad Abduh and Rashid Rida', *Islamic Quarterly*, vol. 30 no. 3 (1986), pp. 159–64.

Chapters in Edited Works

Abu Amr, Ziad, 'The Gaza Economy: 1948–1984', in G. Abed, *The Palestine Economy* (London & New York, 1988).

Dakkak, Ibrahim, 'Back to Square One: A Study in the Re-emergence of Palestinian Identity in the West Bank,' in Alexander Scholch (ed.), *Palestinians Over the Green Line: Studies on the Relations Between Palestinians on Both Sides of the 1949 Armistice Line since 1967* (London, 1983).

Donohue, John. J., 'Islam and the Search for Identity in the Arab world', in J. Esposito (ed.), *Voices of Resurgent Islam* (New York, 1983).

Haddad, Y., 'Sayyid Qutb: Ideologue of Islamic Revival' in J. Esposito (ed.) *Voices of Resurgent Islam* (New York, 1983).

Heller, M., 'Political and Social Change in the West Bank since 1967', in J. Migdal (ed.), *Palestinian Society* (Princeton, 1980).

Kalkas, B., 'The Revolt of 1936: A Chronicle of Events', in I. Abu Lughod (ed.), *The Transformation of Palestine* (Evanston, 1970).

Legrain, J. F., 'A Defining Moment: Palestinian Islamic Fundamentalism', in J. Piscatori (ed.), *Islamic Fundamentalism and the Gulf Crisis* (Chicago, 1991).

Mayer, T., 'The Military Force of Islam, The Society of Muslim Brethren and the Palestine Question, 1945–1948', in E. Kedourie and S. Haim (eds), *Zionism and Arabism in Palestine and Israel* (London, 1982).

Stein, K., 'Rural Change and Peasant Destitution: Contributing Causes to the Arab Revolt in Palestine 1936–1939', in F. Kazemi and J. Waterbury (eds), *Peasants and Politics in the Modern Middle East* (Florida, 1991).

Tamari, S., 'The Palestinians in the West Bank and Gaza, the Sociology of Dependency', in K. Nakleh and E. Zureik (eds), *The Sociology of the Palestinians* (London, 1980).

—— 'The Transformation of Palestinian Society: Fragmentation and Occupation', in M. Heiberg and G. Ovensen (eds), *Palestinian Society in Gaza, West Bank and Arab Jerusalem: A Survey of Living Conditions* (Oslo, 1993).

Taraki, L., 'The Development of Political Consciousness Among Palestinians in the Occupied Territories 1967–1987', in J. Nassar and R. Heacock (eds), *Intifada: Palestine at the Crossroads* (New York, 1991).

Newspapers, Magazines (English, Arabic, Hebrew)

al-Ahram,
al-Arabi
Arabia
Associated Press
Crescent International
al-Fajr
Falastin al-Muslima

The Guardian
Ha'aretz
Harpers Magazine
al-Hayat
Koteret Rashit
International Herald Tribune
Islam wa Falastin
al-Jami'a al-Arabiyya
al-Jami'a al-Islamiyya
Jerusalem Post
Jerusalem Report
al-Jihad
Koteret Rashit
Middle East International
Middle East Mirror
Midstream
al-Mukhtar al-Islami
New Outlook
New Republic
The Observer
Palestine Post,
Palestine Report
al-Quds
Reuters
al-Sharq al-Awsat
al-Tali'a al-Islamiyya
The Times
al-Wasat
Washington Post

Index